RACE, CLASS, AND POLITICAL SYMBOLS

Rastafari and Reggae in Jamaican Politics

ANITA M. WATERS

Transaction Publishers
New Brunswick (U.S.A.) and London (U.K.)

Paperback edition published 1989. Second printing 1999.
Copyright © 1985 by Transaction Publishers
New Brunswick, New Jersey 08903

Library of Congress Catalog Number: 84-16264

ISBN: 0-88738-024-7 (cloth)
ISBN: 0-88738-632-6 (paper)

Printed in the United States of America

Library of Congress Cataloging in Publication Data

Waters, Anita M.
   Race, class, and political symbols.

   Bibliography: p.
   Includes index.
   1. Symbolism in politics—Jamaica. 2. Elections—Jamaica. 3. Political parties—Jamaica. 4. Ras Tafari Movement. 5. Reggae music. I. Title.
JL639.A15W37   1985   324.97292'06   84-16264
ISBN 0-88738-024-7
ISBN 0-88738-632-6 (pbk.)

Contents

Acknowledgments

Space does not permit me to express my full appreciation to the numerous individuals without whose assistance and cooperation this research would not have been possible. Among them:

Professor Herbert Passin guided what might be called the "dub" version of the manuscript in its various stages of completion and made innumerable helpful suggestions. Professor Seamus Thompson, the man with the partisan monogram, gave me considerable assistance in the earliest, and most difficult, stages of the research process. The comments and suggestions of Professors Eviatar Zerubavel and Lambros Comitas helped in putting the research report in its final form. All this book's shortcomings, of course, are my own.

Would that I could here acknowledge the generous assistance of one or another wealthy foundation! This research was impulsively supported by guaranteed student loans, a fact that may enhance its credibility in direct proportion as it depletes my pocketbook.

Thanks are especially due to the Jamaicans who graciously gave their time to be interviewed for the research, and to the staff members of the Center for Policy Research, the Institute of Jamaica, and Dreadnut Cultural Arts, the institutions that provided organizational support. I would also like to thank those friends who encouraged me along the way, including Earl Panton, M.G. Mahon, Winston Thompson, Lorrel Brinkley, Doris Kitson, and my family: Henrietta, Karen, and O. Waters.

I would also like in particular to mention Neville Livingstone, with whom I never had the opportunity to speak, but whose work provided inspiration for this research and at whose indirect invitation I share my words with my fellow beings. Thanks and praises to all the singers and players of instruments.

This book is fondly dedicated to my husband, Fragano Ledgister, without whose love, patience and persistent urging it would truly never have been written.

List of Tables

1

Introduction: Half the History

Preacher man don't tell me heaven is under the earth
I know you don't know what life is really worth
It's not all that glitters is gold
Half the history has never been told
And now that the children have seen the light
They're gonna stand up for their right.
        —*Bob Marley, "Get Up Stand Up"*

The report was true which I heard in my own land
of your affairs and of your wisdom, but I did not
believe the reports until I came and
my own eyes had seen it, and behold,
the half was not told me;
your wisdom and prosperity surpass
the report which I have heard.
        —*Queen of Sheba to Solomon, 1 Kings 10: 6-7*

Scanty history, when revealed as such, is oppressive in retrospect. The consequences that the revelation triggers often demonstrate how deeply patterns of social interaction, justifications of dominance and submission, religious ideas, the very meaning of social existence, are rooted in historical consciousness.

Such a revelation, without taking account yet of its relative "truth," gradually emerged in the island of Jamaica, in the 1930s and thereafter. It became apparent that when the Europeans enslaved the Africans, they

1

appropriated the Amharic history of the African peoples. In their inept fumbling with that complex language, and recognizing the opportunity to deceive the slaves about their true origins and history, the Europeans omitted large and important tracts in the English version. As one of those cognizant of the revelation said, "The white man buck up words that he can't really translate. So in the Bible only half has been told. Still there's a half that you never really know" (quoted in Owens 1976, 31).

Deep study of that document and of prophesies made since further revealed that the true Messiah was not Jesus of Nazareth but the Emperor Haile Selassie I of Ethiopia, the descendant of King Solomon and Queen Makeda of Sheba, and thus a living man of the House of David, exactly as the Old Testament foretold. This was the crucial "half of the story." Given an almost psychoanalytical propensity for discounting coincidences, the fact that Selassie's forebear herself was the one to hint that there was more than met the eye caused no surprise.

Further corollaries were derived. It became obvious, for example, that the true reason that the British monarch Edward VIII abdicated the throne in 1936 was that he had been present at the emperor's coronation and had recognized in him the rightful ruler of all Africans, including those in the British colonies. Over time a body of knowledge about Emperor Selassie was codified, gleaned from various, incomplete sources: a few books and photographs, a ragged issue of *National Geographic*, a rumor, a prophesy.

The reaction to the revelations varied: there was anger at the deception; withdrawal to await Selassie's call to return to the homeland; an insatiable interest in Ethiopian language, gestures, and artifacts; a growing skepticism about all European "truths" and values; and a deeply felt dissatisfaction with the distribution of power in society. As "yeast in the dough," the implications of the beliefs, if not the beliefs themselves, shook the society, and a means of disseminating the beliefs eventually reverberated throughout the world.

This book is also a partial history, an examination of the consequences that these revelations and developments had for the politics of one Third World nation, especially its electoral politics.   International reportage about these political developments has truly told somewhat less than half the story; raw voting statistics and simple statements of electoral outcomes give no indication of the colorful and complex machinations that determine them.

Jamaica is a postcolonial, "plural" society with a high degree of economic inequality.   Its two political parties, the Jamaica Labour Party (JLP) and the People's National Party (PNP), are highly competitive and enjoy comparable success in the electoral arena.

Beginning in 1972, it has been noted, Jamaican political parties have frequently used Rastafarian symbols and reggae music in their electoral propaganda.   The Rastafarians are the millenarian cult that accepts Selassie as the Messiah and constitutes about 3 percent of Jamaica's population; reggae music is an indigenous popular art form associated with, and frequently propagating the beliefs of, Rastafarians.   Two students of Caribbean political science noted this trend after Michael Manley's electoral victory in 1972.   The group that inherited political power after independence, they wrote,

> also appropriated very heavily the cultural forms of the Rastafarians, the most alienated group in the society, particularly their music and their terminology.   In the 1972 election the PNP came to victory after ten years in opposition using the Rasta language and music in an almost undis- guised form. (Singham and Singham 1973, 281)

If the Singhams' formulation is correct, that the People's National Party came to victory partly on account of its aligning itself symbolically with the Rastafarians, in the Singhams' words the "most alienated" group in Jamaica, what made such an unlikely strategy succeed?   Why would a political party identify itself with a millenarian cult whose beliefs are sharply at odds with a majority of the electorate, whose membership never exceeded about 3 percent of the population, and whose members exhort each other not to participate in politics at all?   How did such a cult take on so much importance that a modern political party felt that it had to be addressed at all, much less embraced in propaganda?

This study explores the reasons that political parties chose to utilize these symbols and music in their campaigns, how such utilization changed over time, how the use of such symbols represents political parties' perceptions of the nature of relevant social groups in the electorate, and the relative effectiveness of the symbols used.

In this chapter I will first briefly describe the use of lower class symbols by politicians and the nature of social groups in Caribbean society. Key questions will be generated about the use of Rastafarian symbols by politicians. Finally, the sources of data and the methods employed in this study will be discussed and the study's significance will be estimated.

Although Coleman reported that African leaders in emergent states generally "avoid religious issues or sectarian identification" because "most of them confront a religiously heterogeneous electorate" (1960, 279), many studies of electoral politics in the Third World describe the use of religious or secret society symbols by politicians. In a study of elections in Kenya in 1960, Bennett and Rosenberg reported that Kenyatta frequently used the symbols of Mau Mau and other secret societies of the Kikuyu (1961, 8-11). Martin Kilson reported that the nationalist movement in Sierra Leone made extensive use of the symbols of tribal religious societies; it adopted a burned palm leaf, the Poro symbol of war, to "draw upon Poro obligations" in elections (1966, 257-58).

Examples of the use of religious symbols are also common in Latin America. Primo Tapia, a Mexican leader early in this century, gained support among the peasantry against the national Catholic hierarchy by manipulating folk rituals and symbolism (Friedrich 1966, 192-93). Charles Davis found that Mexico's governing party's "symbolic reassurances," though these were not uniformly religious symbols, were intended to maintain support for the government among the lower class in Mexico City (1976, 656).

In the English-speaking Caribbean, the use of lower class religious symbols and music by politicians is not uncommon. As long ago as 1925, political candidates in Trinidad composed special calypsos to use as campaign songs and organized street parades to sing them (Elder 1966, 126). The earliest meetings of the labor movement in the late 1930s in Jamaica drew upon the rich repertoire of religious song and adopted its best "fighting" songs: "Onward, Christian Soldiers," "Fight the Good Fight," and "Those Who March to War" (Sewell 1978, 43).

A journalist who visited Trinidad during its most recent election reported that the lower class Baptists there supported George Chambers of the People's National Movement.   Chambers had said of the rival Organization for National Reconstruction (ONR) that "Them too wicked! Not a damn seat for them!"   When the journalist visited Trinidad he attended an ONR rally and noticed that the rally was circled by a large number of Baptists, dressed in white robes, who marched unceasingly around the rally's periphery.   When he approached one marcher and asked what the group was doing there, he received the curt reply: "Not a damn seat for them!" (Smikle 1982.)

Beginning in 1955 with George Simpson's "Political Cultism in West Kingston," an impressive body of literature has been published about the Rastafarians.   The major works (Simpson 1955; Smith, Augier, and Nettleford 1960; Kitzinger 1971; Nettleford 1972; Owens 1975. 1976; and Barrett 1977) will be drawn upon in the description of the movement in chapter 2. Here we will confine ourselves to what these works say about the use of Rastafarian symbols by politicians.

Smith, Augier, and Nettleford, in "Report on the Rastafari Movement in Kingston, Jamaica" (1960), reported that some Rasta brethren repeated a story about the 1959 general elections. Agents of the PNP supposedly

> promised spokesmen of the Ras Tafari movement repatriation to Africa if the latter voted for the PNP and this Party was returned to power. PNP spokesmen assert that this story is a complete fabrication... Clearly such allegations are politically profitable to those persons interested in discrediting the PNP, and to others who are interested in discrediting both parties and the

two-party system with them. (Smith, Augier and
Nettleford 1960, 17)

This team of university researchers also discovered resonance between the Rastafari brethren and communism.
The brethren did not regard the Jamaican government as
their own, and many refused to vote (Smith, Augier, and
Nettleford 1960, 21). Some expressed interest in one-party
states and said that "the Communist system is far prefer-
able to the present capitalist system of the white and
brown Babylonians" (Smith, Augier, and Nettleford 1960,
21). The research found "no evidence that Ras Tafarians as
a group are being manipulated by non-Ras Tafarians with
violent beliefs such as Communists" (Smith, Augier, and
Nettleford 1960, 27) but did encounter groups of Rastafarians among whom "Marxist interpretation and terminology
predominated over the racial-religious" (Smith, Augier, and
Nettleford 1960, 28).

The researchers warned that the political aspect of
Rastafari would spread rapidly "unless Government takes
positive steps to meet the legitimate needs of the lower
classes, including the Ras Tafari group" (Smith, Augier, and
Nettleford 1960, 28). Some of the recommendations made
by the researchers address the problems of the lower class
rather than the subgroup of Rastafarians. These included
improvements in the number of low-cost housing units
available and in the facilities available to residents of
squatter settlements like Back-o'-Wall, where Rastafarians
and other poor Jamaicans lived without water or sewage
systems.

In a thoughtful work on Jamaican culture, Nettleford
examined the interaction between the Rastafarians and the
larger society. His thesis was that Rastafarian commentary on society provoked defensive responses from middle-
class observers at first, but was accepted and reiterated by
them later:

The wider society's conception of a harmoniously
multi-racial and stable nationalism is challenged
fundamentally by the Rastafari. The movement
was objectively to inform the wider society of the
inherent incongruities of the Jamaican social sys-

tem in which the poor grew poorer and the rich more prosperous. By the late sixties these incongruities were to become the stock-in-trade of many commentators on the social system including those who ten years before would have regarded the stating of these as intolerable if not subversive. (Nettleford 1972, 61)

He predicted that the Rastafarians' philosophy would "in form the thinking and even the public policy of the nineteen seventies" (Nettleford 1972, 111).

One of the interesting parallels Nettleford pointed out between the Rastafarians and the large number of Anglophiliac Jamaicans is that both look outside Jamaica, one to Ethiopia and the other to England, for the legitimation of authority and for inspiration. It was this aspect of Rasta doctrine that led Frank Hill, a journalist, to refer to Jamaica's upper class as "white Rastas" (Nettleford 1972, 44). Nettleford reported that in 1966, soon after the visit of Haile Selassie to Jamaica, JLP Senator Wilton Hill presented a motion that Jamaica's constitution be amended to make Selassie king of Jamaica in place of Queen Elizabeth II: "He justified his motion on the grounds of racial ties between Jamaicans and the Emperor and the fact that the people of Jamaica had shown greater affection for His Imperial Majesty than for 'our alien Queen'" (Nettleford 1972, 64).

After the university report of 1960 was issued, Premier Norman Manley made "bold attempts" to carry out the report's recommendations, including the most controversial one, which was to organize a mission to Africa to explore the possibilities of repatriating the Rasta brethren (Barrett 1977, 100). Barrett also recognized the gradual acceptance of Rastafarian ideas by others in the society when he wrote that "what Ras (Sam) Brown boldly attacked in 1961 is the same philosophy Michael Manley seeks to destroy at present" (1977, 152).

Owens's research concentrated on the Rastafarians' theology more than their political influence. He does point out that Rastas with whom he worked expressed positive feelings for Fidel Castro (Owens 1976, 38, 233).

None of these works directly addresses the problem at hand here, why political parties in Jamaica make use of Rastafarian symbols, but they do link Rastafarians with the majority racial group, blacks, and the majority socioeconomic stratum, the lower class. It will be argued here that these two linkages made the use of their symbols attractive for politicians seeking solutions to a number of key problems that they faced after attaining independence.

The legacies of colonialism and plantation society created a society divided on two closely coinciding axes: race and class. Analysts of stratification in Jamaica and the Caribbean characterize these societies as "plural." One of the primary proponents of this model defined pluralism as a society in which members are distinguished by fundamental differences in their institutional practices. Two or more groups, because of historically rooted cultural differences, form distinct aggregates within their society and are characterized by deep social divisions among them (M. G. Smith 1969, 27). In a seminal work on the plural character of Jamaican society, Smith discerned three distinct sections that are called White, Brown and Black sections (1965, 163ff.) Membership in one or the other section is not determined by one's actual racial appearance or genealogy but, rather, is based upon what Smith called "associational color," the color of one's associates, or "cultural or behavioral color," which is defined as "the extent to which an individual's behavior conforms to the norms associated with one or the other of the hierarchically ranked cultural traditions of the societies, as these norms themselves are associated with color-differentiated groups" (1955, 52-54). Members of each cultural section participate, according to this theory, in qualitatively different sets of social institutions, including religion, property, and kinship, and hold correspondingly different sets of norms and values.

Although pluralist theory is usually expressed in cultural terms, the organizing principle that allows for the persistence of pluralistic institutions is race (Bahadoorsingh 1968; Depres 1967). Even those embroiled in the so-called Great Debate between pluralists and "consensualists," who emphasize the common values to all groups in the society, agree with R. T. Smith that "creole society imposed a rank order upon ethnicity which must in itself have led to frustrations and dissatisfactions" (1967, 240).

Most of the leaders in the Caribbean who inherited power from their colonial masters were members of the "Brown section," that group of individuals whose forebears include both Europeans and Africans, as will be discussed in chapter 2. But universal suffrage brought a Black majority to the electorate. One problem faced by a Caribbean political party that is composed of members of the Brown section is overcoming the animosity between the Brown and Black sections of the society. The Rastafarians were among the first champions of "Black power" in Jamaica, and were followers of the first Jamaican Black nationalist, Marcus Garvey. Therefore the symbols that they provided may have been manipulated by politicians to gain the support of members of the majority Black section.

Other social scientists agree that Jamaica is a divided society but differently define the parameters of division. They argue instead that discontinuities based upon socio-economic class supersede those of race and culture (Lewis 1968; Gronseth 1978; R. T. Smith 1967, 240; Austin 1974, 112). Shortly after independence, Jamaica held the distinction of having the world's highest level of inequality, with the most wealthy 5 percent of the population receiving 30 percent of the national income, and the poorest 20 percent receiving only 2 percent (Lowenthal 1972, 298). Because an overwhelming proportion of the electorate in Jamaica is lower class and many politicians are of the middle class, the political parties may have used Rastafarian symbols to identify their parties with the plight of the poor, thus providing a response to a second problem.

A third problem is unique to postcolonial countries, especially those that gained independence without a mass national liberation movement (Lindsay 1975). This is the postcolonial nation's leadership's need to dissociate its political power from that of the colonial power structure. Nettl wrote that the newly independent nation's leaders face a paradoxical task: "The need for continuity with the past ... coupled with the desire for maximum dissociation from it" (1967, 205). This is especially true for leaders who have negotiated independence from the metropolitan power after a period of "training" for self-government (Munroe 1972, 29) that led them "away from creative activity and toward emulative behavior" (Munroe 1972, 34). Others called it the metropolitan country's "theory of maturity" (Toure 1960) or "preparation" (Schaffer 1965). Pye expressed the paradoxical task this way:

> The psychological dilemma in political development is obvious: to gain respect and dignity in the eyes of the world there must be advances in political development, yet the very content of the specifics of development are inescapably seen as having been the unique attributes of European civilization, or the white man, of those who once humbled and humiliated one's own society. It is precisely the conflict between the need to adopt from others and also to assert the uniqueness, and hence superiority of one's own culture ... that makes us talk about an identity crisis rather than just nationalism. (1966, 103)

One way of accomplishing the task of dissociation is revival of traditional culture. In studying political ideologies of developing countries, Sigmund found that "reassertion of traditional culture is psychologically necessary to balance the overwhelming technical, economic and military superiority of the West" (1967, 31-32). Bernard Lewis suggested that the former colonial territory may try "to rewrite the past — first, to reveal the imperialists in all their well-concealed villainy, and second ... to restore the true image of the pre-imperialist past which the imperialists themselves had defaced and hidden" (1975, 96-97).

Although the Rastafarians do not represent the traditional culture of precolonial Africans, they sought to adopt as many of the elements of the traditional culture as they could, and called attention to the history of precolonial Africa. It was this aspect of Rastafarian ideology that may have been used by politicians to dissociate their rule from that of the British before them.

Our main purpose here will be to explore the use of Rastafarian symbols and music, with attention to the symbols' resonance with the interests of certain groups in the society. Politics is an arena in which group interests are articulated, and the way these symbols and music are used may shed some light on the relative salience of racial and class distinctions among the population. How did the use of such symbols change over time? What can be learned about the impact of racial and class distinctions on the political development of a relatively new democracy? "Viewed as indicators," wrote Karl Deutsch,

> political symbols and their ... distribution can tell us something about the flow of messages between political groups and organizations.... Such flows of messages can tell us something, in turn, about the distribution of attention of the individuals, groups, and organizations concerned. Thus they may help us understand political meaning and political perception at different times. (1953)

To answer these questions a number of factors must be explored: the kinds and number of Rastafarian symbols and music used in each election; the audience to which these were projected; the context in which the symbols or music was presented; which party and which part of the party used the symbols and music more frequently than others; whether or not the symbols and music were used to highlight certain policy issues more than others, and if they were tied to policy issues at all; and the other symbols of race, class, and colonialism that were available and were used by politicians.

The period of time covered by this study includes five general elections: 1967, 1972, 1976, 1980, and 1983 (See Table 1.1). I chose 1967 as the first election to study because the use of Rastafarian symbols in that election was not noted in the literature. Therefore it could serve as a baseline year against which to compare the others. As will be shown in chapter 3, such symbols were not entirely absent in 1967, but 1972 did mark the first election in which they were used by a political party for its national campaign.

Data Sources and Methods

The methods used in this study were selected with three aims in mind. First, to ascertain the viewpoints of several groups of people cutting across the spectrum of race and

---

Table 1.1
Distribution of Parliamentary Seats
in Five Elections

	1967	1972	1976	1980	1983
Jamaica Labour Party	33	16	13	51	60
People's National Party	20	37	47	9	0
Total	53	53	60*	60	60

* The total number of seats in Parliament increased before the 1976 election from 53 to 60.

---

class categories. Many studies of Jamaican politics concentrate only on the Jamaican "elite" (e.g. Stephens and Stephens 1983). This makes the researcher's task less onerous but takes into account only a small proportion of the electorate. Rosenblum warned that the degree of comparability between elite and mass political culture should be regarded as a question to be investigated and never as a "given" in the research (1975, 27). Second, because the greater part of the campaigns consisted of mass meetings, complete information about which never reached the printed page, to learn about the symbols of the oral and unofficial campaigns as well as printed advertisements and party statements. This requirement ruled out a strictly content-analytical study of symbols such as is more feasible in developed countries (Pool 1951). Finally, to gain a clear understanding of the meaning of the symbols used by politicians, as well as the prevalence of their use.

To fulfill these requirements, a variety of data-gathering tools were employed. These fall into three broad categories: documents, interviews, and personal observation. These sources of data will be described first, in order of their importance to the study.

Documents

As an historical study, documents of various types provided the bulk of the data, and of the several types,
newspapers were most important.   For the first four
elections studied, 228 issues of newspapers were reviewed.
(see Table 1-2). More than half of these were issues of the
Gleaner. (For purposes of convenience and simplification, I
do not differentiate in the text between the *Daily Gleaner*
and the *Sunday Gleaner*, nor between the *Daily News* and
the *Sunday Sun*, its Sunday equivalent. In the text, the
following abbreviations are used when newspapers are
cited: DG = *Daily Gleaner*, WG = *Weekly Gleaner*, DN =
Daily News.) For each of the first four elections, the *Daily
Gleaner* was reviewed for one month before election day.
In some cases, respondents alerted my attention to items
that did not fall into the month immediately before the
election, and when these were reviewed, the extra issues
were excluded from the counts of advertisements in the
tables at the beginning of each substantive chapter.   To
bring the research up to date, the *Gleaner* and other
newspapers and periodicals were monitored for the months
before the election in 1983.

The *Gleaner's* advantages as a source of information
about electoral symbols are these: it was published during
all elections, unlike the *Daily News*, which began publication in 1973 and closed in 1982; it contained most of the
paid political advertisements; it contained some descriptions of parties' mass meetings; for three of the five
elections, it published the statements of both political
parties.   Its disadvantages arise from the fact that the
Gleaner, as an established Jamaican institution, is an
organizational actor in electoral contests.   Its extreme
anti-PNP bias from 1975 to the present and its overall
middle- and upper-class orientation have been frequently
noted by researchers (Lacey 1977; Stephens and Stephens
1983; Kopkind 1980).

The *Gleaner* has a circulation of about 50,000 (#7;
Kopkind 1980), and a generous estimate of readership is
250,000. It is not known what proportion of the electorate
reads the *Gleaner*.   However, advertisements in the
Gleaner were often also party posters that were mounted
in public places.   Texts of radio broadcasts were occa-

sionally reprinted partially or entirely in the pages of the *Gleaner*, and these reached a wider proportion of the electorate as broadcasts. In 1973, there were about 633,000 radio receivers in Jamaica, enough for about 28 percent of the total population (Hammond Almanac 1979).

Table 1.2
Newspapers Reviewed
for Four General Elections

Before Election of:

Newspaper	1967	1972	1976	1980	Total
Daily Gleaner	30	42	36	36	144
Weekly Gleaner	5	0	7	0	12
Weekend Star	5	10	10	7	32
Daily News	0	0	0	29	29
Abeng	0	11	0	0	11
Total	40	63	53	72	228

Three types of information were sought in the *Gleaner*. First, the paper served as a source of information about potential respondents. Second, detailed notes on all paid political advertisements were gathered. Third, a review was made of articles, letters to the editor, columns, and editorials about election activities and about Rastafarians, their symbols and music.

In a pilot study of election-related documents, a review was made of twelve *Weekly Gleaners* that appeared before the 1967 and the 1976 elections. Data gathered from these were occasionally used in the substantive chapter, but were omitted in those tables in which comparisons of numbers of items were made. The *Weekly Gleaner* is a tabloid published primarily for Jamaicans abroad. The edition that I reviewed was for distribution in North America and was a compilation of news and features from a particular week's *Daily Gleaners* and *Stars*, the evening tabloid published by the Gleaner Company. Because it contained features from the *Star*, the *Weekly Gleaner* had more information about music than the *Daily Gleaner*. Therefore, for each election, the Friday (Weekend) edition of the *Star* was also reviewed for one month before each election day.

The Gleaner Company reference library compiles scrapbooks of election-related items on a regular basis. These scrapbooks were also reviewed for the first four elections.

In 1980, for reasons that will be fully explained in chapter 6, it was necessary to review the *Daily News*, a state-owned tabloid, for the month before the election, to review one party's paid political advertisements.

Finally, I found it useful to review several months' issues of *Abeng*, a newspaper that will be discussed in chapter 4.

Documents from the political parties themselves were sought and obtained for the more recent elections. These included party manifestos, campaign literature, booklets used by campaign workers, and other documents. Some were reviewed at the headquarters of one of the two parties and are listed separately in the bibliography. These are cited in the text as Documents I through X.

Given Jamaica's oral tradition and the focus of this research on Rastafarians and reggae music, recorded music was included among the documentation for this research. An effort was made to collect the lyrics for all songs directly used by politicians; very few were unavailable. Other songs that illustrate or exemplify trends in symbol use and in Rastafarian political perspectives were also transcribed.

Miscellaneous documents also included are reports of speeches, recordings of speeches, and interviews in periodicals (e.g. Hayes 1980).

Interviews

To grasp fully the meanings that certain symbols had for various groups of Jamaicans, open-ended interviews with individuals in key structures and groups were sought. In all, forty interviews with thirty-eight Jamaicans were conducted. Six of the thirty-eight were representatives of the 1982 "elite" as defined in a recent study (Stephens and Stephens 1983) that followed the methods used by Bell (1964) and Moskos (1962). Eight respondents were Rasta-

farians; seven were journalists. Fifteen respondents identified themselves as supporters of the People's National
Party; nine as supporters of the Jamaica Labour Party.
Nineteen in all had been involved directly in political work,
either as candidates or as holders of party offices. Ten
respondents had their origins in the lower class; twenty-
five in the middle class; and three in the upper class (see
chapter 2 for definitions of Jamaican classes). Three
respondents were White; sixteen, Brown; and nineteen,
Black. Respondents are identified in this report by number
(e.g. "#6"); the appendix provides background characteristics for all respondents. Their identities are not be
revealed in this work to protect their privacy. Occupation,
class, race, and political affiliation if any appear in condensed form in the appendix.

Respondents were not interviewees in the survey methods sense of the term. Although the interviews were
guided by a basic schedule, not all interviewees were asked
to provide opinions on identical questions. Rather, they
were informants as the term is used in anthropological
field research. The interviews were designed to tap each
respondent's particular field of expertise. Most of the
interviews were conducted in Kingston between May and
September 1982.

Personal Observation

This research is informed partly by five years of working
closely with and observing the Rastafarian and the more
general Caribbean communities in New York City, as well
as by several excursions and one extended period of fieldwork in Jamaica. In New York I had the opportunity to
interview about twenty reggae musicians who toured the
city; two of the interviews (#36, #37) are used in this
research. I attended several ceremonial festivals sponsored by the Twelve Tribes, a Brooklyn branch of the
Kingston-based Rastafarian organization. In May 1981, I
attended the Kingston funeral of a reggae musician, Bob
Marley. There I had the opportunity to observe the curious
relationship between Jamaica's major politicians and Rastafarians. That event was a major influence on the
formulation of the research questions discussed in this
book.

The fieldwork for this research was conducted in Kingston from May through September 1982. During that period, I attended two party conferences, the JLP's annual conference in May and the PNP Women's Movement conference in August. Apart from formal interviews, I was able to speak informally with a number of people about the research, and I monitored both newspapers for items relevant to the thesis. Not surprisingly, the two biggest controversies of the summer were related to music. One was occasioned by Harry Belafonte's anti-JLP remarks at a PNP-oriented function, and the second was in regard to the song that won the Annual Festival Award; many *Gleaner* columnists and letter writers found the song objectionable. I was fortunate to have an opportunity to read and hear people's opinions about the proper role of an artist in the case of the Belafonte issue, and to observe the furor that a simple song can instigate in Jamaica in the case of the Annual Festival Award.

Methods

All information gathered via documents, interviews, or personal observation was classified first by election period: before February 1967; February 1967 through February 1972; March 1972 through December 1976; December 1976 through October 1980; and November 1980 through December 1983. All information from each of these periods was collected in five election "resource books." Sources of the information were noted to judge credibility during the analysis phase. Each resource book was further coded and cross-referenced for five categories: (1) reference to class, (2) reference to race, (3) reference to colonialism, (4) use of Rastafarian symbols, and (5) use of music.

"Reference to class" was defined as any mention of categories within the society created by classifying people by socioeconomic status. Catchwords that fall into the category "reference to class" included *rich/poor, sufferers, small man* or *little man, cost of living, taxes, capitalists, landlords, unemployed, the masses, exploited, upper, middle, lower,* and *working class.*

"Reference to race" was defined as any mention of categories based on color or national origin of forebears. Words that fall into the category included *minority groups,*

Black, White, Brown, Chinese, Syrian, East Indian, Arab, creole, African, slavery, and any reference to Black nationalism, Marcus Garvey, and Martin Luther King, Jr.

"Reference to colonialism" was defined as any mention of Jamaica's history as a British colony or to its current dominion status, or to Jamaica's status as a member of developing and dependent nations. Catchwords included in this category included *Third World, imperialism, Britain, foreign investment, bauxite,* and *aestabilization.* References to Cuba and Cuban domestic and foreign policies were also included here from 1976 on for reasons that will be explained in chapter 5.

"Rastafarian" is defined here as any individual who professes to believe in the divinity of Haile Selassie, and Rastafarian symbols are those colors, words, phrases, objects, places, and persons that have been adopted by Rastafarians as meaningful in relation to Selassie's divinity. Catchwords here included *Selassie,* "*I*"-*words* (see chapter 4), *Ethiopia,* Ethiopian colors and national symbols, "*dreadlocks,*" clothing such as the tam, words and phrases such as "*one love,*" "*reasoning*" and "*high-up,*" *Back-o'-Wall,* and *repatriation.* I familiarized myself with the symbols of Rastafarians by reviewing the literature and by asking respondents (especially #1, #2).

Before each election, photographs of all candidates are presented in the *Gleaner,* and these were coded by race as a continuous variable from 5 (Black) to 1 (White). These data are discussed in chapter 8.

Evaluation of Data

The data gathered for this study vary somewhat for the five elections, but an effort was made to obtain *equivalent* data for the five elections because the same data were unavailable. For example, the *Gleaner* changed considerably over the sixteen years. In 1967, election news consisted mainly of brief accounts about who had been nominated for which constituencies. There were relatively few reports of what the candidates said at mass meetings, and relatively few advertisements. In 1972 and 1976, coverage of rallies improved and political advertising became more plentiful. By 1980, the *Gleaner* had become markedly partisan, and it was necessary to review issues of another newspaper.

Respondents' recollections improved the more recent the election, as did the availability of documents such as campaign literature. One of the strengths of the data is the number of relevant pieces of music that were made available through a number of sources, particularly one respondents (#2) who is a former disc jockey and a reggae music collector.

The major drawback about the data is the paucity of information about early partisan contests in certain constituencies, especially Western Kingston, the birthplace of Rastafari. In 1967 and 1972, most of the constituents in that area were probably illiterate, and no documentation of the "oral campaign" survived. A second drawback is the underrepresentation of respondents who supported the Jamaica Labour Party. This was the party in power during the fieldwork; minor officials were somewhat reluctant to be interviewed, and referred me to their superiors.

The work of Carl Stone, a Jamaican political scientist, was especially helpful for this research. He has studied Jamaican elections for many years and has conducted opinion polls that regularly appear in the *Gleaner*. His data on class-based voting behavior, available until the 1980 election, proved to be particularly germane to this research. It is unfortunate that equivalent data about race and voting behavior were not available, but inferences from the available data can be made.

The photographs of candidates from the *Gleaner* that were coded by race represent only a rough estimate of the racial composition of the party teams.

The Significance of the Research

Because of the relative scarcity of research and the complex configuration of the problem, an exploratory approach is taken here. Its results, therefore, are unlikely to challenge any major theoretical perspective or debunk any long-held perceptions of Caribbean politics.

The research will, however, provide a perspective on the content of electoral propaganda in one postcolonial nation. With regard to its history as a British colony and as an independent member of the Commonwealth, Jamaica's experiences are not unlike those of many other developing nations, notably the nineteen former and eight current British colonies in the Caribbean and Africa. Jamaica and other new nations were for centuries "industrial" colonies, "fitted to European needs with peculiar intensity and pervasiveness" (Mintz 1971, 36); each must now become a nation for itself, fitted to the needs of its own people.

This research aims to be a contribution to two growing, if modest, bodies of literature: case studies of Caribbean politics and studies of the Rastafarians. Jamaica's last contested election, 1980, so deeply polarized the society that many social scientists felt compelled to take sides; therefore, the researcher's non-Jamaican status may enhance rather than limit the credibility of the results. The most impartial research about Jamaican elections had tended to be quantitative; rigorous qualitative research is needed.

A number of fine ethnographies about Rastafari have been published over the years, concerning Rastafarians in Jamaica as well as in England (Cashmore 1979; Garrison 1979; Hebdige 1979; Noyce 1978). The movement's contributions to art and music have been well documented, but research into its impact on political culture has been lacking. This book will, I hope, begin to fill the void.

Chapter 2 is a brief summary of the historical development of Jamaica's racial and class structures, and of lower class religion and Rastafari. Definitions of the terms used throughout the research for Jamaican classes and racial and ethnic groups are presented.

The following five chapters are the substantive ones on each of the five elections. Finally, chapter 8 delineates the conclusions that may be drawn from this research.

2

Race, Class and Politics in Jamaica

Jamaica is one of four major islands in the northern Caribbean that form the Greater Antilles. Ninety miles south of Cuba, it is the largest island of the former British West Indies, with an area of 4,411 square miles. Of a population of 2.1 million (DG 2/12/83), approximately 30 percent live in Kingston, the capital since 1872, and St. Andrew, the adjoining parish to the north, which together form the major urban area of Jamaica. Administered jointly by the Kingston-St. Andrew Corporation (KSAC), the district is known as the Corporate Area. In the remaining twelve parishes there are only three towns that have populations over 25,000: Montego Bay (42,800 in 1970) in the parish of St. James, Spanish Town (41,000 in 1970) in St. Catherine, and May Pen (26,000 in 1970) in Clarendon.

The recorded history of Jamaica begins in 1494, when Christopher Columbus landed on the island, but there was no permanent European settlement until 1509, when Diego Columbus, son of the explorer, sent a delegation to Jamaica. The island was held by Spain until 1660, when, after five years of struggle against an English invasion, the last of the Spanish troops fled from the coastal area now called Runaway Bay (Morales Padron 1952). The native Arawaks had been enslaved by the Spanish and did not survive; the entire indigenous population of about 60,000 was exterminated within fifty years. The Spanish settlers imported slaves from Africa, but there was little development of the island before the arrival of the British.

   With the victory of the British invaders, the development
of the colony began in earnest. The population grew from
4,205 in 1662 to 17,272 in 1673. In a single year more than
1,000 settlers arrived from Barbados. Land was meted out
to the new settlers and cultivation of sugar cane and cocoa
was encouraged (Gleaner Company 1973).   In less than a
century, the colony of Jamaica became prosperous. The
European planter has been described as "a machine for
making money" (Lowenthal 1972, 33). Most of the property
and slaves were owned by absentee proprietors, who dis-
posed of the profits in Europe. A detailed account of one
Jamaican sugar plantation indicates how profitable sugar
was.   The total expenses of maintaining the plantation
amounted to some 36 percent of total income, and between
1775 and 1800 it brought about 5,000 pounds in annual
profit to its proprietor (Craton and Walvin 1970, 118).
   Ample returns depended upon an abundance of slave
labor. Africans were imported to the colonies at stagger-
ing rates; over 1 million were brought to Jamaica between
1655 and 1808 (Gleaner Company 1973, 58). By 1793, the
Black population outnumbered the White by 6 to 1 (Augier
and Gordon 1962, 22), and on the plantations themselves
the ratio was even higher. In 1690 the governor of Jamaica
notified the planters of a slave revolt that had been suppressed. He wrote: "This rebellion might have been very
bloody, considering the number of negroes and the scarcity
of white men. There were but six or seven whites in that
plantation to 500 negroes, and that is the usual proportion
in the island, which cannot but be a great danger" (Augier
and Gordon 1962, 124).
   Because of the slaves' superior numbers and relatively
frequent revolts, the planters took deliberate measures
against rebellion. As a strategy of deculturation, slaves of
the same tribal origin were deliberately separated to
prevent free conversation (Augier and Gordon 1962, 123),
and cultural practices, including African music, were suppressed (Beckford and Witter 1980, 39-40; Augier and
Gordon 1962, 121). Punishments for even minor infractions
were severe (Augier and Gordon 1962, 122; Lowenthal
1972, 42).
   The origins of the Jamaican peasantry are to be found in
the custom of provision grounds, small plots of land worked

by the slaves to raise their own food. The excess produce of these gardens was sold at regular "Sunday Markets," and some slaves were able to accumulate savings with which they could buy, in rare cases, their freedom or, more frequently, a small piece of land after emancipation (Beckford and Witter 1980, 39-40) for two or three pounds an acre (Augier and Gordon 1962, 74). Emancipation had devastating effects for some of those slaves who had depended on provision grounds and were denied access to them by their former masters.

From 1663 to 1738, planters were plagued by attacks on their estates by the Maroons, descendants of the Spaniards' former slaves who had escaped to the mountains and forests of the interior when the British took the island. The Maroons had constructed an isolated society in the mountains and returned to some of the African customs that they had so recently been forced to abandon. Masters of guerrilla warfare, the Maroons regularly fought the British planters. Two Maroon groups signed a treaty with the British in 1738 that allowed the Maroons certain lands and the rights of self-government. In return, the Maroons helped the planters to track down runaway slaves (Gleaner Company 1973, 52). The Maroons of Trelawny Town fought the British again in 1793, and the British deployed about 5,000 troops against them. The Maroons surrendered on the promise that they would be allowed to remain on the island, but were deported to Nova Scotia and thence to Sierra Leone. Other groups of Maroons, however, continued to enjoy the privileges they had won previously (Gleaner Company 1973, 58) and still live today in four Jamaican villages.

The early nineteenth century saw the slow demise of the sugar plantations as money-making machines. Pressures of the nascent industrial capitalists in Britain and the attrition caused by frequent slave revolts eventually led to the abolition of the trade and finally of the institution of slavery. The British found 1808 an opportune time to abolish the trade because, as Lord Castlereagh, then responsible for colonial affairs, informed the colonial governor, there was "too great an increase of colonial produce, the markets of the world are overstocked, and the price proportionally reduced" (Augier and Gordon 1962, 126).

Despite opposition in Jamaica's House of Assembly, the trade was abolished. The abolitionists in England, in alliance with missionaries in the colonies, pressed for the abolition of slavery and won the fight in 1834. Although some former slaves became wage laborers on the plantations, a large number fled the plantations and either bought marginal land that the estate owners had deemed unsuitable for sugar or "squatted" on crown land or abandoned estate land. Bigelow, an American who visited Jamaica in 1850, remarked that by that year Brown and Black landowners numbered 100,000 (Bigelow 1970, 116). Lowenthal reported that the number of resident plantation laborers declined rapidly, from 42,000 in 1832 to 14,000 in 1846.

Planters in the postemancipation period complained of the high wages they had to pay workers and of a labor shortage, for which the importation of free Africans in 1841 and of indentured laborers from India and China from 1845 on could not compensate. Bigelow denied that there was a true labor shortage but argued instead that low wages had driven former slaves from the plantations. He wrote:

> To my utter surprise I learned that the price for men on the sugar and coffee plantations ranged from eighteen to twenty-four cents a day, and proportionally less for boys and females. Out of these wages, the laborers have to board themselves. Now when it is considered that in the largest market on the island, flour costs from sixteen to eighteen dollars by the barrel, butter costs thirty-eight cents a pound, eggs from three to five cents a piece, and hams twenty-five cents a pound; does not the cry of high wages appear absurd?" (1970, 125).

The number of estates declined as the less efficient ones fell into bankruptcy (Beckford and Witter 1980, 40ff.). Between 1832 and 1850, the number of sugar estates declined from 653 to fewer than 500, and more than 500 coffee plantations were abandoned (Bigelow 1970, 54-55).

Another blow to the planters was the adoption of the policy of free trade by the British in 1846, throwing the

British colonies into competition with Cuba and other non-British sugar producers (Augier and Gordon 1962, 68). The serious economic crisis contributed to the difficulties that led up to the Morant Bay Rebellion of 1865, which will be discussed below.

The agricultural industry diversified somewhat in the later nineteenth century. Bananas were shipped to the United States beginning in 1870, and cocoa, citrus fruits, ginger, and coffee continued to be produced. A number of major sugar estates remained in operation, first with indentured labor from Asia, later with wage laborers. Sugar remains an important export crop, accounting for 10.6 percent of total exports' value in 1970 (Gleaner Company 1973, 26).

Since emancipation, when former slaves purchased small parcels of land for their own use, small farming has been an important sector of the agricultural economy. In 1961 farms of fewer than twenty-five acres occupied half the island's cultivated land, and were owned by 154,000 individuals in an estimated resident population of over 600,000 (Edwards 1973, 28). But the trend toward rationalization and economies of scale has caused a number of small farmers to give way under the pressure of competition with larger, more mechanized farms. As a *Gleaner* headline succinctly put it, "Small Men Being Squeezed Out Of Bananas" (Lacey 1977, 24). The small farmers remain a significant constituency in electoral politics, however, and the issues of feeder roads and crop prices are usually addressed in political campaigns.

The first major diversification in the Jamaican economy was the exploitation of bauxite deposits, beginning in the 1940s. The demand for aluminum increased dramatically in the United States during World War II, and aluminum was designated as one of the seventy-four metals to be stock-piled after the war (King and Girling 1978, 4). Jamaica's rich deposits of bauxite, its supply of cheap labor, and its political stability beckoned the aluminum companies, which bought huge tracts of bauxite-rich land during the 1940s. Six companies, including Kaiser Aluminum, Reynolds Metals, and Alcoa, are involved in the industry today, and bauxite accounted for 67 percent of total exports' value in 1970 (Gleaner Company 1973, 26).

The arrival of the aluminum companies had a critical impact on Jamaica's economy and society. The companies did not by and large reinvest their profits in other industrial sectors as the government had hoped, and most of the equipment used in the mining process was heavy machinery that had to be imported. The construction industry, however, enjoyed an unprecedented period of growth. As a result, according to two economists, "members of the old oligarchy began to diversify their economic activities into construction and related supplier industries, forming the nucleus of a new industrial bourgeoisie.... Through the new industrialists' influence, the Jamaican government sponsored a program of 'import substitution'.... The program opened Jamaica's doors wide to foreign investors" (King and Girling 1978, 10).

Some of the companies that availed themselves of the incentives were Goodyear, Colgate-Palmolive, and Mead Johnson. Some foreign investors produced items for the domestic market; others took advantage of the cheap labor force to establish "screwdriver" industries in which components are imported, assembled, and exported (King and Girling 1978, 10). Manufacturing accounted for about one-third of Jamaica's gross domestic product in 1968 (Nettleford 1972, 237).

The bauxite industry created a small, relatively well paid stratum of industrial workers in the rural areas. Bauxite workers received about J$4.09 an hour in 1976, compared with J$0.71 in the garment industry and J$1.43 in the building trades (King and Girling 1978, 13), but employment in the industry that year was less than 7,000 or about 0.6 percent of the labor force.

Jamaica's class structure today reflects its history as a colonial plantation society and its beginnings of industrial development. It is mainly characterized by a high rate of inequality and a great deal of poverty. About 10 percent of the population enjoy almost half the national income (Phillips 1977, 10).

In this report, Carl Stone's formulation of Jamaican class structure will be utilized (1976, 179). Stone discerned seven class categories; in this report they will be grouped to yield three main categories: upper/upper middle (1 percent of the total population), lower middle (20 percent),

and lower (79 percent). Each class has a particular significance to parties seeking success in electoral contests.

Stone's classification has a number of drawbacks. First,
classes are defined by mixed criteria, a combination of
occupational prestige, income, and ownership of productive
capital. Second, the scheme is vague with respect to the
placement of specific occupational categories. Third, it
does not differentiate between rural and urban categories
of workers. However, the classification is more useful for
the purposes of this research than any other formulation of
Jamaican classes. It is particularly useful in the study of
elections because its author has analyzed voting data with
respect to classes using this formulation. Thus, comparative data on three of the four elections are available and
will be reported in the substantive chapters.

The upper/upper-middle category consists of two groups,
each 0.5 percent of the population. The first Stone calls
the "capitalists"; it includes owners and managers of large
and medium-scale privately owned enterprises and farms
that employ wage labor in significant quantities. The
second, which Stone calls the "administrative upper-middle
class," is composed of the public sector's top bureaucrats
and technologists, but also includes independent service
professionals, politicians, and clergymen. For the sake of
convenience, this group will be referred to as the *upper
class*; it numbers about 20,000 individuals.

The upper class is a significant social group for politicians seeking elections because of its contributions to
political parties and its control of information dissemi-
nated to the middle class. Parties' dependence on their
wealthy contributors was recently demonstrated when two
top PNP officials, D. K. Duncan and Beverly Manley, quit
their posts because of objections to them from wealthy
Jamaicans who were potential contributors (DG 1/9/83).
Those who control the *Daily Gleaner*, the Jamaican newspaper of record that began publication in 1834, are members of the upper class. The *Gleaner* has long been
recognized as the voice of the "national bourgeoisie"
(Lacey 1977, 28) and of "capitalist enterprise, alliance with
the West and a conservative sensibility" (Kopkind 1980, 41).
Its chairman and managing director, Oliver Clark, a White
member of the upper class, told Andrew Kopkind that "the

business community ... looks to the *Gleaner* to be its advocate" (Kopkind 1980, 42).

The lower-middle class in Stone's formulation also consists of two groups. The first, 5 percent of the population, is independent property owners and middle-level capitalists. Shopkeepers, people in small business, middle farmers, and landlords form this sector. The second group is the "labour aristocracy," about 15 percent of the total population. Included here are semiprofessionals, technicians, white-collar workers, and high-wage and skilled workers, such as bauxite workers. This 20 percent of the total population (400,000 individuals) will be referred to in this study as the *middle class*.

While the upper class controls the top levels of private media institutions, the middle class is the consumers of media information. Because the *Gleaner* has a daily circulation of 50,000 (Kopkind 1980, 43) and a generous estimate of readership would be no more than 250,000, it can be assumed that most of the readership is within the 400,000-plus membership of the middle class.

Members of the middle class participate directly in elections by running for office, staffing campaigns, and supporting parties financially with small individual contributions. The "labour aristocracy" is the mainstay of the two major trade unions, the Bustamante Industrial Trade Union (BITU), an affiliate of the Jamaica Labour Party, and the National Workers' Union (NWU), an affiliate of the People's National Party.

The remaining four-fifths of Jamaica's people form the *lower class*, sometimes referred to by politicians as "the masses." In Stone's formulation, it includes three groups. Thirty-four percent of the total population are own-account workers or petty capitalists: small farmers, "higglers," and small contractors. Twenty-five percent are low-wage manual workers, and 20 percent are chronically unemployed.

Because the middle and upper classes are concentrated in the Corporate Area, the lower class is the most important class in terms of sheer numbers of votes in most constituencies. The electorate was composed of 990,417 voters in 1980 (Director of Elections 1980); all parties must appeal to this vast group to achieve electoral success

(Ayearst 1954). Another role that some members of the chronically unemployed class play during election campaigns is participation in "tribal war." Politicians provide ghetto youths with weapons and sometimes with salaries and other privileges in return for their services as "soldiers" for political street battles (Lacey 1977, 32).

Race in Jamaica

The racial hierarchy of plantation society proved to be an enduring one. The dominant position of Whites and the importance of shades of color can be traced to Jamaica's colonial past; the role of some ethnic minority groups is a more recent development.

Economic power in Jamaica still resides to a great extent with White and fair groups (King and Girling 1978; Lowenthal 1972; Campbell 1980; and others). Lowenthal estimated that in the late 1960s, the median wage for Whites was almost twice that for Browns, and thirteen times that for Blacks (1972, 81). With status as well as wealth, Whites have the most and Blacks the least. Lowenthal reported that of sixty Jamaicans identified as influential in 1961, twenty were White, while only about one percent of the population is White (1972, 82). Over the 1960s and 1970s, the number of Whites identified as influential was less than one-third of the total list of members of the "elite" as determined by similar methods, but of fourteen members of the business-sector elite, eight are White and the rest are Brown (Stephens 1982). In a study of the forty-two companies listed in Jamaica's Stock Exchange Report of 1969-1973, Reid found that twenty-one Chinese and White families accounted for 125 of the 219 directorships and nearly 70 percent of the chairpersons; no corporate firm was controlled by Blacks, and only 6 of the 219 directorships were held by Blacks. Two of the 6 were government appointees (Reid 1977, 25). Likewise, Robotham reported 1943 census data indicating that at that time Whites owned less than 1 percent of the farms, but these accounted for 30 percent of the total farm acreage. Of farms larger than five hundred acres, 46.1 percent were owned by Whites, 39.4 percent by Browns, 13.7 percent by Blacks (Robotham 1977, 55).

Paul Blanshard, an U.S. Department of State official assigned to Jamaica in the early 1940s, reported in 1947 that:

> there is a striking correlation between race, income and residential location. The great stores, banks and commission houses are, of course, owned by whites; the chief subordinates positions are held by browns. The residential sections of the suburbs rise gradually toward the Blue Mountains, and as they rise, the temperature falls about one degree for each hundred feet of elevation, the income rises about $500 a year, and the racial complexion of the residents changes with the elevation. The whites and wealthy browns live above the 500 foot level, while the black workers who constitute the great majority of the population live in congested slums in the lowlands. Some of the white men's homes are residences of considerable elegance, and some of the brown men's homes are only slightly less elegant. (1947, 86-87)

The importance of shades of color usually strikes White North Americans as unusual. The Brown stratum was well established in the early days of plantation life, the result of miscegenation by White planters with their female slaves. Unlike American slaveholders, West Indian Whites recognized their colored children and often had them educated in Europe (Lowenthal 1972, 48). In his *History of Jamaica*, published in 1774, Long observed:

> It has long been the custom for every father here, who has acquired a little property, to send his children, of whatever complexion, to Britain for education. They go like a bale of dry goods, consigned to some factor, who places them at the school where he himself was bred or any other that his inclination leads him to prefer. The father, in the meanwhile, sends remittance upon remittance, or directs a liberal allowance, that his son may learn the art of squandering from his

very infancy; and, not infrequently, to gratify a
little pride of heart, that little master may appear the redoubted heir to an affluent fortune.
(Augier and Gordon 1962, 107)

A nineteenth-century will reprinted by Augier and Gordon indicates the way in which some Brown offspring
gained their freedom, and were heirs to the property of
their White fathers, and illustrates as well the importance
of shades of color. The will, dated August 1811, read in
part:

I give and bequeath the following money legacies
... unto each of my quadroon reputed daughters
Mary Ann Campbell and Christiana Campbell 100
pounds, unto my reputed quadroon son Duncan
Campbell 200 pounds and each of my reputed
mulatto daughters by Esther ... 100 pounds, and
unto my reputed mulatto son William Campbell by
the same mother 300 pounds; and the last named
four mulatto children I will shall be immediately
manumised.... (Augier and Gordon 1962, 17)

No less than six statuses were recognized for African
parentage of varying degrees. A *Negro* was of pure
African blood; a *Sambo* was three-fourths African and one-
fourth European; a *Mulatto*, one-half African; a *Quadroon*,
one-fourth African; a *Mustee* or *Octaroon*, one-eighth
African; a *Musteefino*, one-sixteenth African (Augier and
Gordon 1962, 128; Phillipo 1969, 144). The offspring of a
Musteefino and a White was considered legally White.
    The resulting Brown stratum and its place in society is
one of the most absorbing problems in Caribbean stratification. The stratum's relations with both the higher-status
White stratum and the lower-status Black stratum have
been conflictual.   West Indian Whites saw the "free
coloureds" as allies to protect White hegemony in a society
where the Black masses far outnumbered both Whites and
Browns (Lowenthal 1972, 47), but at the same time Browns
were discriminated against and denied full civil rights and
equality. As Lowenthal wrote:

> Up to the eve of emancipation, law as well as custom discriminated against the free coloured, who were precluded from participation in government. When civil rights were at last accorded, they were designed to ally coloured with white against free black and the mass of blacks soon to be freed. But the free coloured remained ... an inferior social order. And the small white minority exercised absolute power over social institutions that everywhere discriminated against nonwhites. (1972, 50)

According to the same author, color increased in importance as a determinant of social status after emancipation because the difference in status between the free Black and the enslaved Black disappeared: "Although colour distinctions were less absolute, the distances and grievances between white, brown and black widened after emancipation. Whites who had formerly wooed free-coloured support now rebuffed them, intolerant of coloured equality" (1972, 71).

The distances among the color groups were thrown into relief in the Morant Bay Rebellion of 1865. The friction between the White planters and some newly franchised Brown men was reflected in the role of George William Gordon, the wealthy Brown son of a White planter and a slave, and in the vengeance of Governor Eyre against him. Because the heroes of the rebellion became important symbols for later politicians, an account of it is presented here.

A number of disasters had struck Jamaica within the two decades before the rebellion. Asiatic cholera had claimed the lives of 32,000 in 1850; smallpox struck two years later. A drought from 1863 to 1865 increased Jamaica's already high dependence on food imports, just when the American Civil War had caused an increase in their prices. In 1865, Edward Eyre, an unpopular and dictatorial man, became governor.

At the time, most capital was invested in the production of sugar, rum, and coffee, and, as Bigelow reported, "the island is compelled to import nearly everything it consumes... all its flour, its meal, its rice and immense quantities of peas and beans for the consumption of its own population" (1970, 107). In 1849, the island imported more than 70,000 barrels of flour and nearly 5 million pounds of rice (Bigelow 1970, 108).   The high proportion of food imports remains a problem today.

One of Eyre's bitter and most vocal enemies was George William Gordon, then a representative in Jamaica's House of Assembly. Although baptized in the Anglican Church, Gordon had adopted the religion of his mother, a Baptist. He was critical of the abuses of the Church of England in Jamaica as well as of Jamaica's government. The bishop of Jamaica was an absentee like so many planters; resident in Europe, he regularly received a generous portion of the tithes of Jamaican peasants (Williams 1972, 110).

Gordon's outspokenness provoked Eyre, who had Gordon removed from his post of magistrate on flimsy pretexts. Eyre was reprimanded by the British Colonial Office for what Eric Williams called "his tendency to deal with the private characters of persons who assailed or defended his policies." Williams quoted one such reprimand from the Colonial Office: "I desire to caution you against rejecting Mr. Gordon's complaints as unworthy of attention. When a serious amount of abuse is proved to have existed and evidence has been suppressed, the information obtained from such a person may be useful as indicating the direction in which enquiries should be made" (1972, 111).

Gordon had in St. Thomas a political supporter and religious follower, a Black man named Paul Bogle. Both Gordon and Bogle had spoken out on behalf of the peasants and laborers of St. Thomas who held a number of grievances against the planters of the area. In the summer of 1865, Gordon spoke publicly at Morant Bay:

> Poor people!   Starving people!   Naked people! You who have no sugar estates to work on, nor can find other employment, we call on you to come forth. Even if you be naked, come forth and protest against the unjust representations made against you by Mr. Governor Eyre and his band of custodes. You don't require custodes to tell your woes; but you want men free of Government influence — you want honest men. People of St.

> Thomas ye East, you have been ground down too
> long already; shake off your sloth.... Remember
> the destitution amidst your families and your
> forlorn condition; the Government have taxed you
> to defend your own right against the enormities of
> an unscrupulous and oppressive foreigner, Mr.
> Custos Ketelholdt. (Williams 1972, 117)

He went on to accuse the custos (the local representative
of the Governor) of a variety of misdeeds, including
withholding and unjustly distributing smallpox relief
money.

Bogle and his congregation protested before the custos in
October of that year. While the custos and the vestry, or
local council, were in the Court House trying a Black man,
a number of Blacks intending to rescue their comrade if
convicted approached the building, "armed with bludgeons
and preceded by a band of music" (Williams 1972, 117).
After five days of intermittent skirmishes, rebellion broke
out. As Bogel and his followers demonstrated outside the
Court House, the custos and his men fired upon the crowd.
Bogle and his men rushed the Court House, eventually
setting it afire and killing the custos and others.

Governor Eyre sent a warship to Morant Bay and suppressed the revolt with terrifying severity. Nearly six
hundred people were shot or hanged and over a thousand
huts were burned. Eyre took the opportunity to rid himself
of his chief critic. Gordon was arrested in Kingston and
charged with instigating the rebellion, but there was no
evidence that he was directly involved. He was trans-
ported illegally to Morant Bay, where martial law was in
force, and hanged within hours of his arrival. Bogle, who
insisted the Gordon knew nothing of the incident, was also
tried and hanged.

A British commission sent to study the incident found
that the punishments inflicted by Eyre were "excessive,"
"reckless," and "barbarous." Eyre was recalled and dismissed from the Imperial Service (Gleaner Company 1973,
66). The incident sparked some important changes in the
way the colony was governed, which will be discussed
below.

Eyre's execution of Gordon came to represent the widening gap between the Whites and the Browns, who were relatively new to the government but who filled a number of important administrative posts and had been elected to the Assembly since the early 1840s (Bigelow 1970, 157). Gordon, a wealthy Brown man who had married a White woman, exemplified his stratum's gains since emancipation toward Brown-White equality, the goal of the stratum.

Fifteen years before the rebellion, Bigelow described the relations among the three major groups:

> While the *entente cordiale* between the whites and the colored people is apparently strengthening daily, a very different state of feeling exists between the negroes or Africans, and the browns. The latter shun all connection by marriage with the former, and can experience no more unpardonable insult than to be classified with them in any way. They generally prefer that their daughters should live with a white person upon any terms, than be married to a negro. (1970, 26)

The death of Gordon, described by Eyre's defenders as a "brown-skinned, canting, disreputable agitator" (Williams 1972, 151), was a blow to the *"entente cordiale."*

But the Brown stratum did not cease trying to collaborate with the White. In the 1940s, Blanshard described a relationship similar to that of the 1850s:

> The Caribbean has a large mulatto middle class which has worked its way into the fringes of the owning class, and the members of this brown middle class agree with the whites in many of their economic and social relations. They share in the white man's spoils and eagerly accept the white man's badges of imperial conformity. They are colored in the American sense of the word, but white in every other sense.... While there are many exceptions, the general practice of the successful brown men in the Caribbean is to disassociate themselves as completely as possible from the lowly blacks in order to strengthen their

precarious position in a white-dominated society. (1947, 52)

The Anglophilia of this group is often noted and earned them the epithet "Afro-Saxons" (Lindsay 1975; Allum 1973; Campbell 1980). Smith reported that Brown Jamaicans even began to regard the local Whites as inferior to the "true whites" who remained in Britain (1967, 237). Barrett described how the orientation to things British permeated language and clothing styles:

> Few middle class Jamaicans would consider themselves dressed up unless they are suffocated in Scottish tweed and mohair clothing made for cold climates and not for weather that is close to ninety degrees most of the year.... Despite the fact that most Jamaicans know their dialect -- English being a second language — few middle class or aspiring middle class Jamaicans dare to use what is properly theirs in public. Their grammar may be atrocious, but they will insist on the "proper accent," meaning the accent of the BBC news reporter .... In other words, to copy England is good; to speak Jamaican is bad. (1977, 175)

The relative political apathy of the Black stratum in the period following the Morant Bay Rebellion (Barrett 1977, 65; Foner 1983) has been interpreted by some as a tacit agreement with the values of the racial hierarchy. Smith, for example, described plantation society in terms of Goffman's total institution, which he said helped to explain "why the hierarchical structure of society, coinciding largely with race, came to be *accepted* to the extent that it did" (1967, 231; emphasis Smith's). An early psychological study of class in the U.S. Virgin Islands supports the "consensus" theory: "Lower class workers prefer to have a white employer and find it easier to take orders from him than from one of their own race. They are pleased to have a white person engage them in conversation, and friendship with such an individual is a matter of pride" (quoted in Blanshard 1947, 53; see also Lowenthal 1972, 258).

One of the informants for this study, a brown profession-
al, agreed:

> It is entrenched that to be a little lighter meant
> to be a house slave rather than a yard slave. The
> brown class got more education. For leadership,
> the broad base of people want a little whiteness.
> With a foreigner in charge of any organization in
> Jamaica, a minority will resist, but two-thirds
> will work harder. With a black in charge, people
> will slack off. We still haven't gotten over that.
> We've never had a real black/white problem. But
> we have a shade problem. (#9)

One major exception to the period of relative political
apathy within the Black stratum was Marcus Garvey's
Black nationalist movement of the 1910s and 1920s. Garvey
was born in the parish of St. Ann in 1887, reputedly the son
of a Maroon. He founded the United Negro Improvement
Association (UNIA) in 1914, but its New York City branch
was to enjoy much greater success than the Kingston
chapter. The aim of UNIA was "to champion Negro
nationhood by redemption of Africa" (Garvey 1963, 32), and
its slogans were "Africa for Africans, at home and abroad"
and "One God, One Aim, One Destiny" (Garvey 1963, 202,
272). Garvey predicted a final collapse of European
civilization and a reunification of the "scattered Race" of
Africans, with West Indian Blacks spearheading the reunification (Garvey 1963).

Garvey founded a shipping company, the Black Star Line,
in New York in 1918. It was intended to be an exemplary
institution, and its aim was to create and consolidate Black
economic power, but it became Garvey's "Achilles heel."
Numerous suits brought against the firm and charges of
misuse of company funds caused Garvey to be deported
from the United States to Jamaica, and later from Jamaica
to the United Kingdom.

Because Garvey's intellectually formative years had been
spent in Jamaica, his philosophy reflected the Blacks'
resentment of the brown stratum. His antiwhite sentiments attracted some light-skinned American "Blacks" who
were subsequently appalled when he derided people of their

color as some of the "bitterest enemies of their own race"
(Lowenthal 1972, 286). When Garvey returned to Jamaica
in 1914, he found that "I was a black man and therefore had
absolutely no right to lead; in the opinion of the 'colored'
element, leadership should have been in the hands of a
yellow or a very light man... There is more bitterness
among us negroes because of the caste of colour than there
is between any other peoples" (quoted in Lowenthal 1972,
72).

Given the interest in Garvey among later-day Brown and
White politicians, it is ironic that Norman Manley, the
founder of the People's National Party, was among those
Brown men who harassed Garvey while he was in Jamaica.
Although the main political opposition to Garvey came
from the White stratum, represented by the Jamaica
Imperial Society and its secretary H. G. DeLisser, then
editor of the *Daily Gleaner*,

> it was that class of Afro-Saxons just below the
> ranks of the Jamaica Imperial Society which felt
> most threatened by Garvey's call for self-govern-
> ment, for breaking with the sycophantic imitation
> of everything British. Typical of this class was
> King's Counsel Norman Manley, then an attorney
> for the United Fruit Company, and involved di-
> rectly in one of the many legal cases against
> Garvey. This class supported the continual at-
> tempts to harass and silence Garvey. (Campbell
> 1980, 5)

One of the first Jamaican political parties was founded
by Garvey in 1929. It was called the People's Political
Party, and Garvey ran on its ticket for a vacancy in the
Legislative Council in the January 1930 elections. The
course of his electoral campaign is illustrative of the way
the political establishment hindered his activity,

Garvey began the campaign in September 1929 with a
Fourteen-point manifesto calling for a minimum wage, a
greater degree of self-government, and land reform, as
well as a Jamaican university, an opera house and a
national park "similar to Hyde Park in London" (reprinted
in Garvey 1963, 208). The tenth plank of the platform

called for "a law to impeach and imprison judges who, with disregard for British justice, and Constitutional rights, dealt unfairly" (reprinted in Garvey 1963, 208). Immediately after the opening speech in the campaign, Garvey was arrested and charged with contempt of court because of the tenth plank. Garvey claimed that his party was simply proposing legislation, but the chief justice, declaring that there was already a such a law on the books, sentenced Garvey to three months in prison and a fine of one hundred pounds. There were only a few weeks left in the campaign by the time he was released. He lost the election.

A sample of Garvey's campaign speeches indicates that he did not stress racial discord among the Black, Brown and White strata of Jamaica, and that he used "races" and "classes" interchangeably:

> I am not prejudiced against any class in Jamaica. I love all Jamaicans — white and black — and all those who have made Jamaica the country of their adoption, but all classes should cooperate for the common good. We want Jamaica to stand out as a beacon of Race tolerance and goodwill.... My opponents say I am against white and fair-skinned people. This is not so. I am against the class system here, which keeps the poor man down, and the poor are mostly black people. (Garvey 1963, 211-12)

Although Garvey is known as the founder of Black nationalist philosophy, his statements in Jamaica seem relatively mild. He avoided offending the Brown and White minorities, and even deferred to the Anglophilia of his society by accepting as given that "British justice" and "Hyde Park" were standards worthy of emulation.

Other Ethnic Groups

As Table 2.1 indicates, there are several ethnic minorities in Jamaica: Syrian, Chinese, and East Indian. These groups are characterized by their segregation in one or more occupational niches in the economic structure. Lowenthal argues that because European and Afro-European elites denigrate entrepreneurial activities, they chose not to compete in those fields. Commerce in the West Indies is dominated by the ethnic minorities (Lowenthal 1972, 194).

Table 2.1
Population of Jamaica By Race

Category	%	Summary Category	%
African	76.8	Blacks	76.8
Afro-European	14.6		
Afro-East Indian	1.7		
Afro-Chinese	0.6	Browns	20.0
Other mixtures	3.1		
European	0.8		
		Whites	0.9
Syrian	0.1		
East Indian	1.7		
		Asians	2.3
Chinese	0.6		

Source: O.C. Francis, *The People of Modern Jamaica* (Kington: Department of Statistics, 1963).

One of the earliest and most influential groups in Jamaica is now so small numerically that it does not appear in Table 2.1: the Sephardic Jews, who constitued one-third of the White population in the mid-1800s. Lowenthal reports that the House of Assembly adjourned for Yom Kippur in 1849 in deference to its eight (of forty-seven) Jewish members (1972, 195). By the late 1960s, their numbers in Jamaica had dwindled to about six hundred.

Although a tiny ethnic group, Jamaican Jews today wield considerable power. Closely aligned with, but distinct from, the European and Afro-European elites, Jewish families control many of the larger economic enterprises (Reid 1977). Before the socialist policies of the Manley administration caused the redistribution of control over key sectors, Jewish families controlled the single cement factory, the Gleaner Company, the independent radio station, the largest rum company, and the telephone company (Lowenthal 1972, 196).

The Chinese came to Jamaica as indentured estate laborers in the 1850s and 1860s and as migrants from other Caribbean territories in later years. They are closely associated with the small retail industry, especially groceries. The Chinese owner of a grocery store is a ubiquitous stereotype in the Caribbean; grocery stores are locally called "China shops" (Lowenthal 1972, 203). In 1963 the Chinese controlled 95 percent of Jamaica's grocery stores (Lacey 1977, 26).

The African and Afro-European sections of society often characterize the Chinese as greedy, miserly, and clannish (Lowenthal 1972, 206-7). The latent hostility against the Chinese came to the surface in August 1965 in the so-called Anti-Chinese Riots. Set off by a dispute between a Chinese bakery owner and a Black employee, crowds beat a number of Chinese and set afire or stoned several Chinese-owned shops (*New World* 1965). The *Gleaner* attributed the disturbances to "ragamuffins and hooligans," and, according to one observer, the middle class agreed. Laborers of the lower class expressed the cause of the riots in economic terms, a "resentment against particular Chinese business-men and anger toward the wealthier classes in general" (*New World* 1965).

The Syrians, also a merchant group, migrated to the Caribbean in the 1890s. They eventually dominates the import and dry goods trades, and owned the largest department store and a high proportion of hotels, restaurants, movie houses, and soft-drink plants (Lowenthal 1972, 208). Their phenomenal economic success in the West Indies was described by a Guadeloupean social scientist:

"Poor as Job, going on foot along the roads carrying his suitcase full of notions, the day soon comes when he has a small store. Here in the midst of an indescribable jumble, the Guadeloupean woman can at one and the same time find flowered prints for dresses, a tire for her bicycle, and casseroles for her kitchen. Within a few months, the Syrian imitates patois well enough to make himself understood; at the end of a few years, the former pedlar has become a well-to-do tradesman with a house of his own ... and a Dodge or a Studebaker. Marrying generally among themselves, the Lebanese and Syrians together tend to form a closed group, encysted on the country, draining out of it the wealth that the often nonchalant and unorganized Creoles fail to exploit." (Lasserre, quoted in Lowenthal 1972, 208)

As Table 2.1 indicates, East Indians form one of the largest minority groups in Jamaica, but there are far fewer than in many Caribbean territories. In Trinidad and Tobago and Guyana they form up to half of the total populations. The East Indians arrrived in Jamaica in the postemancipation period as indentured estate labor and, unlike East Indians in Trinidad and Guyana, did not retain their distinctive family structure and religious traditions. Today they remain substantially rural and lower class (Lowenthal 1972, 146).

In summary, ethnicity and class are inextricably linked in the Jamaican social structure. Racial and economic classifications are often joined in everyday speech, such as "the Brown middle class," or used interchangeably. While there are dark-skinned persons of power and wealth, Whites, ethinic minorities, and fair-skinned people dominate the upper class. Stone estimates that most of those he calls the "capitalists," the top 0.5 percent of the population, are Europeans, Jews, Lebanese, Chinese, and fair-skinned mixed persons (1974, 180), while the administrators, also 0.5 percent, is mostly brown-skinned.

Likewise, there is a small number of lower-class Whites, notably in Seaford Town, a rural, relatively isolated village in Westmoreland. The town is populated by the patois-speaking descendants of German indentured laborers, who originally migrated to Jamaica on the promise, later broken, that they would receive land of their own when their tenure as indentured laborers was finished (#5).

Lower-Class Religion in Jamaica

The religions of lower-class Blacks in Jamaica are rooted in slave society. While French and Spanish planters had their slaves converted, the British resisted, with the rationale that once a slave became a Christian, the planter could no longer consider him or her a slave (Augier and Gordon 1962, 94). Missionaries' work with the slaves was discouraged and finally prohibited in some British territories. A law passed in Jamaica in 1807 forbade "the practice of such pretended preaching, teaching and expounding the Holy Scriptures" to "persons of colour, and negroes of free condition, and slaves" (Augier and Gordon 1962, 95-96). The humanitarian movement in England that pressured the government to abolish first the slave trade and finally slavery itself was led in part by members of the sects dissenting from the Church of England, and as its effectiveness increased, so did planters' hostility towards the missionaries in the colonies.

Thus slaves were not exposed to alternatives to African religions until quite late. Although the slaves came from diverse tribes in Western Africa, some common beliefs and practices formed the basis of a folk religion. Two types of powerful individuals were among the slaves that were imported. The first was the Obeah-men and -women, who were capable of sorcery or black magic. The second were priests and priestesses capable of exorcizing the spells of the Obeah, and these became known as Myal. The ritual dance supervised by the Myal is known as the Kumina, and the rituals followed are similar to the Vodun of Haiti, Santeria of Cuba, and the Shango cult of Nigeria (Barrett 1977, 17).

Christianity was introduced to the slaves through the efforts of missionaries representing the Moravians, who came to Jamaica in 1734; the Methodists, in 1736; the Baptists, in 1783; and the Presbyterians, in 1823 (Barrett

1977, 20). The slaves recognized the efforts of the missionaries in the abolitionist movement and joined these denominations in considerable numbers (Barrett 1977, 21). But the missionaries never completely converted the slave population. Instead, some elements of Christianity fused with some elements of Myal to create the wide array of religious cults characteristic of Jamaica's lower class today. The Afro-Christian syncretic cults range from Pocomania (or Pukkumina), an almost purely African religion, through the Revival Cult and such denominations as Native Baptists, that combined elements of the two, to the more mildly syncretic fundamentalist sects.

The Great Revival of 1860-61 consolidated Afro-Christian syncretism. The revival occurred during the period of severe deprivations that had also contributed to the Morant Bay Rebellion. The missionaries were suddenly unable to cope with the demand for their services, but, as Curtin wrote, "What appeared to have been a missionary hope, turned out to be a missionary's despair" (1955, 68). It had become clear that Kumina influences were gaining the upper hand in the mixture of elements and the new syncretic cults were attracting more converts than the European missionaries.

The Revival Cult was a product of this and later revivals, and is still strong in Jamaica today (Simpson 1955, 1970; Seaga 1969). It is practiced in groups of twenty to two hundred followers, called a "band," that is led by a "shepherd." His or her assistants include a warrior shepherd, who protects the band from evil spirits, and the water shepherd, who presides at baptisms. Revival services include singing, dancing, drumming, preaching, and communion. Spirit possession and healing services reminiscent of Kumina are not uncommon among Revivalists (Barrett 1977, 23-24).

In the 1930s, the Pentecostals in the United States began to send missionaries to Jamaica, and these sects have made some headway in Jamaican religious life. The later Evangelical churches that proselytized in Jamaica in the late 1970s have done as wll.

The crossing of religion with politics has a long history in Jamaica. It was said that Sam Sharpe, leader of a slave rebellion in 1831, initiated his warriors into the Myal cult before the rebellion (#13), just as the Jamaican-born slave leader, Boukman, had done with Vodun before leading a rebellion in Haiti in the mid-eighteenth century (Courlander and Bastien 1966). Paul Bogle, who led the Morant Bay Rebellion, was a Native Baptist lay preacher and his tremendous following was attributable to his religious as well as his political leadership. In the era of organized politics, meetings frequently took on the character of religious gatherings. As we will see in chapter 6, the Evangelical preachers took an active role in the 1980 election.

One theme that was often present in the syncretic religions was "Ethiopianism," by which is meant an attention to and fascination with biblical references to Ethiopia. The first Baptist church in Jamaica, founded in 1784, was called the Ethiopian Baptist Church (Barrett 1977, 76), and Ethiopianism reappeared in many of the syncretic cults. It reached a high point in the teachings of Marcus Garvey, who frequently referred to Ethiopia. Garvey described the UNIA as the representative of "'the hopes and aspirations of the awakened Negro. Our desire is for a place in the world; not to disturb the tranquility of other men, but to lay down our burden and rest our weary backs and feet by the banks of the Niger and sing our songs and chant our hymns to the God of Ethiopia'" (Quoted in Barrett 1977, 79). He consistently stressed Psalm 68, which prophesied that "Ethiopia shall stretch forth her hands to God." In an editorial in his newspaper, *Blackman*, he wrote:

> "We have great hopes of Abyssinia in the East -- the country that has kept her tradition even back to the days of Solomon.... They are part of the great African race that is to rise from its handicaps, environments and difficulties to repossess the Imperial authority that is promised by God himself in the inspiration that the Princes shall come out of Egypt and Ethiopia shall stretch forth her hands." (quoted in Campbell 1980, 6)

Before Garvey left Jamaica he allegedly told a Kingston congregation: "Look to Africa for the crowning of a black king; he shall be the Redeemer" (quoted in Barrett 1977,

81). On 2 November, 1930, Ras Tafari was crowned Emperor Haile Selassie I of Ethiopia and accepted the titles dictated by Ethiopian tradition: "King of Kings, Lord of Lords, Conquering Lion of the Tribe of Judah." Several lower-class spiritual leaders in Jamaica began to preach that Selassie was the Messiah, based on Garvey's prophecy and on the fifth chapter of the Book of Revelations, which predicts the loosening of the seven seals and the opening of the book by "the Lion of the tribe of Judah," and Revelations 19, which contains the titles "King of Kings, Lord of Lords." The early followers of these preachers adopted the precoronation name of Selassie and called themselves Ras Tafari. The name was altered by nonmembers to "Rastafarian" or simply "Rasta."

The hope for a speedy repatriation to Ethiopia struck fertile ground in Jamaica. The depression had created social and economic conditions not unlike those of the time of the Great Revival of 1860. Leonard Howell, a Jamaican worker in the Western Kingston area, was among the first to preach the doctrine. Once established in Kingston, he undertook a trip across the island, financed by sales of photographs of Selassie. These were to be people's passports to Ethiopia, and, according to Barrett, Howell sold five thousand at one shilling each in a very short time (1977, 85). Howell was arrested in St. Thomas and charged with sedition, abuse of the governments of Great Britain and Jamaica, and inciting contempt for the king of England. He was jailed for two years, but the activities of his followers continued in secret.

By 1940, Howell was the chief of a Rastafarian commune called Pinnacle, about twenty miles from Kingston. The police raided the commune in 1941 and imprisoned 28 Rastas, including Howell (Barrett 1977, 87). The commune was revived later, and during its second period the men began to wear their hair like the Masai warriors of East Africa, uncombed and uncut. The commune cultivated ganja (marijuana) as a cash crop and began to use it ritually. In 1954 the police raided the commune again, arresting 163. Many of the followers then returned to Western Kingston, the birthplace of the cult, and settled in the Back-o'-Wall section. They became known as "dreadlocks" because of their frightening appearance, and were constantly in conflict with the police. They "roamed the streets like madmen calling down fire and brimstone on Babylon, using the most profane language to shock the conservative establishment. Their wild behavior attracted large audiences and their Rastafarian rhetoric of defiance made their presence felt in Kingston. Although many were shocked by their appearance and behavior, hundreds of the dispossessed began to receive their message..." (Barrett 1977, 89).

The Rastafarians are a largely unorganized group united only around a few central beliefs. First and foremost is the belief in the divinity of Haile Selassie. He is considered by some as the reincarnated Christ and by most as the invincible man and the living God. Because Selassie's family supposedly descended from King Solomon and the Queen of Sheba, his ascent to the throne was considered a fulfillment of the Old Testament prophecy that the Redeemer would be of the House of David. Rastafari is millenarian in the sense that Selassie is believed to be preparing Ethiopia for the repatriation of the Rastafarians and other African and non-African people.

Second, the Rastas believe that the Bible is the purloined history of the African race, taken by the Europeans at the time of enslavement and deliberately mistranslated in an effort to deceive the slaves. The fact that the British had outlawed the teaching of the Scriptures to the slaves lends credence to this claim among the brethren (#36). When the Europeans finally did teach the Scriptures, they taught Blacks "sky-gazing" religion; that is, looking for redemption after death rather than here on earth. As one Rasta told Owen: "'What did hide from the wise and the prudent, it now reveal to I-n-I (us), the babe and the suckling. Because what them did tell the people of sky-gazing and Jesus, they can't come tell I-n-I that in this time'" (quoted in Owen 1976, 268). Reggae songs by Rastafarian musicians sometimes express similar sentiments against Christianity. For example, Bob Marley in a 1974 song called "Talking Blues," sang:

> *I'm gonna take just one step more*
> *Cause I feel like bombing a church*
> *Now that you know that the preacher is lying.*

In a 1978 song, Peter Tosh called Christian preachers the "devil in disguise" and their doctrines "fantasy, a whole pack of ignorancy."

Third, the Old Testament history of the Israelites' captivity in Babylon is interpreted as prophecy of the period of African slavery and continuing Black poverty in the New World. The Rastas consider Blacks the true descendants of the ancient Hebrews. Jamaica and the West in general are "Babylon"; Ethiopia is "Zion"; and Rastafarians are "strangers in a strange land" (Exodus 2:22).

The Rastas believe in a special significance of the African race, but White Rastafarians became accepted into some Rastafarian groups during the 1970s. Some Rastas believe that the chosen include a "remnant of every nation" and the chosen remnant of the African nation consists of the Rastafarians themselves.

The symbols of the Rastafarians include, most noticeably, the long, uncombed locks by which they are readily identified. The reasons given for the locks are first that the laws of the Nazarites in the Book of Numbers (6: 1-7) forbid cutting the hair; second, that it is the style of Ethiopian tribal warriors and priests; and finally, it is a symbol of the lion's mane. A non-Rastafarian may be referred to as a "baldhead," but not all Rastas wear the locks. The hairstyle also has local significance. Black and Brown Jamaicans who were concerned about emulating British ways often straightened their hair, and a mulatto child was considered particularly lucky if he or she had "good" or straight hair. In contrast, dreadlocks are a veritable celebration of the very characteristics of African hair that Anglophiliacs considered "bad." It is interesting to note that a very common method of police harassment of Rastafarians was and is to cut off their locks, indicating that the hairstyle had some significance for the agents of "Babylon" as well as the Rastafarians.

Other symbols used frequently by the Rastas are those of Ethiopia, such as the national colors, red, gold, and green, and the lion that appears on that country's flag. Many Rastafarians are strict vegetarians and follow the dietary laws of the Bible. Food that is acceptable under the laws is called "Ital," meaning natural. Language is an important Rasta symbol in itself, and will be discussed in chapter 4.

Rastafarians smoke a good deal of ganja or herb (marijuana), for which they also find Biblical justification (Gene-
sis 1:12, 3:18; Exodus 10:12; Psalms 104:14).

In the late 1950s or early 1960s, a document called "The
Foundation of the Rastafarian Movement" or the "Twenty-
one Points" was circulated widely in Kingston (Lewis 1977;
Barrett 1977, 148). Using this document as a platform, a
Rastafarian named Sam Brown ran for the Western Kingston seat in Parliament in 1962. He won very few votes,
but, as Barrett argued, his campaign drew the attention of
the elite to the movement. One of the informants for the
present study, a White middle-class journalist, befriended
Sam Brown at the time and mentioned that he thought his
campaign was financed with the proceeds of ganja sales
(#17). A Rastafarian remembered of Sam Brown:

> He was a real original. He ran as an independent.
> People didn't want to have anything to do with
> him. I saw him on his campaign. He wore a
> dashiki; he was into a Pan-African thing, and that
> was the first time I ever saw a dashiki. I didn't
> know what it was called. Usually when a candi-
> date was campaigning, everybody rushes up to
> shake their hand, even people from the other side.
> But nobody was much interested in Sam Brown.
> He lost badly, but he wrote some beautiful poetry.
> (#2)

"Twenty-one Points" presents the Rastafarians as "the
most advanced, determined and uncompromising fighters
against discrimination, ostracism and oppression of black
people in Jamaica," and condemns not only White supremacy but also "Brown-man supremacy." The document
rejects vulgar racialism; a man may be "Black as night" but
"his colour is in our estimation of no avail if he is an
oppressor and destroyer of his people." It commits the
Rastafarian to political activity: "16. The Rastafarian
Movement therefore has decided to actively join the political struggle and create a political movement with the aim
of *taking power* and implement measures for the uplift of
the poor and oppressed" (quoted in Barrett 1977, 149;
emphasis in the original).

The status of the Rastafarians will be updated in the background discussions pertaining to each election (chapters 3 through 6). It may be safely said, however, that at the time of Jamaican independence virtually all Rastafarians were members of the 79 percent of the population that are classified lower class, that the vast majority were of the chronically unemployed section of that class, and that virtually all were Black rather than Brown or White.

Political Institutions

The Morant Bay Rebellion of 1865 sparked a major reorganization in the way that Jamaica was governed. The House of Assembly had been established in 1664 and consisted of twenty members elected by the planters. The body had frequently dissented from the proposals made by the British government, notably those concerning slave reform (Augier and Gordon 1962, 129-30). Eligibility to vote for Assembly representatives was based on property ownership, and by 1865 a number of Brown men, formerly "free coloureds," had become participants in the system. The electorate was still only about 0.5 percent of the population (Curtin 1955).

After the unfavorable report of the British commission studying the Morant Bay Rebellion, the House of Assembly agreed to surrender its rights and privileges and consented that Jamaica should be governed directly by the British crown. The territory became a crown colony, a status it retained until 1962. The Legislative Council was established; it consisted of the governor and nine members appointed by the crown. In 1883, the council was reorganized to include sixteen appointed members and fourteen elected members. Again, property was the eligibility criterion (Gleaner Company 1973, 69). In 1938, virtually all the appointed members were White and the elected members were chosen by fewer than 6 percent of the people (Blanshard 1947, 91).

In the 1930s the effects of the depression worsened the lives of Jamaican workers considerably. In 1935 it was reported that only 18 percent of the total population earned any income, and 92 percent of those employed earned less than 25 shillings (about U.S.$6.25 in 1935 dollars) a week (Phillips 1977, 4). Coercion on the job, low pay, malnutrition, disease, and unemployment had taken their toll and signs of discontent were beginning to alarm the government. A commission was appointed to inquire into the workers' demands, but before it could make its report, spontaneous uprisings and strikes occurred island-wide during May and June of 1938, particularly on the sugar estates and the Kingston docks.

The two founders of modern Jamaican political parties emerged as leaders from these disturbances. The first was Alexander Bustamante, the son of an Irish father and a Brown mother. He left his birthplace in the parish of Hanover in Jamaica as a youth and lived and worked in Panama, Cuba, and New York City. "Busta," as he was known, was born Alexander Clarke, but changed his name in order to "pass" as a White native of Spain while in New York City. He was very fair-skinned and was successful at "passing" (Blanshard 1947, 95).

Bustamante returned to Jamaica in the mid-1930s and gained acclaim as a speaker of considerable magnetism and as an inveterate writer of letters to the *Gleaner* about the benefits of eating raw vegetables as well as about the conditions of labor in Jamaica (Blanshard 1947, 95). He was involved in the disturbances of 1938 as a champion of the workers' cause and was jailed as a result of his activity. He emerged as a hero and took the lead in organizing the labor union known as the Bustamante Industrial Trade Union (BITU). He appointed himself president-for-life of the union, and published a weekly paper with his own picture on the front of every issue (Blanshard 1947, 96).

The second political leader was Bustamante's cousin and early ally, Norman Washington Manley. Manley was a Rhodes scholar and lawyer whose interests lay more in the causes of self-government and universal suffrage than in the labor movement per se (Nettleford 1971, xxxix). Riding the crest of the wave of activity that the 1938 disturbances had created, Manley founded the People's National Party (PNP) the same year.

Bustamante was detained between September 1940 and February 1942 by the British authorities because of his work with the labor union. During his internment, Manley and the PNP hierarchy continued to look after the trade union and succeeded in bringing the membership up from 8,000 to 20,000 (Hurwitz and Hurwitz 1971, 198), but the sharp differences in style between the autocratic and self-educated Bustamante and the Fabian socialist intellectual Manley soon broke the delicate alliance between the two leaders. When Bustamante was released from detention, he denounced the PNP caretakers of the BITU as "traitors and conspirators" (DG 2/21/42). Manley in turn accused Bustamante of having made a deal with the British to destroy the PNP in return for being released from detention (Nettleford 1971, xl).

The PNP continued to press for constitutional change and universal suffrage, and these were granted in 1944. Bustamante hastily formed the Jamaica Labour Party (JLP) in 1943, but "in the early years (the JLP) was little more than a transformed BITU designed for election purposes" (Nettleford 1971, xxx).

Manley conceived the PNP as destined to play the role that the Congress Party had in India, and modeled it after the British Labour Party. Middle-class professionals and intelligentsia formed its earliest leadership, but a minority of the planters and some urban working class members were among its earliest supporters. The party executive began consciously to build its mass base in 1942, when many members of the party's left wing had gained membership in the General Council (Nettleford 1971, xlv). The unions organized by the PNP in opposition to the BITU were grouped in the Trade Union Council (TUC).

Meanwhile, the JLP drew on Bustamante's enormous popularity among urban and rural workers, but also gained some White supporters, who

> were gratified by his political views. He supported the British Empire as a God-given instrument of democratic rule, and attacked socialism, communism, birth control and atheism with undiscriminating frenzy. Many conservatives supported him privately because they thought that his crude type of mass dictatorship was less dangerous to their property rights than the opposition labor movement led by Norman Manley. Manley was almost everything that Bustamante was not, a scholarly socialist with a mass appeal in the British tradition. (Blanshard 1947, 96)

Neither Bustamante nor Manley could be considered anti-British. Lindsay pointed out that at the founding conference of the PNP, there was "pronounced hostility from both the platform and the floor... because (Sir Stafford) Cripps in his speech had been severely critical of the British colonial government and its oppressive and exploitative practices toward colonies such as Jamaica" (1975, 15). The conference ended with an "enthusiastic" rendition of "God Save the King."

The first election under universal suffrage was held in 1944. The size of the electorate had increased tenfold. During the election, according to Blanshard, it became "apparent that no white conservative would ever have a reasonable chance of sitting in a Jamaica-elected legislature" (1947, 97). The JLP won twenty-two seats with 41.4 percent of the vote; the PNP won five seats with 23.5 percent. Independents and third parties received 35.1 percent of the popular vote (JIS, 1971); five independents won seats, but no seat went to a third-party candidates. One of the third parties was the Jamaica Democratic Party; it was led by Abe Issa, a Syrian businessman, and was composed almost exclusively of merchants. With 14,000 votes, it lost its bid for a seat and dissolved soon after the election. The third party vote dwindled rapidly to 13.8 percent in 1949, and 10.5 percent in 1955, and has not gained as much as 2 percent of the vote since then.

The PNP's organizing efforts to develop a mass base paid off by the next election, 1949, when the party won a majority of the popular vote but a minority of seats. (Constituencies in Jamaica are bounded in such a way that the JLP has a slight edge, "wasting" fewer votes than the PNP. See Hughes 1978.) The JLP emerged from that election with 17 seats to the PNP's 13 (JIS, 1971). Since 1944, each party has won two terms in office followed by two terms in opposition in an unbroken pattern over nine general elections. According to Jamaica's constitution, elections must be held at least within five years; the incumbent party may chose to hold elections earlier.

The PNP declared for socialism in 1940, and throughout the 1940s encompassed a right and a left wing that were increasingly at odds. The Trade Union Congress finally suffered a split in 1951, when the right-wing leadership resigned and formed the short-lived National Labour Congress. That group attacked the "four Hs," the left-wing leadership, that consisted of Richard Hart, Arthur Henry, and Frank and Ken Hill. The PNP finally voted to expel the four Hs, rewrote its program, and abandoned its overtly socialist orientation. The TUC was dissolved and a new trade union affiliate, the National Workers Union (NWU), was formed (Hurwitz and Hurwitz 1971, 207). Between 1952 and 1974, socialism "remained a guiding principle within the PNP, rather than a platform appeal to the electorate" (Hearne 1976, 153).

Under the PNP from 1955 to 1962, Jamaica moved a few steps further toward independence. In 1959 it became self-governing in all aspects except foreign policy. In 1958 it became part of the Federation of the West Indies. The impetus for federation came from the British, who sought to unify Jamaica, Trinidad and Tobago, Grenada, St. Lucia, Barbados, and a number of other territories. The federation held an election in 1958 and the federation-wide party that Bustamante and the JLP supported won the seats from Jamaica but failed to gain a majority in the Federation Parliament. "Busta," said one informant, "hated to be in the opposition" (#14). In 1961 when Norman Manley called a referendum on the question of maintaining Jamaica's membership in the federation, the JLP campaigned against it. The party used the slogan "Freedom," meaning freedom from the domination of Trinidad in the federation (#9). With a vote of 54.1 percent against and 45.9 percent for, Jamaica decided to withdraw from the federation.

Jamaica's party leaders met with the British government later that year and the conference resulted in a date being set for Jamaica's independence: 6 August, 1962. Bustamante was returned to power in April 1962 and led the country to formal political independence.

In his paper "The Myth of Independence," Lindsay argues that independence was "mythical" in the sense that Britain granted independence only after it was assured of the loyalty to the West on the part of the leadership of the two political parties. He wrote that in Jamaica and other colonial territories,

European imperial powers pacified and placated
colonial discontent by offering the myth while
withholding the reality of national political sovereignty....   To ... those who inherit the formal
offices of state, symbolic political independence
is critical as a strategic manipulative device....
(It) strengthens the prestige of incumbent post-
independence leaders vis-a-vis those who seek to
challenge their authority, and increases the capacity of these leaders to maintain a status quo in
which they inherit not simply the titles, but also a
good deal of the benefits and rewards formerly
enjoyed by metropolitan overlords. (1975, 2-4)

It is true that independence was "granted" to Jamaica
rather than won by its people after a long struggle. It was
negotiated by middle- and upper-class descendants of the
"free coloured" section of plantation society who were
unlikely to challenge the Western democratic form of
government or the power of foreign investors.

Race and Class in Jamaican Political Parties

Jamaica's two main political parties are not class parties, nor are they associated more with one ethnic group
than another. The leadership of both the JLP and the PNP
was dominated by Brown members of the middle class.
However, subtle class differences of the two first leaders
of the parties became reflected in characteristics of the
organizations they led.
The JLP leadership was dominated by Bustamante, a
Brown independent property owner (Stone 1976, 182), but,
as one informant said, "the masses" always had had representatives in the JLP. The first minister of agriculture,
Isaac Barrant, was said to be functionally illiterate, and a
number of early JLP members of Parliament (MPs) were of
small-peasant stock (#13). The JLP was seen as the "little
man's party" (#9) or the "small man's party" (#26).
Bustamante was a populist leader in the sense that he
presented himself as a representative of the "common"
people without a rigorous ideology that challenged the

economic status quo. Although he had a sizable income, he was known to be uneducated. One oft-repeated story tells of his making a speech in which he did not excel in spelling out the people's demands. He shouted from the platform, "My people want bread! B-R-E-D, bread!" (DG 10/26/80, 24). One Rastafarian informant remembered Busta as the "champion of the grass roots" who had increased sugar workers' daily wages from ninepence to one shilling six (#1).

A JLP supporter implied that the JLP was more representative of the African section of Jamaica, when he used the word *Quashi*, meaning a "poor, ignorant Black, usually from the country" (#7), to describe JLP supporters: "The PNP used to refer to the JLP as 'Dutty (dirty) Labourites,' the party of the ignorant, which by implication made the JLP the party of the African creole. Obviously, in a democracy there is a limit to the extent that that characterization is feasible. If the Labour Party is the 'Quashi' party, the masses are 'Quashi' in this country" (#5).

The "small-man" orientation was evident in the symbols that the JLP used. The party's original election symbol was the hand, interpreted by informants as representative of unskilled, manual labor (#9, #13, #29). The earliest party songs were adapted from digging songs and Revivalist hymns (#6).

The JLP or, more accurately, the Bustamante Industrial Trade Union, won the support of the poorest sector of society in the early days of universal suffrage, as well as that of the wealthiest sector, which feared Manley's socialism. The PNP gained ground among the sectors between those two groups, especially in the Corporate Area among the urban working class.

The PNP leadership was also a product of the middle class but the party differed from the JLP in that it attracted the intelligentsia, who are considered members of the middle class on the basis of the prestige of their educational status rather than wealth alone. Almost all of the PNP's nineteen candidates in 1944 had received secondary education, an advantage enjoyed by only 2.8 percent of Jamaicans in that time (Phillips 1977, 5). With Norman Manley, the erudite lawyer and Rhodes scholar, at the helm, the party was identified as the party of intellectuals. One JLP informant said that the PNP was associated with "the well-to-do elements in society, essentially scholars and middle class white collar workers, who had studied in England and who felt that only they had acquired a fitness to rule, having sat at the feet of scholars of the Mother Country" (#29). The PNP was the "middle class, more intellectual urban party" (#9) and "the party for people who wanted to be considered respectable, decent and intelligent" (#5). The head was seen as an apt ballot symbol; it "signified the brainy party" (#25). "The head meant the brain. They used to say Use your head, vote PNP and Wise men vote PNP, fools vote JLP" (#29).

Just as the PNP used the JLP's "small man" image against it, by denigrating its supporters as "dutty labourites," the JLP took advantage of the PNP's affiliation with the educated middle class and characterized the PNP as the "brown man government," even though, of course, many leaders of the Labour Party, including Bustamante, were Brown as well. One informant said that Bustamante had campaigned in 1944 and 1949 with the slogan "Self Government Means Slavery":

> what he implied was "Self government meant brown man slavery." The masses distrusted the brown men. The JLP's slogan "freedom" meant "freedom from brown man oppression." The average Jamaican worker sees the brown man as the oppressor, because he sees the brown man every day. They would rather have "Missus Queen," who freed them from slavery, than the brown man whom they are constantly in touch with. (#13)

From the early days of universal suffrage, the PNP had had the support of the middle class, particularly the civil servants and the "intelligentsia." But, as the party discovered in the 1944 election, these groups alone could not sustain the party when the electorate was overwhelmingly lower class. By 1949, the PNP had made significant gains in support among the urban working class in Kingston and in towns across the country. In 1959, for example, the PNP won 58.6 percent of the small-town vote and 57.7 percent of the main-road rural areas, while the JLP won the majority in the rural areas that were not close to the main roads (Stone, DG 6/8/80, 7).

In 1967, the first election under study here, the JLP retained the support of the richest and the poorest communities in the Corporate Area. Those in between, including the better-off section of the lower class and the groups defined above as middle class, supported the PNP (Stone, DG 6/8/80, 7). The changes in class support of the parties since then is a major theme of this research.

Besides the slogans, promises, and symbols of the political parties, preelection periods have long been characterized by political violence. Intimidation of the other party's supporters, disruption of political meetings, and other forms of violence are tactics that have been employed in elections since 1944. Especially in the mid-1960s, a number of members of the lower class were armed with guns and were paid retainers by the parties to "protect" other party supporters (Lacey 1977, 32ff.). In some cases, entire gangs were co-opted by the parties. The factional violence they perpetrated was mostly confined to Western Kingston at first but gradually spread through the slum areas in the late 1960s. By 1976 and 1980, there were many incidents of violence outside these areas, in rural areas and in other sections of the Corporate Area. In the everyday speech of Jamaica, the phenomenon is known as "tribal war."

One informant (#40) explained in detail the tactics used by the party "thugs." In a neighborhood with mixed political affiliation, individuals employed by party A would paint slogans on the zinc fence walls of dwellings occupied by suspected supporters of party B. If the slogans were washed off or painted over, the house would be firebombed or its residents otherwise terrorized. People were told that the ballot paper was thin enough that their choice of candidate would be discernible, and that retaliation would be forthcoming if they voted the wrong way. As a result of the use of these tactics over a period of ten or fifteen years, some neighborhoods are party strongholds; those who deviated were driven out or moved on to more compatible surroundings.

Space permits only a brief background of Jamaica's history and present social structure. It is hoped that the material presented in this chapter is sufficient background to give the non-Caribbean reader a sense of the historical context of the five election campaigns that are the main subject of this book. The changes in class and race relations, in the status of Rastafarians, and in political party leadership, that preceded each election, will be presented within the chapters on the elections themselves.

3

The 1967 Election

Jamaica's first general election as an independent nation was not a "critical" election in the sense that it involved major realignments of large groups or categories of voters, but the parties were clearly in transition, from the founding leadership to a younger leadership and perhaps from traditional class coalitions to new combinations of support. The results of the election are summarized in Table 3.1. Compared with the 1962 election, the JLP gained only 0.7 percent more of the popular vote, but its percentage of parliamentary seats rose from 58 percent to 63 percent.

Information from respondents was weakest for this election, for understandable reasons. Many were school-children when it took place, and those who were politically aware do not recall as much about this election as about later ones. Several respondents who are JLP supporters now backed the PNP in 1967, and were reticent about their involvement during the period. Two left-wing activists were abroad in 1967 precisely because the political situation at the time impeded their living and working freely at home.

The *Gleaner* offered little election coverage; only eight reports about party meetings appeared over the month

Table 3.1
Results, 1967 General Election

Electors on roll 543,307

Ballots cast 446,815 (82.24%)

Accepted ballots 442,472

Party Share	Popular Vote	Percentage	Seats
Jamaica Labour Party	224,180	(50.65%)	33
People's National Party	217,207	(49.08%)	20
Independents	844	(0.19%)	0
Three minor parties	341	(0.08%)	0

Source: Chief Electoral Officer's Report, 1967.

before the elections. Columnists who wrote about politics usually wrote anonymously, but respondents who were familiar with the *Gleaner* were able to identify them.

Paid political advertisements were plentiful and are summarized in Table 3.2. Although the PNP had a greater total number, most were small and only three full-page advertisements were placed in the *Gleaner*, compared with the JLP's twenty-eight. Of the constituency ads, the PNP made a special effort in Central Kingston, where the party leader's son, Michael Manley, was standing elections for the first time.

The plan of this chapter is to present, first, a brief historical review that will update the changes in political leadership and the cast of characters involved in the election, the advent of recorded indigenous popular music, and the changing status of Rastafari. The campaigns will be then examined with respect to their use of class, race,

Table 3.2
Summary of 268 Election Items in
Daily Gleaner, January-February 1967

	People's National Party	Jamaica Labour Party
Reports of Meetings	8	3
Advertisements		
General		
Full page	3	28
Large, not full page	20	3
Small	9	0
Fund-raising (small)	16	0
Broadcast Announcements	18	14
Specific Constituencies		
Western Kingston	6	0
Central Kingston	20	7
Eastern Kingston	0	2
W.R.St.Andrew	5	0
S.W.St.Andrew	9	4
N.St.Andrew	1	5
W.C.St.Andrew	3	1
E.C.St.Andrew	4	5
S.St.Andrew	0	5
Others	2	6
Other Ads	1	3
Total Advertisements	117	83
Other Items		57

anticolonialism, and Rastafarian symbols and music.   A discussion follows.

Historical Background

The Parties in 1967

The period preceding the 1967 elections saw the ascent to powerful positions of several young politicians who would later become leaders in their parties. Bustamante had long dominated the JLP and the BITU, and was apparently secure enough in his position as "The Chief" to recruit able administrators without feeling his own power base threatened. As one respondent put it, "No one questioned who was leader. Busta could bring in anyone. If Churchill had been in Jamaica, Busta would have tried to bring him into the JLP" (#6).

Bustamante's illness in 1965 and consequent retirement from active politics created a power vacuum; no single member of the JLP leadership was unambi guously second in command. He remained the symbolic head of the party, but several others assumed important duties. Ascending to the post of acting prime minister was Sir Donald Sangster, a solicitor and former minister of social welfare from a well-to-do, rural, Brown family. He became prime minister after the 1967 elections, but died suddenly two months later.

A more important figure of the period was Edward Seaga, who was in charge of publicity for the JLP in 1967. A Boston-born product of Syrian-Jamaican (White) parentage, Seaga had returned to Jamaica after graduation from Harvard College. Seaga had been a student of sociology and folklore, and had undertaken studies of Revival cults and other aspects of Jamaican culture, during which he resided among the peasants of St. Catherine and among the urban poor in the slums of Western Kingston. He joined the JLP in the late 1950s and was appointed by Bustamante to the Legislative Council in 1959.

In 1962 Seaga was the successful JLP candidate for the constituency of Western Kingston, one of the most troublesome constituencies in the Corporate Area and probably the poorest, and blackest, constituency in Jamaica.   It encompassed a large squatters' district called Back-o'-Wall, where Rastafarians lived in considerable numbers. Although most very poor districts in the Corporate Area tended to support the Labour Party, Back-o'-Wall was one that supported the PNP.

During Seaga's fieldwork he had gained the respect and admiration of the Revivalists with whom he had come into contact, and he had become a consecrated shepherd of the Revivalist cult (DG 10/5/80, 15). Two respondents who knew the period stated that Seaga had presented himself as a "roots man" and a Revivalist (#6, #12). Seaga was the owner of a recording company that produced some of the earliest reggae music, West Indies Records (#2). Bustamante was said to fear Seaga's alleged involvement in Obeah (#6). Although Syrian-Jamaicans tended to marry within their ethnic group, Seaga married a Brown Jamaican woman, the winner of a "Miss Jamaica" beauty contest that Seaga, as minister of development and welfare, had organized. The Seagas adopted a Black child and have two children of their own. Thus their family portrait provides a symbol in itself of multiracial harmony.

Besides Seaga's mastery of Afro-Jamaican culture, his Boston upbringing and Harvard education are traits that are appealing to some other Jamaicans. One respondent reported a conversation that he had had with Donald Sangster in the early 1960s. Sangster had said that Bustamante had recruited Seaga because the JLP needed "brains" (#6). Seaga was reportedly responsible for the introduction of several Western symbols into the JLP repertoire; the party changed its electoral symbol from the hand to a liberty bell copied directly from the Philadelphia version in the early 1960s.

Seaga became minister of development and welfare after the 1962 election, and as such was in a position to permanently change the face of his constituency. In 1966, under an ambitious development plan, Back-o'-Wall was completely destroyed; its inhabitants were driven out of their homes without notice by bulldozers and a regiment of 250 well-armed police, according to one eyewitness (Barrett 1977, 156-57). The razed and burned squatters' camps were replaced by a planned lower-class community housing development called Tivoli Gardens. Tivoli won the praises of the United Nations Educational, Scientific and Cultural Organization (UNESCO) as a model of "womb-to-tomb" community development, and reaped the rancor of the displaced residents, including two major groups of Rastafarians. The period was characterized as the height of political patronage, and it is not denied by JLP respondents that the apartments in the Tivoli Gardens complex were granted exclusively to JLP supporters.

The success of Seaga's "empire-building" (#7) is reflected in the unprecedented electoral success he enjoys in the Western Kingston constituency. In a district in which no incumbent had ever been reelected, Seaga has been re-elected four times since 1962; in 1980 fully 99.6 percent of the voters in the Tivoli Gardens area, and 94 percent of all voters in the constituency voted for the JLP (Director of Elections 1980). One respondent, possibly exaggerating somewhat, said that Seaga has not held a single political rally in his constituency since 1962; it has not been necessary to the maintenance of his support (#5).

In 1959 Seaga made a budget speech in Parliament that won him considerable national publicity. He condemned a society that perpetuated divisions between the "haves" and the "have nots." As a result of that speech and his reputation as minister of development and welfare, one respondent said, "Seaga was seen as a champion of the poor man. The PNP was supposed to be a socialist party but had tried to drop that image. Seaga was seen as a symbol of hope, and as a radical" (#13). Although Sangster was chosen to succeed Bustamante as the leader of the JLP, it was clear by 1967 that Seaga was part of the party's inner circle.

Another rising notable in the Labour Party was Hugh Shearer, another Brown Jamaican, who succeeded Sangster as prime minister in April of 1967. Shearer's political career began in 1944, when he campaigned for Bustamante in the first general elections based on universal suffrage. Unlike Seaga, Shearer had a source of power in the Bustamante Industrial Trade Union (BITU), of which he was island supervisor in 1953 and vice president since 1960. The BITU was particularly important because it formed the JLP's only organizational base; the party has no branch structure (#13). Rather than Sangster, it was Shearer who shared Bustamante's union orientation and who seemed his natural successor. As one supporter put it in a letter to the editor of the *Gleaner* in 1972, during the 1930s "the Lord looked down from his throne above and saw the need of His people. He sent a deliverer to deliver us out of our bondage... Our Moses is still alive today ... and his great knowledge, wisdom and understanding have been passed on to Mr. Hugh Shearer" (DG 2/26/72; 18).

Although Norman Manley remained healthy and in control of the People's National Party, his son Michael gained growing recognition as a trade unionist. Michael Manley was educated at the London School of Economics and worked briefly in London for the British Broadcasting Company before returning to Jamaica in 1951. In 1955 he was elected first vice president of the National Workers' Union (NWU), and in 1962, president of the Caribbean Bauxite and Mineworkers Union. In 1964, he led the striking staff of the Jamaica Broadcasting Corporation (JBC) in colorful and dramatic acts of civil disobedience, which won for him the sobriquet "Joshua," by which he has been called since. The strike also marked the beginning of a lasting personal rivalry; the minister responsible for the firings that precipitated the strike was Seaga (Manley 1975, 153ff.). The 1967 election was Michael Manley's first; he had been appointed to the Senate in 1962.

Michael Manley is frequently perceived as White by foreign journalists and indeed could "pass" as White without difficulty. His mother, Edna Manley, is a White British-born woman, and Norman Manley was a Brown Jamaican. The Jamaican electorate is, of course, intimately familiar with the younger Manley's family background, and he is considered Brown in Jamaica, just as Alexander Bustamante, with a similar racial phenotype, was.

Another party development that preceded the 1967 election was the founding of the "Young Socialists." The PNP had almost always had a left wing despite its expulsion of the "Four Hs" in the early 1950s; it had never completely disavowed socialism and some of its members identified with Marxist ideologies. One respondent said that the "communist faction" of the NWU comprised organizers with "a first class approach to working class organising. They didn't preach communism, but they really got the

PNP across to the working class through the trade union" (#14).

In 1963-64, several PNP members formed the Young Socialist Alliance, and some members of this group were expelled from the party after being critical of the direction of Norman Manley's leadership (#6). During and after the 1967 election, there were negative references to the PNP's Left tendencies, some focusing on this group. A JLP supporter wrote a letter to the *Gleaner* that claimed if the PNP won, it would mean "goodbye to American handouts" and that American tourists would stay home because of the PNP's "communist" philosophy (DG 2/6/67, 16). A JLP advertisement asked, "Who trusts the PNP? Not You, Not Me! The country cannot trust their socialism" (DG 2/17/67, 32).

Rather than seek to apologize for the JLP's lack of a coherent ideology, Sangster accused the PNP of dealing in "fairy tales" and "dreams of a socialist or communist economy," and said that the JLP had "no wish to dissipate the energies of the Jamaican people... in a will-o-the-wisp chase after doctrinaire theories and outmoded and, indeed, discarded methods" (DG 2/15/67, 29).

The Advent of Indigenous Recorded Music

Most popular music in Jamaica before 1967 was imported rhythm and blues from the United States (Clarke 1980, 60ff.). Records by Black American artists such as Percy Sledge, Joe Tex, Otis Redding, and Fats Domino were broadcast on Jamaican radio shows, and occasionally the artists made personal appearances in Kingston (e.g. DG 1/22/67, 17). Many of the early records by Jamaican artists were remakes of American songs with minor lyric changes to add a local flavor.

Throughout the 1960s most popular music reached its consumers through a unique arrangement called the "sound system." Because few could afford their own records and equipment, record store owners took powerful equipment — an amplifier of three hundred or more watts and five to ten speakers — and set up the systems in yards and villages for community dances, charging two to five shillings admission (White 1967, 42).

In the early to mid-1960s, the sound system owners turned to local talent. They began to produce records in two-track recording rooms in record shops and electronic equipment stores. Although the sound systems were in the hands of no more than a dozen or so owners, popular music was a decentralized activity. The majority of records, even successful ones, were first recordings by artists who never made a second. And countless records, cheaply manufactured of poor quality materials, were produced. As one respondent, a Rastafarian reggae musician, remarked: "Everyone in Jamaica can go and do a record. It's not like America where people don't know how it happen. In Jamaica you can just go ask any man 'pon the street how fi (to) make a record, and they know. They all do it. No more secret" (#36).

A novel about Jamaican hard times, based on a movie made in 1972, reflected several aspects of the music industry. The hero, a poor youth from the country, comes to Kingston with a dream of becoming a reggae superstar. He records a hit record, but the producer will not release it to the radio stations until the artist signs a contract by which he will receive $20 and no royalties (Thelwell 1980). One of the best and most popular reggae artists reported that his band had had ten singles on the charts in 1966, for which the band was paid a total of sixty pounds (Davis and Simon 1977). A collector of reggae records, who grew up in the slums of Kingston, said that at that time people sold records out of paper bags on the street, and that these were sometimes ten times better than what could be bought in the stores, and cheaper because the musicians sold the records at wholesale prices. "If they were hungry," he added, "even cheaper" (#2).

The first type of urban popular music to evolve in Jamaica was "ska," a jazz-influenced dance music. Although most early ska was instrumental, some selections, such as "Gun Fever," "Rude Boy" by the Wailers, and "Copasetic," were reflections of a subculture of urban lower class youth, called "rudies" or "rude bwais" (boys). One observer wrote in 1967:

Ska is one means of expression of the "lower class." It is propagandistic music and with in-

creasing force it has acquired the role of commentator on the society. It is now reflecting the
increased militancy of the class it generally represents.... Whatever the middle and upper
classes may have to say about the quality of ska
presentations, their usefulness as indicators of the
thought of the other society -- predominantly
Black — cannot be overemphasized. (White 1967,
41-42)

In 1966, factional fighting between gangs who supported
one or the other of the major parties had increased to such
a degree that the government felt justified in calling a
state of emergency (DG 1/8/67). The themes of both the
fighting and the government's reaction to it appeared in
ska songs of the period. The Rulers in their song "Copasetic" (i.e. correct, proper) call attention to the state of
emergency. "Gun Fever" by Baba Brooks also noted the
presence of "blam-blam-blam":

> Did you read the news, I'm a bit confused
> The gun fever is back
> Rudeness and guns, is the talk of the town
> The gun fever is back
> Every time you read the Gleaner or Star
> Is man shot dead or rudie make war
> It's the fever, the gun fever
> The simplest thing is blam-blam-blam
> What is this on our little island?
> It's the fever, the gun fever

"Carry Go Bring Come" by Justin Hinds and the Domi-
noes may be called a mild protest song. It chose the
biblical quotation "The meek shall inherit the earth," and
ends with the cryptic question, "How long shall the wicked
reign over my people?" The title is a patois phrase
meaning rumormongering, which, according to the song,
"brings misery." This song, particularly its last line, was
used often in the campaigns. "The Train Is Coming" by Ken
Booth, another song that was used by politicians, has
something of a millenarian aspect to it. It promises: "We

are leaving on the train / And we will roam this land /Where we all will be free."

Shortly before the 1967 election, the beat slowed down. Musicians began to play what was called "rock steady." The first rock-steady record released, in my respondents' memories, was "Sounds and Pressure" by Hopeton Lewis. It was very successful and was followed by a second in the same style, called "Take It Easy." Both tunes were about music: the first described a dance; the second was about the new, slower, "easier" rhythm itself. These songs were the first and sixth most popular in Jamaica at the time of the 1967 election, (DG 1/22/67, 6) and both played a role in the campaigns.

The Status of Rastafarians in 1967

Rastafarians in 1967 were still subject to the derision and scorn of the Jamaican middle class and rural lower class (#9, #20), despite two events that heightened their visibility and corrected some myths about their subculture. When Simpson studied the cult in 1955, he found that the attitude of most middle-class Jamaicans toward the Rastas was one of "contempt and disgust." "There seems to be no fear of a Ras Tafari uprising, but it is widely believed that members of this cult are psychopaths and dangerous criminals. Rastafarians are often referred to as 'those dreadful people'" (Simpson 1955, 144).

The first improvement of the status of the Rasta was the publication of a University College of the West Indies (UCWI) report about the movement. In 1960 a number of Rastas living in Kingston appealed to the college to assist them in various ways and to publicize accurate information about their doctrines. In response, and with Premier Norman Manley's encouragement, three UCWI staff members spent two weeks with the brethren. Their published report included recommendations that the government of Jamaica send a mission to Africa to arrange for the immigration of those Rastas who desired to return to the Mother Continent, and that the police "cease to persecute peaceful Ras Tafari brethren" (Smith, Augier, and Nettleford 1960, 38). As one respondent, a JLP councilor, said, the report had an impact on the attitudes of the middle class:

> The Rastas were frowned on until the 1960 study. The study presented Rasta to the public as something other than criminals. I grew up in a house near a Rasta, and I always thought of him, and any locksman, as a thief. He was said to steal chickens, and he may have — he probably needed to. For most of the middle class, we don't bother to probe much. The professors pointed out that Rastas have non-criminal qualities. (#9)

A second event that brought the Rastafarians to the attention of the public in a positive light was the visit of Haile Selassie to Jamaica on 21 April 1966. An estimated 100,000 Jamaicans, many of the Rasta brethren dressed in white, greeted the emperor at the airport. Their sheer numbers created a potentially dangerous situation. A journalist who covered the event for the *Gleaner* described it this way:

> The Rastas had been there all night and you could get high just smelling the airport. When the plane came in, the crowd just imploded around the plane. Legitimate authority was helpless. Selassie was paralyzed with fear. He realized they were adoring him, but he also knew that he could be loved to death. Busta, Shearer and N.W. (Norman Manley) all tried to get them under control. It was the most terrifying demonstration of mass good nature I'd ever seen. Finally, two Rasta leaders escorted Selassie out of the plane. (#17)

The lack of trouble and the show of cooperation during the visit helped create an atmosphere of tolerance, if not goodwill, extended to the Rastas by the middle class.

When the 1967 elections took place, Rastafarians had yet to achieve the political role and the visibility that they took on one or two years later. Many of the followers of the doctrine kept their hair trimmed, instead of wearing dreadlocks, to avoid persecution by the police. Only in 1968 and 1969 did many young people begin to grow locks (#2).

The 1967 Election Campaigns

Overall Strategies, Slogans, and Symbols

The symbols used by the parties in the 1967 election were mostly those relied upon in past elections. The bell of the JLP, the silhouette head of the PNP, and the PNP's broom symbol and slogan "Sweep them out!" had all been in existence during the previous election (WG 2/8/67, 8).

The JLP depended on the charisma of its chief, Bustamante. The decision about when to hold elections, the prerogative of the party in power, had depended on his health. When it became clear that he would not be well enough to run for Parliament again, the JLP faced elections for the first time since 1944 without the dynamic leadership of its founder. The JLP chose to hold elections three days before Bustamante's birthday, announcing that the party wanted to give him a birthday present in the form of a JLP victory (WG 2/1/67, 1). The *Gleaner's* political reporter called the JLP's choice of an election date "basically expedient," and noted that nothing impeded the use by a party in office of any sentimental circumstance to strengthen its election prospects: "Charismatic leadership is still a factor in Jamaica's politics and the JLP ... is making the fullest use of the prestigious political personality of its old 'Chief' in the elections next month" (WG 2/8/67, 8).

Both parties used similar means to get their electoral messages across. Both used paid political advertising in the *Daily Gleaner*, although, as noted already, the PNP used many small advertisements and many for particular constituencies, while the JLP used many full-page advertisements. Both used printed stickers, and shirts, buttons, and placards with slogans, and both organized mass meetings, called "monster meetings." Both utilized religious themes and proverbs, and both borrowed slogans and symbols from the American civil rights movement. Each party also played upon the slogans of the other party. For example, a current PNP song was "We Shall Overcome,"

which of course includes the words "Deep in our hearts /We
do believe / That we shall overcome one day." In the JLP
advertisements, the slogan "Deep in your hearts you are
satisfied with the JLP government" appeared frequently,
and in a broadcast Seaga said, "I love to hear the PNP sing
'We shall overcome' while their followers say, 'We shall
come over'" (DG 2/15/67, 8).   Sangster, warning of the
coming elections, said, "We have overcome" (DG 1/17/67).
Likewise, a primary slogan for the JLP was "The JLP has
done more for you since nineteen hundred and sixty-two."
PNP advertisements replied, "More for WHO?   More for
government ministers" (DG 2/2/67, 9).

Similarly, each party utilized the symbols of the other in
its own propaganda to denigrate the other party. The JLP
had long used the V-sign, signifying victory. In one public
meeting the PNP's Ken McNeill said the V-sign of the JLP
meant "Violence, Victimization, and Vandalism" (DG
2/16/67, 27), and P.J. Patterson said that bell ringing
indicated the death of the JLP (DG 2/2/67, 5). A common
PNP symbol was the broom, along with the slogan "Sweep
them out!" The broom was a household object that any
lower-class family owned and could bring along to a rally,
which PNP supporters did in large numbers (WG 2/1/67,
24). According to Jamaican folklore, when one wished an
unwanted spirit or human to leave one's house, one sprinkled a broom with salt and turned it upside down behind the
door (#14). But a letter from a JLP supporter reminded
readers of the broom's Western symbolism. He said the
broom was "connected with the legends of witches in the
older days.... The broom-carriers in this political campaign
remind me of those witches that were being destroyed and
burnt for their ungodly misdeeds. I would like to appeal to
the voters not to be bewitched by false promises from the
PNP" (DG 2/14/67, 20). In a radio broadcast, Seaga said
that PNP meant "Promise 'N' Propaganda" (DG 2/15/67, 8).

The PNP used the slogan "Vote to be Free, Vote PNP,"
although "Freedom" had become a JLP catchword during
the federation referendum. In short advertisements of few
words, the PNP attempted to tie the JLP to the image of
the "Big Man Party." The promises the PNP made were
often extravagant: to abolish hunger and want (DG 2/4/67,
9) and to free the people from inequality (DG 2/10/67, 11).

The opposition party tried to use Bustamante's retirement and the rise of diverse new JLP leaders to demonstrate that the JLP was a divided party. "Without Busta," one advertisement read, "no one is certain who will be boss of the JLP. A party divided within itself cannot govern! We are united!   PNP — The only hope for Jamaica!" (DG 2/7/67, 10).   Bustamante in turn denied the split and expressed confidence in Sangster (DG 2/11/67, 22). This issue emerged as a major theme in the following election.

The JLP campaigned on its accomplishments, presented in such a way as to reverse the traditional characterization of the PNP as the "brainy" party. Its advertisements were often in newspaper-page format entitled "Election News," with long and detailed descriptions of government programs. The advertisements often compared activity of the JLP government from 1962 to 1967 with the PNP government's activity from 1955 to 1962, which, as PNP supporters pointed out, was comparing preindependence with postindependence conditions. Each "edition" of "Election News" featured one sector, such as farming, industry or culture. A repeated theme was of "modernization": "More and better roads ... JLP improves and modernizes the postal system.... Bigger and better river control works" (DG 2/6/67, 8), and an artist's rendition of a skyline of tall office buildings planned for the New Kingston area was presented (DG 1/29/67, 9). Some advertisements made use of "sophisticated" visuals, such as bar graphs, but close examination by this researcher revealed that the size of the bars did not vary from graph to graph and bore no relation whatsoever to the numbers they purported to represent (DG 1/28/67, 16).

One respondent mentioned that Sangster had told him that the JLP of the early 1960s was deliberately "looking for brains" (#6) and had found them in the persons of Seaga and D. C. Tavares. The party's sensitivity to its image as the not-so-brainy party is evident in some JLP advertisements. Candidate Victor Grant, who became attorney general, was dubbed "The Bigger Brain" (DG 2/17/67, 15), and a variety of projects, some of them Seaga's, were described in "Election News" as "Forty-two Big New Projects from JLP Brains in Four Years" (DG 2/16/67, 22).

The use of religious symbols had always been important in partisan contests in Jamaica, as in other Caribbean countries. One respondent, a JLP campaign manager, said that the use of biblical quotations and hymns, as well as the "transformation of a political meeting into a religious service ... implies that what you are saying is approved by God" (#31). Both parties had long used hymns and biblical readings as standard features of group meetings (Sewell 1978, 44). Some hymns come from the standard Anglican hymnal (*Hymns Ancient and Modern Revised*), and others are "Sankeys," hymns collected by Dwight Moody and Ira Sankey and used by Revivalists and Baptists in Jamaica since the time of the Great Revival.

Norman Manley's favorite hymn was a Sankey entitled "Ninety and Nine," and it was frequently sung in PNP meetings (Sewell 1978, 44). It appears in the PNP's songbook along with sixteen other hymns and nineteen songs. The JLP had been known to begin rallies with "Onward, Christian Soldiers," and the PNP with "Blest Be the Tie That Binds" (Sewell 1978, 44).

Biblical references were appealing to politicians because of their universality. Virtually every Jamaican had some knowledge of the Bible, which was, and is, frequently the only book in a family's possession. Quoting the Bible had appeal for most Jamaicans, both Rastafarians and the Protestant majority.

Many of the phrases used in 1967 were millenarian ones. A broadcast by Norman Manley was entitled "Praise the Lord for the Day of Deliverance Has Come" (DG 1/29/67, 2). An advertisement for Dudley Thompson read, "Thine enemies shall become thy footstool" (DG 2/1/67, 8), and another PNP advertisement read, "Weeping endureth for a night but Joy cometh in the morning" (DG 2/10/67, 25).

The JLP proved just as adept in finding apt biblical support. When Norman Manley first praised, then criticized, the JLP government's National Insurance Scheme, the JLP called it "the voice of Jacob but the hand of Esau" (DG 2/18/67, 30). In paraphrase of an Anglican prayer, E. K. Powell was advertised as the man who will "Lighten your Darkness" and who promised that "the wishes of the wicked shall not prevail" (DG 2/7/67, 4).

The Use of Class Symbols and Class Conflict

In 1976 sociologist Carl Stone wrote that the PNP's new democratic socialism resembled the populism of Bustamante's JLP, "except that it is informed by a greater sense of the existence of class enemies" (WG 11/30/76, 15). Bustamante seemed to have a notion of classes, but no sense of conflict or distinction among them. In his statement upon retiring from political life, for example, he promised to continue to fight "for the improvement and the protection of working people of all classes" (WG 2/1/67, 25).

An examination of the campaign materials of 1967 indicates that the traditional characterization of the JLP as the "small man party" and of the PNP as the party of the middle class had already begun to erode, and that the PNP introduced notions of class conflict into campaign propaganda more often than the JLP. References to class in the JLP materials are rare and are nearly always euphemistic. One JLP candidate is described as "the People's Man" (DG 2/13/67, 2) and the JLP government was said to have assisted "small farmers" by introducing modern agricultural methods (DG 1/27/67, 16). On the twenty-fifth anniversary of his release from detention, Bustamante stated that he had "no regrets for the sufferings I underwent in the interests of the underprivileged people of this country" (WG 2/15/67, 26). Only once, in a broadcast by Seaga that was partially reprinted in the *Gleaner,* was the word *poor* used: a claim that the PNP "forgot the poor" during its previous administrations (DG 2/15/67, 8). In JLP written materials, there was no use made of the words *rich, wealthy or capitalist.*

The sole item in JLP propaganda that may be construed as an oblique allusion to class conflict is one of its major slogans, which appeared in many meeting announcements and incorporates a line from an American union song: "Because we have served this nation, we shall not be moved." In that context, however, it retained little of its original meaning, and it was probably used only because it had been popularized by the civil rights movement in the United States.

The campaign managers for the opposition discovered one useful reference to Jamaican classes in the JLP's party organ, *The Voice*, and reprinted it in one of their own advertisements. It was evidently originally written to encourage campaign contributions from those who could afford to make them:

> The JLP is fighting a battle for many selfish rich people in Jamaica ... who can sit in comfort knowing that a prudent government elected by the little people will protect them and their interests.... Let those wealthy people admit and learn that this election is in their behalf, more than or on equal terms as of the small country folk, and I hope they play their part. (DG 2/14/67, 11)

The PNP advertisement in which the quotation appeared continued simply, "No need for us to add anything to this. The truth is out."

This is one example of the effort that the PNP made that year to present the JLP as the "Big Man Party" and to reverse the traditional association of the JLP as the representative of the poor. In another example, Dudley Thompson promised the people of Jones Town, a slum, that the PNP would spread the wealth and that a JLP victory would mean a nation of unsafe streets and wealthy government ministers (DG 2/16/67, 9). Bustamante's central role in the JLP and his retirement from politics enabled the PNP to credit him as the sole champion of the poor in that party while condemning the newer JLP figures as uninterested in the plight of the poor. Michael Manley, for example, said in one mass meeting that rich people had captured the JLP and were behind the violence in the lower class areas, which Bustamante would never have condoned (DG 2/13/67, 8).

Norman Manley emphasized the continuity between colonialism and the current situation in Jamaica, especially regarding the status of the poor. "It's the same colonial road we are traveling ... (we) need to find a new road of justice and equality based on socialist principles" (DG 2/17/67, 15). Likewise, Ken Hill, one of the members of the PNP's left wing, indicated his familiarity with one of the more radical writers of the day when he said at a mass meeting: "Shall we continue under the shadow of British colonialism ... or change Jamaica into a free independent society? Jamaicans want to be free from poverty, from the grosser aspects of a dying colonialism, from the exploitation of the poor by the rich. Join this mighty crusade!" (DG 2/17/67, 15)

Probably the most effective way that the PNP demonstrated the JLP's "Big Man" orientation was in calling people's attention to the life-styles of the JLP ministers. It was this aspect that was most frequently recalled by respondents. The ministers of the JLP government lived at government expense in residences in the traditional planter style; the awareness of their life-styles by the poor of Kingston undoubtedly caused some resentment. The PNP took advantage of the contrasts. Among the PNP campaign promises was "abolishing privileges of luxurious living by ministers" (DG 2/11/67, 8). The PNP played on the JLP slogan and said, "JLP ministers have done more for themselves alone since 1962" (DG 2/16/67, 9), and "The JLP has done more for WHOM? More for the rich man, more for foreign interests" (DG 2/2/67, 19).

In one advertisement, the PNP conveyed the same message by using a folk proverb; it read in its entirety, "Some people are licking their fingers but too many are sucking salt.   What about you?" (DG 2/6/67, 17). The proverb alluded to describes any unfortunate person as one who must "suck salt through a wooden spoon" (#7).

As will be described later, there are few references to Rastafarian symbols and music in 1967, but one reference is made that is related to class conflict. In a letter to the editor of the *Gleaner,* the writer describes the JLP government as one under which the rich get richer, and then says that he would like to ask the same question that the singer of a popular song asked: "How long shall the wicked reign over my people?" (DG 2/15/67, 19). The song is one mentioned earlier, "Carry Go Bring Come," which also uses some Rastafarian language in other lines.

The Use of Race Symbols and Racial Conflict

In 1962 C. L. R. James accused the Brown ethnic section of the British West Indies of an insidious cover-up: "That anywhere in these islands we have achieved racial har- mony," he wrote, is one of "the greatest lies of our society" (James 1962, 140). If a lie, it was one told with relative impunity until the Black Power movement took hold in the Caribbean between 1968 and 1970. In 1962 a JLP-domi- nated committee chose "Out of Many, One People" as the motto of the newly independent nation. While the country prepared for the 1967 election, the British Broadcasting Company was filming a documentary about, according to the *Gleaner*, "the way in which the coloured people in Jamaica had found a solution to the problem of integra- tion" (WG 3/1/67, 4). At the same time, Donald Sangster characterized relations among the races in Jamaica this way: "We regard ourselves as a symbol of the United Nations in that in our country our people represent all the races of the world.... Our people have ... settled here and made themselves into one, representing most of all the common humanity of man" (DG 1/28/67, 17).

During which election, if any, race became a factor in the campaigns was a matter of debate among the infor- mants, but many asserted that it was not 1967 (#6, #14, #15, #25, #31). References to race are rare and almost never indicate conflict among racial groups. Even indirect references are infrequent. These take three forms: sym- bols borrowed from the American civil rights movement, references to Africa and to Jamaica's African heritage, and symbols representing early Black nationalists of Jamai- ca, notably Marcus Garvey.

Of the first type, the PNP used songs associated with Martin Luther King, Jr., who coincidentally vacationed in Jamaica during this period. "We Shall Overcome" was a popular song at PNP rallies, as it still is today. The JLP, as mentioned above, used the phrase "We shall not be moved," also popularized in the civil rights movement. Since the 1961 referendum on the West Indian Federation, the JLP had used the slogan "Freedom," and in 1967 called its candidates "Freedom Fighters" (DG 1/23/67, 4).

One respondent mentioned that he thought that the JLP never used "culture" except under Seaga's influence, who, he said, understands the symbols of Jamaican Blacks better than Manley because of his studies of Revivalism and folklore (#33). During the 1960s, Seaga was responsible for a number of cultural development programs, including the establishment of the Jamaica Festival, the National Heroes Award, and National Heritage Week. In a 1967 advertisement, the JLP listed these achievements as programs to help Jamaicans learn about their "cultural roots" (DG 2/14/67, 10). The word "roots" usually connotes Jamaica's African heritage (#7, #13), but here it is sufficiently ambiguous not to offend Jamaicans disdainful of things African.

One accomplishment remembered by several respondents as a shrewd symbolic move was Seaga's recovery of the remains of Marcus Garvey. With numerous lawsuits still pending against him, Garvey had died in England in relative disrepute, and had been unceremoniously buried there. Seaga arranged for Garvey's bones to be exhumed and returned to Jamaica, and he had a monument built over the new grave in Kingston. A similar honor was accorded Paul Bogle and George William Gordon, heroes of the Morant Bay Rebellion of 1865.

Only two respondents remembered some details of the Western Kingston campaign in 1967, and it seems from this evidence that symbols of African culture were more frequent there than in the printed materials. This is understandable for two reasons. First, the constituency is one of the poorest and Blackest in Jamaica, and such symbols could be used without fear of offending the middle-class Jamaican who is more European in outlook. Second, the contestants in Western Kingston were particularly well versed in such symbols. Seaga, the JLP candidate and incumbent, had a good command of them, as mentioned earlier. His opponent was Dudley Thompson, a lawyer who had lived in East Africa, where he had defended Kenyatta on sedition charges after the Mau-Mau rebellion in Kenya. Kenyatta had been called "Burning Spear" and Thompson acquired that nickname himself (#13, #20). A reggae musician has since picked up the name. Another respondent remembered Thompson, a Brown man, using the names "Mr. Black" and "Mr. Africa" (#12).

The current situation in Africa was mentioned in some JLP materials. Two months before the election Sangster said that the government intended to help the victims of apartheid, and that Jamaica should cooperate closely with the countries of Africa in their struggle against apartheid (WG 1/25/67, 4). An "Election News" advertisement focusing on foreign policy achievements featured pictures of JLP leaders with Haile Selassie and with President Kaunda of Zambia, both of whom had visited Jamaica. It described Jamaica's foreign policy as one based upon "independence of judgement and vigorous opposition to racialism and colonialism" (DG 2/10/67, 8; see also DG 2/13/67, 13).

A phrase often used by the JLP in announcements of mass meetings was "Big Guns," to describe members of the party leadership. In answer to a criticism of these words, a JLP backer made reference to racial conflict elsewhere in the world: "It was the roaring of the 'Big Guns' that gave us independence! Long may the 'Big Guns' roar! We in Jamaica are fortunate to have our 'Big Guns' to roar for us and we wish that the downtrodden people in South Africa had even a little pistol with which to 'piff' against their oppressors" (DG 2/7/67, 23).

In the printed campaign materials, PNP references to race and to racial conflict are rare. They usually take the indirect form of historical allusions, such as references to colonialism and slavery. For example, a PNP ad promised to "free the people of Jamaica from land slavery" (DG 2/10/67, 11) and from "the plantation system" (DG 2/13/67, 4). In contrast, the JLP print materials rarely made reference to the period of colonialism and slavery, except with regard to Bustamante's struggles as a trade unionist.

The Use of References to Anti-Colonialism

The 1967 election period material revealed numerous references to Jamaica's British heritage, but few negative ones. Although Jamaica has been an independent nation since 1962, it is formally the "Dominion of Jamaica," and the British monarch is its head of state. This is reflected in the ceremonial functions of government; for example, the proclamation dissolving Parliament before the election was made "in the fifteenth year of the reign of Her Majesty Queen Elizabeth II" (WG 2/1/67, 20).

Some attention was called to the British origins of the Parliamentary system, which the Miami *Herald* called the "heritage of centuries of British rule" and Jamaica's "strength as it approaches the most important election in its short history" (WG 2/15/67, 7). Indeed, it was the first election in its history as an independent country. The latter fact seemed to have caused some anxiety for the *Gleaner* editor who wrote: "However camouflaged by parliamentary paraphernalia, Britain stood in previous elections as the ultimate guarantor of the grant of poll and the people's choice." The test of maintaining law and order is the one "which separates the men of independence from the boys of 'chip on the shoulder colonialism'" (WG 3/1/67, 17).

The period marked the twenty-fifth anniversary of Bustamante's release from detention in 1942. A service marked the anniversary, but there was no expression of animosity toward the British. Even at the time of his release, a *Gleaner* editorial noted, there was no "wave of hatred against Britain or the governor" (WG 2/15/67, 25). Lord Milverton, who as governor of Jamaica had had Bustamante detained, called on Bustamante shortly before the elections and reportedly had a "warm meeting" with him (WG 2/22/67, 6). Notes of congratulations and appreciation were exchanged between Queen Elizabeth II and Bustamante on his retirement from public office (WG 3/1/67, 29).

The JLP government claimed in one advertisement that it had pursued a foreign policy that was anticolonial (DG 2/10/67, 8), but that is the sole reference to the subject found in the JLP materials. The PNP, on the other hand, identified the JLP government as a continuation of colonialism (DG 2/17/67, 15). The statements of Ken Hill and of Norman Manley discussed above were both made in public meetings rather than in printed advertisements. Hill's strident anticolonialism, however, cannot be considered the PNP norm. As Louis Lindsay has pointed out, the PNP had been the more Anglophilic of the two parties as Jamaica had approached independence. There was a wide gap between the mainstream PNP ideology of Manley, Nether-sole, and Glasspole on the one hand and the group that came to be known as the "four Hs" on the other (Lindsay 1975, 22). The Four Hs, who had been expelled from the party in 1952, included Hill, who was reinstated.

The Use of Rastafarian Symbols and of Popular Music

One respondent claimed that if there had been a strong, anticolonial movement in the 1950s and 1960s, the Rasta-farian movement would not have been as visible nor would its impact have been as far-reaching. As it was, Rasta filled the void (#8). That void was not apparent in the material from the 1967 elections. Neither anticolonialism nor Rastafarian symbols played an important role. How-ever, precedents were set in the use of popular music and African symbols, and there is some evidence of an appeal to some aspects of Ethiopianism, if not specifically to Rastafari. Although respondents agreed that Rasta was politically marginal (#6, #20, #31), one added that Rastas were "the yeast in the dough" (#10).

Interviews revealed that only two constituency contests in 1967 were remembered for their use of Rasta symbols. These were Western Kingston and Central St. James, which includes Montego Bay. In the latter, one respondent who was a youth at the time remembered that the JLP candi-date, former Health Minister Eldemire, grew a beard just before the elections and adopted the biblical name David. Both have Rastafarian significance, especially the full beard, which was uncommon at the time except among Rastas, who were also called "Beardsmen" (#4).

The other constituency in which Rasta symbols were used was Western Kingston, in the contest described earlier between Seaga and Thompson. Thompson had accompanied Rastafarian leaders on a mission to Africa, and so was known among the Rastas in the area (#15). One JLP respondent said that Seaga used both Revivalist and Rasta symbols as well as popular music and drums like the Nyabinghi drums of orthodox Rastafari (#12). Seaga's recording company produced the records of Byron Lee and the Dragonnaires, one of the most popular, if not the most progressive, groups at the time, and Seaga arranged for free concerts in the constituency with the singers who recorded at the company, West Indies Records (#12). These were not publicized in the *Gleaner*, and only one respondent remembered their taking place. For the most part, these musicians were not Rastafarians.

One of the major tenets of Rastafari is the preparation for the return to Africa. It was this aspect that had been highlighted in the 1961 report on the Rastafari brethren published by the University College of the West Indies. That aspect had received attention in the years since the report was published; an "Ethiopian Fund" was set up in Jamaica by the Ethiopian World Federation to send Jamaican settlers to Ethiopia (DG 1/31/67, 3). One JLP advertisement promised to continue to send Jamaican workers abroad for overseas employment — a proud achievement of the government was the numbers of women it had placed in domestic employment in the United States and in the United Kingdom — and to explore other areas, including Africa, to which Jamaicans might want to go (DG 2/12/67, 9). A letter to the editor from a PNP supporter condemned a JLP candidate's statement to a mass meeting in "one of the troubled areas." "I heard the candidate say," he reported, "'If you want to go to Africa, vote for me.' There was an extraordinary applause for the candidate" (DG 2/10/67, 12).

The JLP government enjoyed the prestige of having arranged for Selassie's visit. Photographs of the emperor were rare and valuable to Rastafarians, and several appeared in advertisements that year, portraying him with JLP leaders. There is little doubt that these made a deep impression. In one, Selassie is holding his fingertips together in a distinctive way, and that posture is meticulously imitated in photographs of Rastafarians taken in the 1970s (e.g. Simon and Davis, 1977). The return of Garvey's remains to Jamaica also would have been favorably viewed by most Rastafarians, who count Garvey as their principal modern prophet.

Other minor items that have Rastafarian overtones include one candidate's nickname. D. C. Tavares, a JLP minister, was called "The Lion of the Southwest" (DG 1/24/67, 3). He was campaigning for Southwest St. Andrew, an urban, lower-class constituency. The lion is a

major Rastafarian symbol, because of the Ethiopian imperial title "The Conquering Lion," but it is also a well-known
European symbol of power.   Finally, a raid on a JLP
headquarters in Central Kingston, also a lower-class constituency, uncovered weapons, stolen goods, and "chillum
pipes" (DG 2/3/67, 1), which are large pipes used primarily
by Rastafarians for ritual ganja smoking.

None of the respondents recalled the JLP's using rock-
steady or popular recorded music in its 1967 campaign,
except for Seaga in Western Kingston.   However, both
parties used the lyrics of popular music in print advertisements, the PNP more than the JLP, and particularly PNP
advertisements for Michael Manley in the constituency of
Central Kingston. The most frequently used "song slogans"
were "Sounds and Pressure," "The Train is Coming," and
"Take It Easy" (DG 1/22/67, 3; 1/29/67, 4; 1/30/67, 5;
2/1/67, 5; and others).   The JLP's candidate in that
constituency, E. K. Powell, used a line from another
popular song in his advertisement as well as a retort to
Manley's use of "Sounds and Pressure."   The advertisement
read: "'The wicked shall not reign over my people.' Their
Sounds Mean Oppression ... Vote Bell to Live Well!" (DG
2/1/67, 4). As noted above, a PNP supporter had also used
the "wicked" line to describe the JLP.   The use of the term
would also recall biblical promises of retribution.

In another JLP advertisement, Stafford Owen, the JLP
candidate running against Norman Manley, used a song title
in the same way, as an eye-catching slogan: "What a Bam-
Bam!" referring to the song by Toots and the Maytals that
had recently won the Jamaica Festival Song Contest:

> *I want you to know that I am the man*
> *Who fights for the right not for the wrong*
> *Going here and going there*
> *Talking this and talking that*
> *Soon you will find out*
> *The man I'm supposed to be*
>
> *Bam bam what a bam bam*
>
> *Now this man trouble no man*
> *But if you should trouble this man*
> *It will bring a bam bam bam bam*
> *Can you hear that?*

"Bam bam" was apparently a catchword of the day and a common slogan in the JLP's verbal propaganda (DG 2/10/67, 14). Humorist A. E. T. Henry, writing about the election in the *Gleaner,* uses a biting sarcasm that may reflect middle class snobbery toward popular music: "In the immortal words of the great Jamaican lyric poet, whose name I have forgotten, 'What a Bam-Bam' this is going to be!'" (DG 1/20/67, 8). In a clashing juxtaposition of allusions, a letter to the *Gleaner* exclaims: "What a Bam Bam it will be when (Seaga) shall make his enemy his footstool!" (DG 2/11/67, 12).

The phrases "Sounds and Pressure," "The Train Is Coming," and "Take It Easy" were not from Rastafarian songs, but from the vanguard of popular music in which the Rastafarians were soon to participate. In contrast, Byron Lee and the Dragonnaires represent a different trend in music; the group still performs but has never produced original reggae music. Only one song used in the campaign is unambiguously Rasta, "Carry Go Bring Come." This song includes the lines "Better to make our home in Mount Zion-I / Instead of heaping oppression upon the innocent minds," an allusion to repatriation.

None of the songs mentioned so far was used in connection with any ideology of class, race, or militant anticolonialism, with the single exception of the song mentioned in the letter that described the "wicked" as those who help the rich get richer. The songs that were used were appealing, rather, because they sounded tough (#13), or militant (#2). Furthermore, the songs were "intellectually innocent" (#2), in the sense that their authors were not concerned with partisan politics. One respondent said that if the artists had known what the songs would be used for, they might not have recorded them. It was not that they supported one party over another, and that the wrong party used their songs, but that being identified with any party was dangerous for a youth in the slums of Kingston, which were becoming increasingly racked with the "gun fever" of the political thugs (#2).

Another aspect of the campaign that may have been of interest to Rastafarians was the issue of Back-o'-Wall, the area of Seaga's constituency that had been entirely razed to make way for Tivoli Gardens. The bulldozers wiped out

five entire polling divisions (DG 1/20/67). The father of
one of the respondents had been a Rastafarian resident of
Back-o'-Wall. He claimed it was the single most important
enclave of urban Rastas, and a community that had leaned
toward the PNP (#2). Both parties called attention to the
incident in their campaigns. The JLP boasted that its
government had removed gamblers and criminals from the
area (DG 2/9/67, 27), while the PNP promised to abolish
the bulldozing of people's homes (DG 2/4/67, 9). Dudley
Thompson called Seaga the "Minister of Devilment and
Warfare" (DG 2/16/67, 9) and the PNP's Vivian Blake
promised in a rally that the PNP would end "bulldozing the
homes of the helpless" (DG 2/6/67, 17).

Discussion

Jamaica's first general elections as an independent
nation were transitional for the two major parties. One of
the two leaders that had led the parties for twenty-five
years had retired, and it proved to be the last election for
the other. New, younger leadership was rising in the ranks
and blurring the traditional lines of demarcation between
the parties, which had been based more on the personal
styles of the party leaders than on the ideology that each
party professedly espoused.

Symbols and catchwords were important to the voters
and politicians, and a great deal of election activity
focused on them. Bells were rung in Parliament; hundreds
of supporters took their brooms with them to rallies;
politicians and their constituents extrapolated, and publicized further, negative meanings from the other party's
symbols.

Although some 80 percent of Jamaicans are very poor,
and a small group of individuals control most of the wealth,
conflict among classes was not an overriding theme of the
election campaigns. The JLP, which had traditionally been
considered the representative of the poor, spoke of that
class essentially in euphemistic terms, and maintained that
a government could be run in the interest of all classes
simultaneously. The PNP, on the other hand, handicapped
by a stereotype that characterized it as the party of the
middle class, a relatively small proportion of the elector-

ate, strove to present the party program as one in the interests of the lower class and inimical to the interests of the wealthy, and promised programs that were truly in the interests of the lower class, such as minimum wage and the abolition of the Master-Servant Law.

The results of the election as far as voting behavior and social class are concerned seemed to confirm the parties' traditional class characterizations. Carl Stone took a random sample of polling districts in the Corporate Area and classified these by the social class of the majority of residents into six categories. Three of these represent sections of what is here called the lower class; two, the middle class; and one, the upper class (see Table 3.3).

The JLP gained a majority of the support in two types of community: the upper class and the poorest section of the lower class. The PNP's base of support came from those in between, especially the "better-off working class," i.e. the uppermost section of the lower class, and the "lower middle class." The middle section of the lower class was almost equally divided between the two parties.

Table 3.3
Share of Party Vote in Sample of Urban
Polling Districts
1967 Percentages

		PNP	JLP
Lower Class	Very Poor Working	43.3	56.7
	Poor Working	51.6	48.4
	Better-off Working	80.5	19.5
Middle Class	Lower Middle	81.0	19.0
	Middle	54.4	40.6
Upper Class	Upper Middle	40.0	60.0

Source: Stone, DG 6/8/80.

In the two years following the 1967 election, the myth of racial harmony would be shattered, but in this campaign there was no sign of incipient racial awareness. Some politicians used symbols and expressions from the body of culture that pluralists would describe as Black culture, but there is no evidence that they appealed to that culture's potential hostility to others. Indeed, the one politician who seemed to use such symbols most often was the White Seaga.

Anticolonialism received little attention from either party. Although lip service was paid the topic by at least one of the PNP's more radical left-wing members, when it was used at all by the PNP it was usually used to argue that the JLP government had maintained the preindependence status quo, especially regarding Jamaica's class structure.

Indigenous recorded music was still in its infancy, but certain politicians were already aware of its potential as a means of attracting audiences of lower-class voters. No popular music slogans or Rastafarian symbols appeared in the parties' national advertising, but some were used in advertisements targeted toward specific constituencies. There is evidence that the middle class disdained popular music, but that the government had banned some records from radio play (#2, #36). Indigenous recorded popular music was definitely linked with the Jamaican lower class, as was the philosophy of Rastafari, but the two were not yet associated with one another. Of the popular songs of the year, few used Rastafarian language or ideas, but a number concerned issues relevant to the lower class alone.

The context of the use of the symbols of the lower class, including music, was usually not one of class or racial group conflict or of anticolonialism. If they were used with any hostility at all, it was partisan hostility, that is, "Sounds and Pressure" and "Keep up the Pressure" used tough, militant words but the militancy probably expressed hostility against the other party's ghetto strongmen, rather than expressing class or race conflict.

4

The 1972 Election

The 1972 election was a major landmark in Jamaica's short history. The People's National Party, under the leadership of Michael Manley, was swept into power after a long and colorful campaign. The defeat left the Jamaica Labour Party bitterly divided, and the party did not regain its momentum for five years. Her Majesty's loyal opposition, in contrast to the "racial harmony" of the previous campaign, was now saluting with clenched fists and threatening to "beat down Babylon."

The PNP's thirteen-point margin over the incumbents in the election returns was as impressive as the histrionics of the contest (see Table 4.1). The JLP lost ground in all but two of the fifty-three constituencies (DG 3/1/72, 10), and the PNP won thirty-seven, or 70 percent of the seats in Parliament, to the JLP's sixteen seats.

Many respondents were able to supply detailed information about this campaign. Even those who were in secondary school at the time remembered a number of details, perhaps because of the efforts that both parties made to appeal to youth, a growing, if nonvoting, segment of the population. Although the de facto voting age was over twenty-three years, more than half of Jamaica's population (51.6 percent in 1970) was under eighteen years of age (DG 2/12/83).

The campaign in the *Gleaner* was a fuller one than that of 1967. The paper reported on many more mass meetings, supplying some indication of the symbols that the parties used in speeches but declined to use in print advertisements.

Table 4.1
Results, 1972 General Election

Electors on Roll 605,662

Ballots Cast 477,771 (78.88%)

Accepted Ballots 473,651

Party Share	Popular Vote	Percentage	Seats
Jamaica Labour Party	205,587	(43.40%)	16
People's National Party	266,927	(56.36%)	37
Independents	1,088	(0.23%)	0
Christian Democrats	49	(0.01%)	0

Source: Chief Electoral Officer's Report, 1972.

Both parties spent roughly equivalent amounts on advertisements; the PNP's fund-raising efforts had evidently been more successful than in 1967. Table 4.2 presents a summary of the information collected from the *Gleaner* for 1972. The JLP in particular used printed advertisements more frequently for specific constituencies, especially in the rural areas.

This chapter follows roughly the format of the preceding chapter. First, a brief historical background will trace the growth of Black power ideology in Jamaican culture and discuss the developments in music and in the status of the Rastafarians. Then, an overview of the 1972 campaigns will be presented. Third, specific references to class and race, and the uses of Rastafarian symbols and reggae music will be reviewed, followed by a discussion.

To make sense of the remarkable differences between the campaign styles of 1967 and 1972, some of the events of the period between the elections must be examined. The developments that, in retrospect, seemed to have the biggest impact on the election of 1972 began outside the arena of partisan politics, on the campus of the University

Table 4.2
Summary of 345 Election Items in
Daily Gleaner - February, 1972

	People's National Party	Jamaica Labour Party
Reports of meetings	13	10
Advertisements		
General		
Full page	35	37
Less than full page	17	1
Broadcast announcements	19	10
Specific constituencies		
W.Kingston	2	1
C.Kingston	2	14
E. Kingston	1	0
W.R.St.Andrew	16	0
N.St.Andrew	1	4
W.C.St.Andrew	0	3
E.C.St.Andrew	5	1
S.St.Andrew	16	7
E.R.St.Andrew	2	0
Other Constituencies	0	20
Total advertisements	106	98
Other items		118

of the West Indies and in the crude recording studios of downtown Kingston. By far the most important of these developments was the spread of the Black power movement.

As with any social movement, it is difficult to pinpoint the advent of the Black power movement in Jamaica. Nothing in an event-by-event chronicle of Jamaican history prepares one for the mass outpouring of frustration and bitterness that took place in October 1968, in the so-called Rodney affair.

Although Jamaica had enjoyed a spurt in economic growth during the 1960s, six years of independence had not fulfilled some basic, if unrealistic, expectations. Unemployment was an estimated 30 percent, and 80 percent of those who were employed earned less than $20 weekly (Gonsalves 1979, 1). Foreign interests controlled most of the major sectors of the economy, including bauxite, tourism, and banking (Girvan 1971).

In January 1968, a young radical academic, Walter Rodney, was appointed lecturer of history at the Mona, Kingston, campus of the University of the West Indies. Rodney was a Guyanese graduate of the university who had received his doctorate in England and had taught African history in Tanzania. Rodney espoused the Black power ideology, and soon after his arrival on campus he began to lecture on African history, Black power, and Black "revolution" (Rodney 1969, 14, 63). Rodney's presence at U.W.I. helped to create an atmosphere of conflict not unlike the student protest movements that were taking place worldwide. In the spring the students elected a new leadership for the Guild of Undergraduates (the student government) that had run "on a platform of student power... and was agitating for student representation on relevant University bodies" (Gonsalves 1979, 3). April that year saw the assassination of Martin Luther King, Jr., who had delivered the valedictory sermon for graduating U.W.I. students three years before (Gleaner Company, 1973).

The interest in the philosophy of Black power was greeted with apprehension by the JLP government, particularly by Black Minister of Home Affairs Roy McNeill. As Gonsalves reports, McNeill told the House of Representatives that he had "never come across a man who offers a greater threat to the security of this land than does Walter Rodney" (Gonsalves 1971, 2). Under McNeill's direction, the Importation of Forbidden Publications Act had been invoked to ban such books as *The Autobiography of Malcolm X*, the works of Eldridge Cleaver and Stokely Carmichael, and *The Children of Sisyphus*, a novel by Jamaican sociologist Orlando Patterson (#7).

In October 1968, Rodney went to Montreal to attend the Congress of Black Writers. When he returned to Jamaica three days later, he was confined to the plane and returned involuntarily to Canada. Rodney had been banned. The next day, students from the university led a march from the campus to the Ministry of Home Affairs and to the prime minister's office. Their numbers grew to several thousands as nonstudents, including many Rastafarians and urban youths, joined the march. The march became a protest of racial inequalities; the students chanted "Black power" and brown-skinned people were reportedly harassed. The police attempted to break up the demonstration with tear gas and batons. Although the students retreated to the campus, the march set off a series of incidents throughout the city. Fifty buses were burned, fourteen major fires were started, and windows were smashed. Three persons, probably rioters, were killed and many were injured (Gonsalves 1979, 9; Rodney 1969, 66).

The following day, Prime Minister Shearer spoke in House of Representatives proceedings that were broadcast live on the radio. He accused Rodney of holding "extreme communist views" and of having "engaged in subversive activities" in Jamaica, among which was associating himself with "groups of people who claimed to be part of the Rastafarian movement and also with Claudius Henry who was convicted in 1960 of Treason Felony." Shearer added that Rodney was "actively engaged in organizing groups of semi-illiterates and unemployed for avowed revolutionary purposes" (quoted in Gonsalves 1979, 12).

Minister of Home Affairs McNeill blamed the disturbance on the PNP, citing as evidence of involvement the fact that the student marchers sang "We Shall Overcome," a song long associated with the PNP (see chapter 3). The opposition leader, Norman Manley, came to the defense of the students and condemned the police violence used against them (DG 10/17/68). The *Gleaner* reproached him for making "a party issue out of national security."

There were three important consequences of the Rodney affair. First, it inspired numerous persons in opposition to the JLP government to organize themselves into new ongoing associations, the most influential of which was Abeng, which will be discussed below. One respondent, who was in sixth form at the time, helped to found the Sixth Form Association, which evolved into the first PNP youth group (#13). Second, from the perspective of the middle class, the JLP had lived up to its anti-intellectual reputation by abruptly banning a professor and treating the student protesters brutally (#12, #11). Finally, the spontaneity and violence of the nonstudent protests frightened the middle class. When asked what would have happened if the JLP had won the 1972 election, some respondents answered that massive rioting would not have been inconceivable (#7, #25). One respondent, then a diplomat, had returned in 1971 from abroad and visited a middle-class club. "I was taken aback when I heard people there saying that we must get the JLP out. With the ostentatious living of the JLP, unemployment going up, the party just feathering its own nest, we would have a revolution on our hands" (#14).

Abeng

Immediately after the Rodney affair, an organization was formed that called itself Abeng, after the cowhorn bugle used for communication among the Maroon warriors during their wars against the British in the eighteenth century. The group included several university professors who were sympathetic to Rodney's cause, U.W.I. students who would later hold prominent positions in the PNP government, and members from outside the academic community, in particular, workers and Rastafarians. The group issued the first edition of its weekly paper, *Abeng*, on 1 February 1969. Its editorial, "*Abeng* Sounds a Call to Action," said that the purposes of the newspaper were to call into question the "system," and to expose the issue of racial discrimination, which had been "smothered by other newspapers" (*Abeng* 2/1/69, 2), a direct reference to the *Gleaner*.

Abeng is important for the purposes of this study because in it, for the first time, Rastafari doctrine and reggae music were welded unambiguously with the issues of racial conflict and class conflict. Even the initial editorial claimed common cause with "those Jamaican singers of today — singers whose statements about society ring true" and had become electioneering slogans (*Abeng* 2/1/69, 2).

The primary themes of the paper were those of black nationalism. It featured articles on the meaning of Black power (*Abeng* 3/1/69, 3), photographs of Afro hairstyles and dashikis (*Abeng* 2/15/69, 4), articles by Rodney and Marcus Garvey, Jr., and reports of Jamaicans being refused service in hotels. To a lesser extent, it addressed problems of class, including articles on unemployment and a regular column called "Sufferer's Diary," written in patois. "Sufferers" proved to be the catchword for the poor in the 1972 election, replacing the innocuous "small man." Third, it dealt regularly with issues of Rastafarian interest, such as information about ganja laws (*Abeng* 3/1/69, 1), and reports of Rastas being harassed by the police (*Abeng* 3/1/69, 3,4).

Reggae music of the period received coverage in *Abeng* as well. Lines from songs like "Everything Crash" appeared as headlines; Prince Buster, a reggae singer and producer and an activist, advertised in its pages; and the banning of songs by the JLP government was discussed in its editorials. In one article, the reporter interviewed a Rastafarian owner of a beer joint in Denham Town, a ghetto, about indiscriminate raids by the police. Bongo Neville described his beer joint's juke box as a source of inspiration to protest: "The jukebox is not for entertainment. It is like a Black Power poster, a constant reminder that oppression has to be heaved off. That is why Bob Marley, Heptones and a host of other artists are on the record stack" (*Abeng* 3/1/69, 4).

Abeng was severely critical of both of Jamaica's political parties. The PNP came in for slightly less criticism than the JLP, and ultimately one of the questions that caused the dissolution of the Abeng organization was that of its newspaper's stance on the PNP (#3). When Michael Manley was vying with Vivian Blake for leadership of the party, an *Abeng* headline called it a choice between "Black Dog and Monkey." There was "not much difference" between them, it said; "both men were produced as a result of the split in the PNP that drove the working class from that party ... It is Marcus Garvey who said that 'the traitors among the Negro Race are generally found among the men highest placed in society and education, the fellows who call themselves leaders.'" (*Abeng* 2/8/69, 1). When Manley won the party election, an editorial asserted that "among sufferers the feeling is that the new Leader of Her Majesty's Loyal Opposition is a danger to them. He represents the people who own Jamaica and who therefore control its politics" (*Abeng* 2/8/69, 1). A cartoon in the same issue shows Manley pointing to a weather map; the legend: "The forecast for Jamaica — No change in the system — Continuing oppression together with high unemployment — A new front of irrelevance is approaching" (*Abeng* 2/8/69, 3).

The JLP, particularly the prime minister, received sterner criticism. Shearer was called "Pharaoh" or "Pharaoh Share-out," and it was pointed out that the word *pharaoh* "has always been used by black people to mean oppressor...that is why Prince Buster's record 'Pharaoh House Crash' had to be banned" (*Abeng* 2/15/69, 1). One cartoon shows Shearer as a puppet dancing while foreign capitalists manipulate the strings. The legend reads, "Shearer's reggae to the hit song 'The Higher They Climb'" (*Abeng* 3/8/69, 3). The legend refers to two items of popular culture: a hit song at the time, "The Harder They Come," and a Jamaican folk proverb, "Di higher monkey climb, di more him show him tail," meaning the more he exposes himself (#7). Another cartoon illustrates the "Prototype of the New University Man" who will be "employed to formulate JLP policy and write for a well-known daily newspaper." The man has no eyes, so he cannot see thefts "in high places"; no ears, so he "cannot hear the cries of oppressed blacks"; and a rigid neck, to encourage the narrowest view of society (*Abeng* 9/27/69).

Abeng was published from February until October 1969, when the printery where it had been produced was completely destroyed in a suspicious night fire (#13, #21). It had reached a total circulation of 20,000, and had been distributed weekly all over the island (#21). After the burning of the printery, the group split in many directions. One respondent said: "*Abeng* was the vanguard symbolically. Their symbols led later on. But it was not at all in the vanguard organizationally. When the reactionaries burnt down the printery, we wondered, where do we go from here? The discussions of this question became interminable. Several different directions were clear. By 1970, it was clear that we needed to part and perhaps regroup later" (#21).

Abeng members went in at least eight directions, and formed six new organizations (#13, #21). Some members formed Marxist-Leninist groups, such as the Workers Liberation League, the Communist Party of Jamaica, and the Independent Trade Unions Advisory Council (ITAC). Others formed the PNP Youth Organization (PNPYO) and the Youth Forces for National Liberation (YFNL). Several of the Rastafarians moved to the Twelve Tribes organization. D. K. Duncan and Arnold Bertram moved to the PNP, and "brought their symbols with them" (#3).

Historical Background

Changes in Party Leadership

Upon the death of Donald Sangster two months after the 1967 election, Hugh Shearer was sworn in as prime minister, and led the JLP through the 1972 elections until 1974.

In February of 1969, Norman Washington Manley resigned his posts as leader of the opposition and president of the PNP and later resigned from Parliament. He was succeeded by his son Michael after a party election in which Michael Manley defeated Vivian Blake, a lawyer. Blake, according to one informant, "represented the party's Glasspole tendencies, that is, its right-wing. Michael was a trade unionist, and represented party continuity, because he was the son of NW, but also represented the dynamism of youth" (#7). The election campaign of the PNP began in earnest almost immediately after Michael Manley's election as party leader (#13).

Developments in Indigenous Music

In 1968, rock-steady music gave way to a new rhythm, a synthesis of rock steady and ska called "reggae." Which band produced the first reggae song is a matter of debate, but all the contenders for the honor produced reggae songs that year. The first to use the word was Toots and the Maytals in their hit single of 1968, "Do the Reggay." Toots Hibbert later claimed that the word was derived from *regular*. He has also claimed that the word derives from the patois *stregge*, meaning raggedy. "Reggae mean regular people who are suffering and don't have what they want" (Davis and Simon 1977, 17). It has also been said that reggae is derived from the word *regal*, because it is the king's (Selassie's) music.

Two developments accompanied the advent of reggae music. First, a closer association grew between reggae artists and the philosophy of Rastafari. Artists began to name their bands in ways meaningful to Rastas, such as the Ethiopians and the Abyssinians. They used Rastafarian variations on patois in their lyrics, and, at least in one case, used lyrics in Amharic, a language that Rastafarians value highly and try to learn (Planno 1969). A spate of religious Rastafarian music, hymns to Selassie, was released by popular artists like Max Romeo, the Abyssinians, and the Wailers (*Star* 2/25/72).

Second, reggae songs began genuinely to address social conditions. Strikes, riots, police brutality, and poverty became the topical material on which many songs were based. The most frequently recalled song of the period (#2, #13, #20, #29, #34) was "Everything Crash" by the Ethiopians.

Look deh now -- Everything crash
Firemen strike -- Watermen strike
Telephone pole men too
Down to the policeman too
What bad by the morning
Can't come good a evening
Every day carry bucket to the well
One day the bucket bottom must drop out
Everything crash.

It was one of the earliest and most influential political reggae offerings. Released late in 1968, it was an immediate juke box hit (see below) during Christmas that year (#2). Its opening line, "Look deh now" became an oft-repeated phrase during the next election, sometimes preceding an antagonistic observation of the JLP government. The first half of the song names four of the hundred-odd strikes of that year. Then, with two well known proverbs, the song anticipates that everyday strain and stress will lead to sudden disaster, and warns that what is already decayed cannot become fresh later. It is written in a speech idiom that, according to an Australian musicologist, "is charactistic of the grass roots man. (It) closely resembles the speech accents of the 'common' man" (O'Gorman 1972, 52).

Another song, "Fire, Fire" by the Wailers, according to two respondents, was about the violent aftermath of the Rodney affair (#2, #13). It describes the Kingston scene that week in October, when fires had been set in many parts of the city: "Babylon" was "burning." With a simple ballad tune that derived from an old folk song, it is sung quietly and with a threatening edge:

> Fire, fire -- They have no water....
> Who you gonna run to? -- Who you gonna run to?
> Who you gonna run to? -- They have no mercy.
> Stand up and fight it -- Stand up and fight it
> Stand up and fight your fight
> 'til you give me freedom.
> Come on and tell me true
> Why you been treating me crude
> You see the fire burning
> And you don't know where you turning.
> Fire, fire -- Fire, fire.

A song by the Abbysinians reflected the recent interest in the history of Afro-Jamaicans and its connections with their current situation. Called "Declaration of Rights," the song revolves around a theme not uncommon in the songs of 1968-69: slavery never really ended. Like "Fire, Fire," it urges action:

Look how long they brought us down here
Have us in bondage right through these years
Fussing and fighting among ourselves
Nothing to achieve as well
It's worser than hell, I say
Get up and fight for your rights, my brothers
Get up and fight for your rights, my sisters
Took us away from civilization
Brought us to slave in this big plantation

Other songs that year were milder protests. Alton Ellis's "Lord Deliver Us" simply pleads for food for the hungry and clothing for the naked, and wonders why the civilization that brought us bombs and satellites "still can't help us." Several songs that sound quite political were "innocently" written. For example, Delroy Wilson's "Better Must Come," which figured highly in the 1972 election, expressed the author's personal wish for material wealth (#2), but the title soon became the rallying cry for PNP supporters.

I've been trying for a long long time,
Still I can't make it
Everything I try to do, Seems to go wrong.
It seems I have done something wrong,
Why they trying to keep me down
Who God bless no one curse,
Thank God I'm not the worse
Better must come, one day, better must come
They can't conquer me, better must come.

The Wailers' "Small Axe," also used in the campaign, is a militant and threatening song:

Why boasteth thyself, oh evil men,
Playing smart, and not being clever
I say you're working inequity, to achieve vanity
But the goodness of Jah Jah I-dureth for I-ver
If you are the big tree, we are the small axe
Sharpened to cut you down,
Ready to cut you down.
These are the words of my Master

Telling me that no weak hearts shall prosper
And whosoever diggeth a pit shall fall in it
Whosoever diggeth a pit, shall bury in it.

The song evidently originated in a patois play on words. The Wailers' new producer, Lee Perry, had told the band that the big three record producers in Kingston were bent on ruining him. In patois, "three" and "tree" are homophones, and one of the Wailers punned that if they were the big three, the Wailers were the small axe (Clarke 1980, 104).

The reaction of the government and media institutions to this onslaught of ghetto criticism was one of repression on several fronts. First, *every song mentioned in this chapter so far was forbidden radio play* (#3, #13, #20). Even indigenous music that was not banned received very little broadcast play on the two radio stations, one of which was government owned and the other independent. One music writer expressed the wish that the radio stations would play at least one Jamaican record per show (*Star* 1/7/72, 22), and praised a new radio program as the only all-Jamaican show (*Star* 1/14/72, 12). Interestingly, one of the cohosts of this show was Beverly Anderson, who at the time was campaigning with and later married Michael Manley.

Thus protest songs became juke-box hits, played in slum beer joints and on sound systems in the countryside and in urban dance halls. The dance halls became increasingly an arena of conflict between youths and the police (#2, #13). One Rasta respondent told me that whenever he was at a dance and heard the Wailers' song "Fire, Fire," he ran. The police would be certain to raid, because they heard only the words "Babylon burning" and knew well that *Babylon* was a Rasta term for police (#2). The police frequently made such raids on dances; Western Kingston was particularly noted for it (#13). The phenomenon is described in Max Romeo's song "Three Blind Mice":

I went to a party last Saturday night
When I reached the party everything was all right
Then Babylon raid, them raid, them raid
Me catch me 'fraid, me 'fraid, me 'fraid.

It was like three blind mice
You coulda see how dem run
Baton sticks start flying, man start to bawl
Some jump the fence, some put up defense
But me catch me 'fraid, when Babylon raid.
The beast check the d.j.,
Tell him to turn off sound
The crowd never like that,
They start gathering round
Let the music play, let him play
It was like three blind mice
You coulda see how dem run
It was like three blind mice
No man no wan' go a jail.

The rise of this sort of repression clarifies the meaning the juke box had taken on for Bongo Neville, in the report in *Abeng* quoted above. It was no longer mere entertainment but had become a statement of defiance in the face of government efforts to ban critical songs. Conflict over musical practices was not new, and was not limited to Jamaica.   J. D. Elder reported that from 1838 onward, "Negro singing and dancing" was the center of a "most deadly struggle" between Blacks and planters in Trinidad (1966, 88).   Parallel repression from colonial days when plantation owners outlawed slaves' drumming did not escape the notice of Jamaican youths whose interest in African history and culture had recently been revived (Small 1969, 8).

One respondent tied the banning of records directly to the government's desire to maintain the status quo, which Rastafarians would change: "Our songs got banned all the while.... It was a war at the radio station, a literal going to fight fi get your music played. Cause you know them figure say Rasta is changing society. But that is what we come to do. We come to change things and when them see changes them quarrel and say it's changing. And that's what we come fi do, and them know it" (#36).

In the Jamaican novel about a reggae singer mentioned earlier, a record producer points out the unintended consequences of banning songs to a police commissioner, after the latter had caused a song by a fugitive criminal to be banned from airplay: "It was a damn fool mistake to ban that record. That is what tells the masses that unu desperate. That's what makes dis little bwai a big deal — when Babylon start to mess with the hit parade" (Thelwell 1980, 370).

Changes in the Status of Rastafari

Police harassment of Rastas continued through this period, with increasing publicity if not frequency, and with relative impunity. *Abeng,* as mentioned earlier, reported incidents of police raiding Rastafarian dwellings, stealing Rastafarians' money, cutting their locks, beating them, and in one case destroying valuable Nyabinghi drums with bayonets (*Abeng* 3/15/69, 1). In 1971, police set fire to some cave dwellings in Wareika Hills just outside the city limits, killing at least one Rastafarian (#6). An respondent from the PNP reported that after this incident, several members of the PNP wanted to investigate the matter further, to see if the government could be charged with murder. He reported that a leading right-wing member of the PNP dismissed the incident, saying, "I'm not concerned with those people. My constituency has been pestered by them for years, and if the police want to get rid of them, it's okay by me" (#6). A middle-class respondent told the interviewer that his class viewed Rastas with amusement, "because they are stupid people" (#14).

Rastafarian respondents reported this harassment in the interviews. One explained that this was the primary reason parents were unhappy to see the youths close to them growing locks:

> The pressure come from when shall Rasta in our house, anytime the policeman can kick in the door and come in. People have them one son that them love, them check them son, come back in with all these dreadlocks.... They might feel vex but that is not the thing. The only thing that them fret for is because he is a Rasta, they have to feel him gone to prison soon.... So your people fret for you under the circumstances there, so them say "No

come here Jah Rastafari, policeman come   too.
(#36)

Possession of ganja (marijuana), a sacred plant for Rastafarians, and which is smoked in communion rituals,
carried a minimum sentence of eighteen months' impri-
sonment under the JLP government. Many Rastafarians
were arrested on this charge. One respondent claimed that
false charges were sometimes brought against Rastafarians, and the charges stuck because when a policeman "say
them find herb pon you, cause you a Rasta, there's no way
nobody ever say no" (#36). The association of ganja and
Rastafarians was one source of middle class suspicion of
Rastas (#14).

Because Rastafarians look to Ethiopia as their natural
home and consider themselves "strangers in a strange land"
rather than Jamaicans, their doctrine openly irritated
Jamaicans with strong nationalistic feelings. It was on
charges of lack of patriotism and of an "un-Jamaican
character" that the Jamaica Broadcasting Corporation ter-
minated a series of broadcasts by Rastafarians in 1969
(Nettleford 1972, 62). As will be discussed below, there was
also some amount of resistance to Rastas because of their
rejection of Christianity (see Chapter 2).

Yet despite the continuing harassment of Rastafarians,
respondents agreed that Rastafarians were becoming an
important force in society by 1972 (#3, #5, #7, #9, #11,
#20, #21), and that this was due in part to their association
with black nationalism (#5, #7, #20). One said that Black
nationalism had "legitimized" Rastafari (#6). Another said:
"By 1972 the Rastas were appealing because they were
getting away from downpression, out of Babylon; they were
into love, something lacking in Jamaica due to class
divisions, and into the dignity of the black man. They were
into a strong black nationalism, and that was very appealing to the young" (#7). Some representatives of Jamaica's
established institutions were sympathetic to the Rastafarians. C. S. Reid, for example, then president of the
Jamaica Baptist Union, identified Rastafari as a reaction
against Jamaica's being "run as an annex of Great Britain,
treated as a white man's country which happened to be
peopled by blacks" (*Star* 2/18/72, 18).

Rastafarians were gaining visibility through the articles by them and about them in *Abeng*, through their participation in student groups, through the interest that radical intellectuals were taking in them (#11), through reggae music, and because of their growing numbers. One Rasta who has been dreadlocked since that time said that many of his friends also began to grow locks then, "when Rasta was getting a lot of attention, around 1968 or '69. There was a lot of young blood in Rasta then. After that, you might expect anyone to have dreadlocks" (#2).

Rasta had "to some degree taken over the urban *lumpen* areas," (#5), but it was not only lower- class youth who were locking their hair and espousing Rastafarian theology; to do so was becoming common among middle-class youths as well. The sons of David Coore, a former PNP minister of finance, became Rastafarians around this time. One was active in Black nationalist organizations and later went to live in Ethiopia, where he remains to this day; the other is an accomplished reggae musician of the "uptown" (nonghetto) variety (#11). A campaign manager for the PNP said that around 1971, the Rastafarians' "numbers had swelled. A lot of middle class kids became Rastas. It is also true that by that time, their image had improved. Many were into art, doing creative things. They weren't necessarily a bad element. Their language was gaining currency among the middle classes and the school children. We had the feeling that Rasta talk was understood across the country" (#20).

The same respondent later said that the Rastafarian language was a symbol of Black nationalism in 1972 (#20). The language, which became important in the 1972 campaign, consists of changes Rastafarians add to everyday Jamaican patois. The most important of these is the use of "I"-words. In patois, the first person singular is "me" in all cases, such as "Me have me book." The Rastafarian sees this as an expression of subservience, making the speaker always the object and never the subject, and overcompensates with a preference for "I" in all cases. For example, the title of the song by Max Romeo discussed later in this chapter is "Let the Power Fall on I." A speaker may refer to the person addressed as "the I" rather than "you," and to himself as "I-man." The correct plural form of "I" is "I and I."

The I-words have a number of significant connotations. The letter *I* always appears after Haile Selassie's name in print, signifying "the first" but read by Rastas as "I." "I" is also a homophone for the patois word *high*. Often, the first syllable of a word is dropped and replaced with *I*, as in the song quoted above, "Small Axe," which reads, "The goodness of Jah Jah I-dureth for-I-ver," instead of "endureth for ever." *Jah* is a variant of the Hebrew *Yahweh*, the name of the Judeo-Christian god.

The 1972 Election Campaigns

Overall Strategies

In contrast to the election campaigns before it, the 1972 campaigns incorporated a number of symbols new to party use. Both parties used physical props and had adopted new slogans. It was a dramatic, colorful, and, at times, vituperative contest. Although voter turnout was smaller than in other elections under study, there seemed to respondents to be more interest in the election and more participation in campaign events, such as mass meetings, than in any other election. "It was a carnival," according to one respondent (#11).

The Jamaica Labour Party government seemed to be on the defensive from the start of the 1972 campaign. As in 1967, it tried to choose an election date meaningful to JLP supporters, such as the anniversary of Bustamante's release from detention or his birthday. Only after the date was firmly set did it discover it was the birthdate of Edna Manley, Michael's mother.

Much of the JLP material is in reaction to the PNP's more aggressive campaign. One of its most often used slogans was "A change isn't coming with the JLP. It has happened already." This was a response to the PNP's slogan, "Time for a change." Three large JLP advertisements toward the end of the campaign attempted to convince readers that Seaga had gained possession of a major PNP prop, the Rod of Correction (see below), while its previous advertisements had that the PNP's attention to the rod was blasphemous and anti-Christian. A number of full-page JLP advertisements attempted to discredit the PNP by reprinting a pamphlet supporting the PNP. Thus, the JLP paid for a number of advertisements propagating PNP symbols.

Even those respondents who openly supported the JLP described their party in 1972 in interviews as "arrogant" (#14) and "out of hand" (#12). "By that time," said one, "the JLP had lost momentum. Walter Rodney, a grass roots organizer, had been kept out of Jamaica. The party seemed to be just pro-business, and had split into factions" (#12).

The JLP did revive some of its campaign tactics from 1967. The "Election News" format of full-page advertising was used again, comparing the PNP's preindependence administration to the JLP's postindependence adminstration (e.g. DG 2/5/72, 13) in areas such as loan acquisition, tax relief, and social welfare. Indeed, one advertisement compared the JLP government's performance with the five hundred years of government since Columbus discovered Jamaica. "Older Jamaicans are now saying 'I wish it happened in my time'" (DG 2/16/72, 11). Just how old these quoted Jamaicans were was never specified.

The advertisements that were comparative generally described a situation of preindependence and contrasted it with a description of the current situation. They ended with the slogan mentioned above, that the change "has already happened."

Other JLP slogans were "Jamaicans agree with the JLP," which was made more specific in some advertisements, such as "Young Jamaicans agree..." and "Farmers agree..."; "One Good Term Deserves Another"; "Who Trusts the PNP? Not You, Not Me!" (revived from 1967); and, late in the campaign, "The PNP believe in Michael's Rod; the JLP in Almighty God" (DG 2/24/72, 19).

The single characteristic about the JLP government most often mentioned by respondents was corruption at its higher levels (#7, #12, #13, #14). JLP ministers were known for "ostentatious living" and "feathering their nests" (#14). There were rumors that ministers had enriched themselves with kickbacks, and some party members were severely demoralized. There was some mention that a member of the JLP administration regularly passed information to the PNP, and it was reported that one JLP candidate told a crowd at a mass meeting, "If you don't vote for me, vote for Pagon" (#7). Pagon was the PNP candidate in the same district, and on election day most people did vote for him, rather than for the JLP candidate or for the independent.

The JLP government exposed itself to PNP attack on several fronts, including factionalism, corruption, and disfranchisement. Early in the campaign spokesmen for the PNP were asking if the JLP was Shearer's, Seaga's, Robert Lightbourne's, or Wilton Hill's party. There is evidence that the party was divided. It did not, as indicated above, always present a united picture in its paid advertising; two JLP candidates were allowed to contest the same seat in West Central St. Andrew, both of whom lost; and Seaga seemed to have a much higher profile than the party leader. One of the most effective PNP ads showed the JLP's bell being smashed in two by the Rod of Correction. The headline read, "A House Divided Against Itself Must Fall. The Day of Correction is at Hand" (DG 2/28/72, 27). The same advertisement implied that Minister of Education Edwin Allen had been misappropriating funds, and other PNP material promised to "restore integrity to public life" (DG 2/27/72, 7) and to require members of Parliament to declare their assets publicly (DG 2/27/72, 41).

A very controversial issue was that of youth disfranchisement. The voting age was twenty-one at that time, and the JLP government had not enumerated voters since 1969, resulting in a de facto voting age of twenty-three years, five months. The PNP estimated that 60,000 young adults were disfranchised, and gave the issue a great deal of publicity (DG 2/19/72, 17; 2/21/72, 13; 2/22/72, 8, 15; 2/23/72, 5, 10; 2/24/72,15; 2/28/72, 23) both in the party's own advertising and in advertisements paid for by "a group of disfranchised youth." Several of the advertisements asked, "Will you vote for us this time so that we can vote next time? We cry shame on any government that denies us our right to vote" (DG 2/22/72, 15). Another read, "We have pleaded, begged, protested, but the government has not listened to us. Is your child one of the neglected youths?" (DG 2/24/72, 15). The PNP promised to lower the voting age to eighteen and to institute electoral reforms so that enumeration could be more equitable (DG 3/1/71).

The JLP also referred to youth more than in 1967. For the Central Kingston constituency, Errol Anderson's advertisements accused the PNP of "taking no interest in the education of youths" and ended with the words, "Youthman It's Your Time. Tell Your Parents. On February 29, Vote Like This: Errol Anderson X" (DG 2/25/72, 30). Anderson was advertised as "Young, Gifted and Black" (DG 2/22/72; 13). In a general advertisement, the JLP asserted that "Young Jamaicans Agree with the JLP" because of its record for school and camp places and trade training centers (DG 2/17/72, 24).

It is interesting to note that the PNP made a special effort to appeal to two categories of nonvoters. The first was the youth (#11, #12, #13), a large section of whom were disfranchised. The second was the Rastafarians (see below), who generally profess not to vote. Although one PNP respondent, referring to the Rastas, said that "the smoking class" voted for the PNP in 1972 (#13), given most Rastafarians' expressed contempt for participating in "Babylon poli-tricks" (#18), it is highly unlikely that they voted in significant numbers.

The PNP was well prepared for the election; Prime Minister Shearer had held off elections until four months before the constitutional limit, and Michael Manley had been campaigning since he was elected party leader in 1969. The PNP's fifty-three candidates had been presented a full year before the election (DG 3/1/71).

One of the most significant elements in the PNP campaign was the Rod of Correction. The special meanings of this symbol will be discussed below, but it is useful to briefly discuss its origins here. In 1970, Michael Manley and P. J. Patterson, a leading younger member of the PNP, went to East Africa for a formal visit. Reportedly, when they visited Ethiopia they met with Emperor Haile Selassie, who gave Manley a walking stick in the usual formality of gift exchanges (#13). Patterson had acquired a horsewhip in Kenya, though not as a gift from any state official. According to an eyewitness, when the two returned to Jamaica, the "usual crowd" was there to greet them at the airport. "P. J. stole the show with his horsewhip. This must have inspired Michael to use the rod; his ego could not have taken being upstaged by P. J." (#13).

The rod became known as the Rod of Correction, and was the outstanding symbol of the 1972 elections. Almost half of the respondents cited it as soon as the topic of political symbols was raised (#4, #6, #7, #9, #10, #11, #13, #14, #17, #22,#24, #29, #31, #34). It was reportedly Claudius Henry, a spiritual leader who accepted Selassie as the Messiah, who named it the Rod of Correction and explained its significance to Manley (#13). Manley used the rod with skillful showmanship. When he came onto a platform to speak at a mass meeting, the rod would be in a box with people already onstage. He would go to them and take the rod out of its box, then hold it up and turn slowly to the audience. "He wouldn't say anything at all," a respondent said. "He didn't have to. The crowds would just go wild" (#13). During the speech when Manley talked about, for example, the corruption of the JLP ministers, he would again retrieve the rod, saying, "The Rod, this will get rid of it!" (#13)

The rod had a distinct political message, apart from the other meanings with which it was imbued that will be discussed below. The rod would correct social and econo- mic ills of the country (#4), and it was promised that it would correct JLP arrogance. With the help of PNP members, Clancy Eccles, a musician working for the party, wrote a song about the rod based on an old Sankey about the Baptist preacher of the turn of the century, Bedward. The original was sung, "Dip them, Bedward, Dip them/ Dip them in the healing stream." The Eccles version read, "Lick dem, Joshua, Lick dem / Lick dem with the Rod of Correction" (#7). This song helped to publicize the Rod further.

It is remarkable to note the attention that was devoted to this object. At one point during the campaign, burglars broke into Manley's house. Reportedly for a tense two hours Manley and other party leaders thought the rod had been stolen, but Manley's helper, who believed in the rod's supernatural powers, had hidden it safely away (#6). The next day was one that several informants remembered (#6, #17, #22). Seaga produced a rod that he claimed was the Rod of Correction, left behind by Michael after a tense meeting in Western Kingston. The *Gleaner's* account of the JLP rally where Seaga made the claim reads:

> the highlight of the meeting was the production by the candidate of a rod which he claimed to be "Joshua's Rod" — dropped, he said, in the Coronation Market last Thursday following an incident there. "Now he is a shepherd without his staff —a Joshua without a rod — and a leader without power," declared Mr. Seaga, as he held aloft the alleged rod to the cheers of the huge crowd. He said the rod had been found by a little boy, who had presented it to Seaga. "Any other rod Mr. Manley is seen with is a bogus rod," he declared. On election day (Seaga) was going to dip the rod into the ink and mark his X; then he would send it back to Emperor Haile Selassie.... (DG 2/24/72, 44)

In turn, a few days later Manley held a meeting in his own constituency of Central Kingston, which the *Gleaner* called "The Night of the Rod." Manley said that "a little boy had been caught in a lie. 'Trouble would take him for meddling in Joshua's business and when this little boy awakes on March 1 he'll have salt tears in his eyes.... Let them know that there is only one Rod of Correction in Jamaica and it is I-rod.' ...The crowd cheered and shouted 'Let us touch it' and 'Let us hold the power'" and chanted "Bell Time Done, Rod Time Come'" (DG 2/26/72, 16).

One PNP candidate who was intensely involved in the campaign that year cut a regular walking stick around the middle and brought it to the next PNP meeting. He reported that he said to the crowd: "'This is the stick that Seaga claims is the Rod of Correction. But you know the real Rod of Correction is invincible. And look at this one.' I held it up and cracked it in the middle. The crowd went wild. Michael had only to hold up the real thing and they went wild again" (#6). The same respondent had "no doubts" that the burglary of Manley's house was arranged by Seaga to steal the rod. He also said that he had once falsely claimed to a crowd that Seaga had actually stolen

the rod and that he, the respondent, had sneaked into Tivoli
Gardens dressed like a Rastafarian and stolen it back (#6).

The controversy about who was in possession of the true
Rod of Correction flowed over into the paid political
advertisements in the *Gleaner*.   One by the JLP showed
two photographs of Manley with a rod, but the pictures are
too blurred for it to be certain if it is the same rod in each.
The headline reads, "Which Rod?" and the text goes on:

> These pictures show Mr. Michael Manley with two
> different rods. Everyone knows that he has been
> touring the country with two rods: A rod of
> discovery and a rod of correction. It is significant
> that now he shows in the latest photo the "white
> top" rod of discovery. Where is the real rod of
> correction? LOOK AT THIS. BEHOLD THE ROD
> (photograph of Seaga with a rod). WHO TRUSTS
> THE PNP? NOT YOU, NOT ME. (DG 2/27/72, 10)

The PNP countered with:

> The Rod of Correction vs. the Stick of Deception.
> Seaga's Stick is not Joshua's Rod. (photograph of
> Manley with rod).   Here it is on triumphant
> display at the Coronation Market on Thursday
> night. It has never been out of my possession for
> one day -- nor will it ever be. Seaga's Stick is a
> Childish Trick.   It is the type of stick that is
> commonly used in Jamaica by people who cannot
> help themselves. The Rod is made of carved
> African Ebony, with an Ivory handle and an Ivory
> tip. It has metal clasps at the handle and tip.
> Jamaicans will not be fooled. (DG 2/27/72; 15)

The PNP's print advertising campaign was also a dramatic one, and made effective use of slogans. One respondent
said that the "PNP didn't want to alienate anybody in 1972.
They used slogans that appeared to be saying more than
they were. They seemed to be profound, but they were
really just ambiguous" (#13). Another respondent said that
the symbols and slogans of 1972 "implicitly promised many
things, including social justice. The promises were impli-

cit, and very few explicit promises were made" (#22). The PNP's primary slogans were "Better Must Come," "Time for a Change," "Power for the People," or simply "Power," and variations on "The Day of Correction."

The party ran a series of full-page advertisements that contrasted sharply in their simplicity with the JLP's wordy "Election News" format. They stressed the "time" theme and focused on single issues. All began with the words "It's time"; for example, "It's time to revive agriculture" (DG 2/13/72, 10); "It's time to end crime and violence" (DG 2/6/72, 9); "It's time people get work" (DG 2/7/72, 19).

In retrospect respondents remember the JLP campaign as one of facts and figures, but the PNP print advertisements also used statistics effectively. To demonstrate, one promised a fight against crime and in a simple table showed that annually between 1961 and 1971, murders rose from 57 to 154; rapes and assaults from 217 to a startling 4,142 (DG 2/6/72, 9).

One advertisement illustrates the PNP's use of the corruption issue. "It's time to end graft," it began. A photograph showed one man passing money behind his back to another. Both are dressed in business suits. "It's time to bring back honesty in public life. The growth of graft and corruption will destroy our country. Why should a few get fat and rich at the expense of the many? An equal opportunity must be given to all, not just to those who pay for favors" (DG 2/19/72, 5).

Manley frequently stressed the moral decay of the JLP government and the need for a "moral and spiritual rebirth." The party called for a "new style of government" to effect this rebirth: "We are committed to the idea of involving citizens and the church in democratic decision-making. We call this the Politics of Participation.... Our country has become bitterly divided. On all sides there is evidence of moral decline. Our task is to reunite our country, to inspire a new sense of moral purpose" (DG 2/20/72, 9).

In a letter to the *Gleaner* two months after the election, a church leader summed up the PNP victory:

The weakness of the JLP's electioneering was...
that they failed to answer the moral charges
made against them.... It was not money, but

righteousness which was at stake. In further
support of this is the fact that most of the images
and symbols used by the PNP were religious
symbols, including the Rod of Correction.... The
correction implied was not an economic nor even
a political one, but a moral and spiritual one. (DG
4/16/72)

The Use of Class Symbols and Class Conflict

Although race seemed to be the uppermost subjective
component of the campaign (#21, #20), the distribution of
economic power remained an underlying current. More
than one respondent viewed the interest in Black nationalism as a fleeting expression of class conflict (#3, #21, #34;
Stone 1974, 180). Rough estimates indicate that the PNP
referred more frequently than the JLP to class-related
issues (27 versus 20 references), such as wages, jobs and job
training, free school places, the plight of the "small
farmers," and poverty.

In both 1967 and 1972, the JLP stressed its role in
bringing "Progress and Prosperity" to Jamaica. Shearer,
for example, said in 1972 that unlike the PNP, which had
supported Jamaica's participation in the West Indies Federation and thus had harbored "ugly, unpatriotic doubts," the
"JLP had faith that independence under wise leadership
would bring prosperity to Jamaica" (DG 2/4/72, 9).

In one advertisement, the JLP presented its record in
acquiring money. One small pile of coins represented the
$420 million that the PNP had raised in the seven years
form 1955 to 1962, and a larger pile represented the JLP's
$1,130 million in the five years from 1967 to 1972. The
text ran, "The Money Game.... They say money is the root
of all things.... The rich have too much, the poor have too
little...." After comparing the two parties' success in
attracting foreign exchange loans and capital investment,
it continued, "Astounding you say? Well, the root of
success in the money game is based on two facts --
Confidence and Performance. Performance and confidence
are wonderful things... If you have them, KEEP THEM --
DON'T CHANGE THEM" (DG 2/5/72, 13).

The PNP attacked both the "money game" advertisement in particular and the concepts behind it. Reprinting most of it in an advertisement of its own, the PNP added, "The JLP boasts of the money game. Where has all the money gone?" In that advertisement and others, the PNP accepted the basic claim made by the JLP, that the JLP government had brought a measure of economic success to Jamaica, but attacked the ways the riches were distributed by contrasting the wealth of the ministers with the poverty of most Jamaicans. One advertisement consisted of a photograph illustrating the squalor of a tenement yard and the words "It's time people live better than this. Why should so many Jamaicans exist in poverty and degradation! Is this their share of Jamaica's progress?" (DG 2/8/72, 9). Another asserted, "Hundreds of thousands are not sharing in Jamaica's progress because they can no longer afford the simple necessities of life" (DG 2/12/72, 15). A third pointed out that a farmer's average income was $165 a year, to support a family of four; "Can this be progress?" (DG 2/13/72, 10). The PNP's election manifesto emphasized sharing the fruits of development, rather than producing them (DG 2/24/72).

Both parties made an effort to appeal to the economically unfortunate. Both repeatedly stressed "work for the needy" (PNP: DG 2/2/72, 8; 2/7/72, 19, 25; 2/23/72, 5. JLP: 2/19/72, 24; 2/28/72, 15), and the cost of living was frequently mentioned (PNP: DG 2/18/72, 19. JLP: 2/21/72, 28; 2/27/72, 36). The JLP pointed to the National Insurance Scheme, under which a proportion of the aged received pensions, and said in one advertisement: "No more must the old and the poor go to the Alms House" (DG 2/10/72, 6). The PNP claimed the scheme did not do enough: "It's time for ALL old people to get pensions. Isn't it a shame that so many old people are so callously made to suffer want and deprivation?" (DG 2/16/72, 14). At a mass meeting, a JLP supporter was reported to have made the claim that the PNP gave free school places only to the rich, and now the JLP gives 70 percent of the free places to "the poor" (DG 2/10/72, 5). The JLP did institute an arrangement by which more free places were awarded to needy students. The PNP administration before 1962 had awarded free places solely on the basis of test scores; after

1962, the JLP allocated 70 percent of high school places to children from public primary schools, and reserved 30 percent of free places for middle-and upper-class students whose parents could afford to send them to private elementary schools. The material reviewed revealed no PNP response to this charge, and the 70:30 ratio remained the method of school place distribution throughout the PNP administrations of the 1970s.

Manley and other PNP spokespersons adopted a new catchword for the poor, which had frequently been used in *Abeng: Sufferers*. At a mass meeting, Manley told the audience that he was "a sufferers' man" and that "the government of the PNP which is going to take over on March 1, 1972, will be a government devoted to trying to solve the problems of sufferers" (DG 2/7/72, 1). Although they did not use the word, JLP supporters strove to demonstrate that the plight of sufferers had improved during the JLP government. One advertisement implied that the JLP could improve the condition of the poor without antagonizing the well-to-do: "Where are the barefoot people now? Where is the Jamaica where you could employ household help for one dollar per week? ...Where is the Jamaica in which... workers were still expected to put in long hours for low wages? ...The JLP fought with policies and programmes to change all that... without preaching class or race hatred" (DG 2/28/72, 31).

The PNP's slogan, "Better Must Come," definitely spoke to the desire for a better material way of life for the masses, but it was not a slogan that necessarily implied class conflict. One respondent said it was meant to appeal to the "largest possible group, from the middle class on down" (#20). Manley told a mass meeting, "When a man sings 'Better Must Come,' ... he only means he is suffering and looking forward to a better day" (DG 2/7/72, 1).

Although Manley often condemned the "rich men," implicitly and explicitly it was clear that the wealthy to whom he most often referred were the corrupt bureaucrats and politicians, not the indigenous upper class. On the contrary, the upper class and the middle class were sources of strong support for the PNP. One respondent said that the PNP "was still very much a middle class party, and had an appeal across the spectrum of classes. Manley had a gut appeal for the general masses, but also an intellectual appeal to the middle class" (#11). An educator pointed out that 1972 was the first time "the middle class went out campaigning in large numbers, especially teachers, young teachers, and professionals and businessmen too. There was a great hopefulness" (#12). A third respondent, a PNP supporter, agreed: "Michael was everybody's hope, all classes. The masses thought he was Malcolm X, and the bourgeoisie thought he was John Kennedy. It was an all-class alliance. But really the masses also thought of him as Joshua, who would lead them across the River Jordan to defeat the Pharaoh Shearer" (#13). Rather than division, Manley and other PNP spokespersons repeatedly stressed national unity (DG 2/16/72, 12; 2/20/72, 9).

A letter to the editor of the *Gleaner* from a JLP supporter attempted to throw into doubt the reversal of the traditional class biases of the two parties. The writer said the PNP, which was formed by the middle class, turned its attention to the poor only to receive electoral support. He asked who the "sufferers" that the PNP talked about really were:

> They are the so-called middle class who feel that the lower classes, as they call them, are faring better under the JLP government... Their children are now able to sit side-by-side with their children in the best high schools... They cannot crush them under foot as they used to. This annoys them and they would do anything to destroy the party and bring these poor people again into slavery. (DG 2/27/72, 12)

In one advertisement for the PNP there is a specific reference to the "working class" rather than "sufferers." It was not part of the PNP's advertising campaign but a release by the Trade Union Congress, a union dominated by Marxists in the 1950s that remained supportive of the PNP even after it was "purged" from the party in 1952. The advertisement accused the JLP of factionalism and corruption, and of an orientation against the working class. In 1964, it said, the AFL-CIO offered a loan of $4 million to build one thousand houses for workers, and there was a photograph of Shearer accepting the offer. It continued:

> The Government Betrayed the BITU! The Government Denied the Working Class Low-Cost Housing! Can you understand this action by a labour government? ... This betrayal is only one of the many committed by the JLP against working class people. The Trade Union Congress of Jamaica with its record of service cannot relinquish our role as champions of working class people... He that knoweth the will of the people and doeth not shall be beaten with many X's. Now is the time for change. Vote PNP. (DG 2/27/72, 28)

In one account Manley was quoted as stressing the unity of the "sufferers" that was needed to break the "bond of oppression," but again the "class enemy" of the poor was not defined in the context of a consistent ideology of class struggle and may referred only to corrupt politicians: "I have watched men teach people to hate each other, setting youth against youth, teaching black man to hate black man, and poor to hate the poor. When my people need unity to break the bond of oppression, they are taught to hate" (DG 2/21/72, 18).

Both parties supported increasing the power of "Jamaicans" over economic enterprises, yet the foreign capitalist was not the target of vitriolic propaganda. The JLP prior to the campaign period had pursued what it called "Jamaicanisation," which meant that foreign companies had to give local enterprise a chance to participate. The results of this policy, according to a PNP supporter, were that the local bourgeoisie had managed to buy some shares, but still had no controlling interests (#13). The JLP in 1972 emphasized that it was proceeding slowly but steadily on this task:

> Everyone has their own way to do things. We do our own thing too. We could do it somebody's way, but we do it the JAMAICAN WAY. Take the problem of foreign ownership. First we accept that we want the help of foreign interest... but

> we want Jamaicans to participate in the action
> too. How? Suddenly? Overnight? One, one fill
> basket, Jamaicans say. This is the Jamaican Way.
> "Gradual" is the word. IT'S OUR WAY TO
> CHANGE. (DG 2/7/72, 10)

The PNP promulgated a policy of "Economic Nationalism" that was not very different. The middle class
perceived it as a chance to control the economy, with
fewer foreign interests (#13), but this received little
attention during the campaign.

"Under the JLP," one respondent said, "wealth naturally
flowed to a few." But it was not so much this fact as the
fact that those few were mostly non-Black that contributed to the growing sense that injustice was inherent in
the economy (#25).

The Use of Race Symbols and Racial Contention

The surge of support for Black nationalist philosophies
was evident almost immediately in the People's National
Party. In 1969, P. J. Patterson, who was reputedly a Black
nationalist and radical, won a seat in a by-election with the
slogan "Young, Gifted and Black," the title of an American
song popularized in Jamaica by reggae artists (#13).

In contrast to the JLP government's rejection of a
proposal made during Walter Rodney's days on campus to
teach African history in the schools, Manley proposed it
himself in his 1969 budget speech, his first as leader of the
opposition:

> We are still trapped in the legacy of our history.
> We lack that assurance in racial matters that
> flows from a complete emotional certainty that
> all races accept each other as equals. An epoch
> of brainwashing in a white-oriented society has
> left scars, which, however unconscious, mar the
> inner assurance with which black people accept
> their own norms of beauty and excellence. I
> propose the teaching of African history and of a
> realistic re-interpretation of Jamaican history as
> standard elements of our school curriculum to

help undo the damage of the ages and set our present attitudes in a framework of historical truth. (PNP Document I)

In early 1970, Manley praised the concept of Black power, while rejecting racism and violence. To him Black power meant:

> The acceptance, with joy and pride, of the fact of blackness, of black dignity and black beauty.... Jamaica must restore to her sense of independence and nationhood a basis of pride and hope, respect of dignity and self-confidence which are expressed in that great phrase of "Black Power." I say to those who know how much is wrong in this country and to those who suffer from those wrongs, join together to use political Black Power to make the black man free in his own country to live a decent civilised and happy life. (DG 2/22/70)

When the party presented its candidates at its 1971 annual conference in the National Stadium, the platform was hung with banners proclaiming slogans obviously borrowed from the Black power movement in the United States but deliberately altered: e.g. "Change, Baby, Change" and "Right on with the Change." These particular slogans did not figure in the 1972 campaign a year later, but similar ones were introduced.

Many respondents associated the PNP's 1972 campaign with Black power (#5, #7, #13, #15, #20, #21, #22, #25, #29, #30), yet the party did not associate itself overtly with the philosophy. In 1962 an independent candidate, Millard Johnson, had run and failed miserably on a Black nationalist platform. Three supporters close to the PNP campaign of 1972 said that the party was close to Black power but was loathe to be identified as such because it would alienate a number of middle-class Anglophilic Jamaicans (#13, 20, 26). Two symbols were primarily associated with Black power. First, the party adopted the slogan "Power for the People," deliberately not "Power to the People." Again, the party wanted to come close to taking on but not directly take on a Black power slogan (#13). Second, the party used the clenched fist as a symbolic gesture, which was controversial even within the PNP. There was a move to exclude it from the party's symbolic repertoire shortly before the 1972 campaign, but it was narrowly defeated in the National Executive Council (#13).

These two symbols were apparently very popular. A journalist said that when driving through the countryside she noticed that "the fist was everywhere" (#11). Another respondent who was in the countryside noticed "a lot of clenched fists and shouts of 'Power!'" after the election results were reported (#7). In 1971, key campaign managers for the party wrote a song with Clancy Eccles called "Power for the People" that was used extensively by the party and was sung by the artist during the bandwagon (see discussion below). After the song was already quite popular, another version was cut on which Eccles sings only the chorus and Michael Manley, or "Joshua," as he was introduced on the record, talk-sings his party's philosophy of change as verses of the song. He discusses the "politics of participation," or "collective consultation," which the PNP would institute if it had the chance to form the next government, and stresses that the party's role is one of agent of change.

It is interesting to note that among the campaign materials from the PNP in 1972, apart from the clenched fist and "Power for the People," symbols adopted from the Black power movement, there is virtually no reference to race. Once Manley is reported to have said that the JLP has taught "black man to hate black man" (DG 2/21/72, 18), and there are scattered references to Africa (e.g. DG 2/29/72, 8). The Rod of Correction, because it came from Africa and represented conflict, was associated by some with Black power (#3, #4). Whatever efforts the party was making to associate itself symbolically with Black power, it hesitated to make such commitments in its printed advertisements.

The JLP used references to race occasionally in the campaign. Minister of Education Edwin Allen was portrayed as having been "chief spokesman for human rights for black people in England" (DG 2/1/72, 7), and Errol Anderson adopted Patterson's slogan "Young, Gifted and

Black" (DG 2/22/72, 13).   But the primary thrust of the
references in the JLP's campaign was to discredit the PNP
and to deplore its "injecting race into the campaign" (DG
2/21/72, 18). One pro-JLP respondent said: "The PNP tried
to make race an issue in 1972, which makes the PNP the
world's first socialist-racist party. 'Workers of the World,
Fragment!' That shows you how deep their socialism goes"
(#5).

In one advertisement, the JLP attempted to portray the
PNP symbols and slogans as threatening ones. It is a
simple advertisement, with a full-page photograph of an
angry-looking, bearded Black man with his fist clenched in
the air. The word "Power" is coming from his mouth. The
text reads, in its entirety: "Beware of Power! Beware of
the Fist! Who trusts the PNP? Not you, not me!" (DG
2/23/72, 26; 2/26/72, 30). This sentiment was echoed in a
letter to the *Gleaner* some time later: "Outside the Iron
Curtain and its satellites, the peace loving people of the
world dread the sign of the clenched fist. No literate
person needs to be told what it signifies.... I was threatened with murder for all 'pale' faces when I passed a PNP
meeting two nights ago and was told that the license of my
car would be remembered" (DG 2/27/72, 12).

One way in which the PNP associated itself with Black
power was by using Rastafarian symbols, which will be
discussed below.

The Use of Rastafarian Symbols and Reggae Music

"There is only one man who sets the election date," said
Prime Minister Hugh Shearer in 1971. "And that man is I-
man" (Walters, 1981). So began an election contest replete
with symbols borrowed from the followers of Haile Selassie
I, emperor of Ethiopia. Manley, Rod of Correction in hand,
scoffed at the "man who called himself I-man" and who had
tried to set an election date meaningful to the JLP. The
election date he had set, Manley said, "turned out to be the
birthdate of I-Mother" (DG 2/7/72, 1).

The respondents generally agreed that 1972 was the
highest point in the use of Rasta symbols by politicians,
even though the JLP used them more often in 1976 than in
1972. The types of symbols used fall into several cate-

gories: language and names, props, issues, and connections with specific individuals.

As mentioned earlier, the Rastafarian's distinctive words and phrases were current and popular in the early seventies (#34, #5, #20) and were considered by some to be a symbol of Black nationalism (# 20). Manley used not only the "I-words" but also other phrases associated with Rastas. He began every speech with "The Word is Love" (DG 2/24/72, 7; 2/25/72, 41), which had definite Rastafarian connections (#1, #2, #7, #20). Rastafarians generally use the word *Love* as a greeting and as a farewell. Another Rasta greeting is "Peace and Love," which was also used by Manley. "Hail" and "Hail the Man" were used frequently at mass meetings (DG 2/6/72, 18; 2/18/72, 20) and were also Rasta phrases, valued particularly because of similarity with the name *Haile*. On the day after the election, a song was released by Ken Lazarus called "Hail the Man," in celebration of the victory of "Joshua" (Walters 1981).

The name *Joshua* also had meaning for the Rastafarians, although it had meaning as well for the far greater numbers of Protestants in Jamaica (#9).   Joshua is a biblical hero for Rastafarians (#4) and Blacks throughout the diaspora who traditionally identified themselves with the Jewish captivity in Egypt. Rastafarians refered to Manley as Joshua in songs (e.g. Max Romeo, "No, Joshua, No," 1974). A senior official of the PNP who had campaigned in the lower-class areas of Kingston said that he thought that people sometimes confused the names *Joshua* and *Jah* (#34). Whether or not this is true, there is little doubt that the similarity of the two names did not escape the notice of Rastafarians, who are known to take such nuances of language quite seriously.

Of the physical symbols used, the Rod of Correction is, of course, the most important. The PNP also used the *Abeng*, or cowhorn of the Maroons, at mass meetings; it had been popularized by the Abeng movement and the Rastafarians (DG 2/16/72, 12).

The connections between the Rod of Correction and the Rastafarians were several. First and foremost, the rod was said to have come from Selassie himself. Of the respondents who had opinions about this claim, five believed it (#6, #13, #17, #22, #31) and two thought it was fabricated by the PNP to associate itself with the Rastafarians (#9, #14). It rang true for Rastas who had heard the story of Selassie tossing a rod at the Italian army (#9). Second, such rods were carried by Rastafarians long before the Rod of Correction (#4, #13), probably as a response to photographs they had seen of Ethiopian priests carrying rods. Third, Manley deliberately made a connection between the Rod of Correction and the song "Beat down Babylon" by Junior Byles, which is an overtly Rastafarian song (DG 2/7/72, 1).

Finally, the rod is tied with older, African religious currents in Jamaica. Rods were used in a number of Obeah ceremonies, in which people were beaten with rods to drive out evil. Rods also figured highly in the Myal cult from preemancipation days. Slaves in Jamaica had come from several tribes, and the "men of science" ("witchdoctors") among them did not have the authority to unite the slaves effectively. There was a deliberate attempt to create a new religious order to unite the various tribes in one secret society; it was called the Myal cult. Myal is associated with rebellion; the slave leader Tacky initiated his warriors into the Myal cult before the slave rebellion that he led (#13). The initiation was supposed to make the warriors immortal. The Rastafarians' beliefs derive partly from the survivals of such African religions (Barrett 1977) and the immortality theme is not an uncommon one. Some Rastafarians are convinced that death is for sinners alone, and that they are immortal as long as they follow the laws of the Nazarites. In a discussion of the influence of the Soviet Union in Ethiopia, one Rastafarian said: "The Russians can't take guns and destroy it, you know. Bad man. Dem a idiot. Them say there is no god. And me, I know that there is a god. Cause I know who god is. And the guys come stick me with a gun and say there is no god. I say yes, there is a god. And them fire it! And it miss. And them fire it again and it miss. And them fire it plenty time and it miss, because there is a god" (#36) There are references to immortality in several Rastafarian reggae songs.

In one report of a mass meeting, Manley is said to have claimed protection from above. He said he had been shot at but "there is no way God let a bullet touch me, because my mission is love" (DG 2/21/72, 18). Manley used to make claims of protection for the Rod of Correction as well, saying that no one could steal it because it would evade robbers on its own (#6). Belief in the supernatural powers of the Rod of Correction, therefore, was not discouraged by the PNP. Several respondents felt that a large number of people believed it had such powers (#6, #10, #13, #22).

At times the PNP campaigned on issues that directly affected Rastafarians in a practical, nonsymbolic way. First, rumor had it during the campaign that Manley had promised the Rastafarians that he would legalize ganja (#7). Of course, the PNP government did not do so, but it did abolish the eighteen-month minimum sentence and imposed instead a maximum sentence of three years.

In a report of a PNP mass meeting, victimization and harassment of Rastafarians were mentioned. Curiously, the speaker was Eli Matalon, a Jewish millionaire industrialist. He said that Prime Minister Shearer was styling himself as "I-man," "yet it is his government that has persecuted the Rastafarians by shaving their beards and trimming their hair.... It was only during the building of the Harbour View Housing Scheme (a PNP project) that Rastas were allowed to work unmolested" (DG 2/21/72, 18).

One of the most controversial figures in the 1972 election was the Reverend Claudius Henry (see Chevannes 1977). Henry was a Black nationalist and a Rastafarian of unorthodox beliefs. He gained notoriety first in 1959, when he distributed thousands of cards inviting the bearer to an "Emancipation Jubilee" and promising passage back to Africa. The cards were sold at one shilling each, and hundreds of Rastafarians and other Jamaicans appeared at his church's headquarters, baggage packed and ready for the return trip. Many had sold their belongings. Henry was arrested and fined 100 pounds. The year after, raids on Henry's church revealed a cache of arms, and Henry's son Ronald was reportedly leading a band of Rastafarian guerrillas in the Red Hills outside Kingston. When the son was discovered by Jamaican and British soldiers, two British soldiers were killed in the ambush. Ronald Henry and four of his men were tried and sentenced to death, and Claudius Henry was imprisoned (Barrett 1977, 95-99).

Claudius Henry had long been released from prison in 1971, by which date he had definitely made contact with

Michael Manley. Henry had been mentioned in connection with Walter Rodney as well (Gonsalves 1979, 12).   The *Gleaner* reported that at the PNP's Annual Conference in February of 1971, "As each candidate's name was called, the drums of the Reverend Claudius Henry's Peacemaker's Church boomed across the arena" (DG 3/1/71).   One respondent was certain that it was Henry who first called the rod the Rod of Correction, and was less certain but was under the impression that he had given Manley the name Joshua as well (#13). A song sung in Henry's Peacemaker's Church went as follows:

> *Haile Selassie I is our God*
> *Claudius Henry is our King*
> *Michael Manley is our Joshua*
> *What a peace of mind*
> *Our Joshua has come.*

Instead of singing "Amen" at the end of the song, the congregation would sing "Power" (#13).

In November of 1971, Henry evidently had a handbill printed on which there were three photographs: "Moses and his Rod," under a photograph of Henry; "The King and his Righteous Sceptre," under one of Haile Selassie; and "Joshua and his Staff," under one of Michael Manley. This was the famous "Henry Pamphlet," or, as the PNP called it, "the JLP Bogus Pamphlet Lie" (DG 2/26/72, 5).

One week before the election, the JLP printed its first advertisement calling attention to the pamphlet. It began with the headline, "The voice is the voice of Moses but the hand is the hand of Joshua," and continued with a recapitulation of the Henry family saga. Then it read:

> The year was 1971. Behold!   Claudius Henry returns. He makes common cause with Michael (who calleth himself Joshua) the son of Norman, under whose reign Henry was convicted.... And now it has come to pass that Henry (who calleth himself Moses) recalling that his son was hung by the neck and that he was imprisoned... now proclaimeth before all people that "we have suffered Death and Imprisonment, for this message

of truth and no one came to our refuge, but Mr.
Michael Manley...." And now it has come to pass
that they now support each other with their rods
and drums. Astonishing? But it's true! The PNP
believe in Michael's Rod.   The JLP in Almighty
God. (DG 2/22/72, 28)

The pamphlet was reprinted, and is sufficiently clear for
the photographs, but not the text, to be seen.   A second
JLP advertisement quoted the text of the pamphlet.   It
stated that the time for a change had come, and "this
change will be the greatest religious event to take place
since the beginning of the creation of God." It continued:
"Is the pamphlet saying that the event is greater than the
birth of Christ?   Greater than the Ascension of Christ?
Astonished? But it's true!" (DG 2/24/72, 19).

The PNP received some support on the issue from the
leadership of the Jamaica Council of Churches, which in its
own full-page advertisement in the *Gleaner*, condemned
the "use of the Henry Pamphlet to attack the leader of the
PNP and his party," calling it "personal abuse and a
deplorable dragging of the name of God into the election
fight." It expressed confidence that the leaders of both
parties believed in God (DG 2/26/72, 23).   The PNP itself
retaliated by denying any association with the printing and
distribution of the pamphlet, calling it "blasphemous" and
claiming that it was the product of the "senseless and
deceitful political trickery of desperate politicians" (DG
2/26/72, 5).

The JLP printed two more advertisements about the
pamphlet.   When it lost the election, Shearer, conceding
defeat, described the conduct of "certain church officials"
as "very strange, questionable and disappointing" (DG
3/1/72, 1).   Three weeks later, former JLP Minister of
Education Edwin Allen wrote in a letter to the *Gleaner*
that a "major factor in the PNP victory was the partisan
role played by those church leaders" who had published
statements in the *Gleaner.* He added that he had always
"taken an interest in" the Rastafarians, and when Selassie
visited Jamaica, Allen had asked members of his entourage
to send missionaries to Christianize them (DG 3/26/72).

The use of the Henry pamphlet was not the only sign of JLP resistance to the PNP's use of Rastafarian symbols. At a JLP mass meeting, a constituent paid tribute to the late Norman Manley, but then stated that his son had joined forces with some "strange elements" and "wanted to turn the country into a Rastafarian state" (DG 2/18/72, 22). This theme was repeated in several letters to the *Gleaner* (DG 2/23/72, 17; 2/25/72, 18; 2/27/72, 12). Another said he would be willing to give Mr. Manley a try, but he had doubts when he heard Manley say things like "Hail that man" and "I and I" (DG 2/25/72, 18).

A JLP advertisement went so far as to liken Manley and Hitler:

> Hail the Man or Hail God? The JLP's slogan since 1961 has been "freedom." What about the PNP's?
> In 1962 it was "Have faith in the man"
> In 1967 it was "Follow the man"
> In 1972 they say "Hail the Man"
>
> We thought man should have faith in God, follow God, and hail God, not man. That is what we were taught in church.
>
> Manley's supporters say "Hail"
> Hitler's supporters said "Heil"
>
> Is there a difference?
> Who trusts the PNP? Not you, not me. Vote JLP.
> (DG 2/25/72, 24).

A later letter to the editor mentioned the similarities between "Heil" and "Hail" and added that Mussolini and Castro had both said that they were placing power in the hands of the people (DG 2/27/72, 12).

Music

The aftermath of the 1972 election was filled with hope and reggae. "Better Can't Come Too Soon!" a supporter of the PNP shouted on a country road upon hearing that his party was victorious (#7). "May God's blessings rest on your deliberations," said Sir Clifford Campbell, representing the crown at the opening of Parliament, "and better must come." On the morning of 1 March, a song heard on the radio for the first time, "Hail the Man," proclaimed that "It's a brand new day" (Walters 1981). Clancy Eccles had made a victory song, "Free at Last," that celebrated the demise of "Pharaoh" administration (Walters 1981). It was not surprising that a campaign dominated by music would finish "wid riddim."

Probably the first song used in the campaign was "Everything Crash" by the Ethiopians, which was current when Manley was elected leader of the PNP. It was played at PNP meetings and was adopted as something of a party song during the 1969-70 period. The fact that it had been banned was a help to the PNP (#13). As mentioned earlier, the song was remembered by a number of respondents. Its first line, "Look deh now," appeared in other campaign material, for example, a poem about the election in the *Gleaner* ended with the lines:

> *Michael Joshua Manley coming*
> *Look deh now, Shearer is running. (DG 2/29/72,*
> *18)*

Delroy Wilson's "Better Must Come" was probably the most widely used of the reggae songs. The song, as was mentioned above, was "innocently" written; an reependent who knew the artist said that it had its inspiration in the fact that Wilson himself just "didn't have enough hits" (#2). The song laments that times are hard, suspects others of "trying to keep me down" and "trying to take advantage of me," and looks forward to "better." The song includes a proverb,"Who God bless, no one curse." When the song was released, a PNP activist heard it in a barroom juke box. "I thought that if most people were thinking along the same lines as the people who were making the songs, we would win by a landslide" (#6). He "appropriated" the title in 1971 and had it used as a filler in the party paper, *The New Nation.*

"Better Must Come" became the party's primary slogan, used in most print advertisements and in mass meeting speeches. The slogan spoke to the desire for a better material life; it contained an implicit promise for a more equitable distribution of wealth, according to one political

scientist (#22). A PNP campaign manager said that the
party used the song "because it was clear that the rich
were getting richer and the poor were getting poorer"
(#20).

During 1970, the idea of using songs occurred to several
PNP activists at the same time, and a tape was put
together that included a number of songs that had been
banned by the JLP government (#6). The PNP carried the
Jamaican custom of music at mass party meetings several
steps further by organizing "bandwagons."   Rather than
incorporating a bit of music into one's political meeting,
the PNP kept the political speeches to a bare minimum
during its stage shows.

Once a week during 1971, the PNP held a bandwagon in
some parish capital or country town (#13). With the help
of Clancy Eccles, the musician who was hired by the PNP
and who wrote several songs used in the campaign, the
party hired all the major artists whose songs expressed
dissatisfaction as well as many of the other popular artists
of the day.   Of fourteen artists listed in a bandwagon
advertisement (DG 1/23/72), eight were among the top
twenty-five artists for 1971 (Star 1/21/72) or among the
top ten in the month preceding the election (DG 1/16/72).
The cast included Bob Marley, Peter Tosh, Bunny Wailer,
Clancy Eccles, Ken Boothe (whose song had been used in
1967), the Jamaicans, Max Romeo, Dennis Alcapone, Delroy Wilson, and Junior Byles.   The concerts were free in
the rural areas, and a nominal fee was charged when they
were held in the National Stadium in Kingston. They were
advertised not in the form of a political advertisement, but
as a concert would have been, with pictures of the artists'
faces around the announcement and a photograph of a
crowd at the bottom.   Michael Manley's photograph appeared among those of the singers.

The artists appreciated the work and the exposure. "We
got all the top artists," said a PNP respondent. "They were
naturally opposed to the government because their songs
had been banned.   Anything that remotely smelled of
protest had been banned" (#13). "It was a chance for the
artists," said a musician who had played in the bandwagons.
"It was a service for the politician, but the musicians got

the chance to play to a large crowd, which served to promote them. They also got paid regularly" (#27).

The music was a drawing card, pulling out the crowds and capturing the audience for political speeches. "We were able to attract a wider audience than the JLP," said one PNP spokesperson, "because we had better speakers and better entertainment" (#34). The artist who had played in the events agreed: "People all over love music. We covered every nook and cranny in Jamaica and got good crowds all over" (#27). One PNP activist estimated that the average attendance was 20,000 (#13).

The repertoire of the artists in the bandwagon was not exclusively political but included all the "hit parade" music. However, the protest music that had been banned was particularly striking. The artist that had participated remembered Junior Byles as providing one of the highlights of the concerts with his song "Beat down Babylon." "It really had an impact," he said. "It started some people thinking in different political directions. It wasn't necessarily produced with a political aim, but people attach political meanings to the songs" (#27).

"Beat Down Babylon" was associated with the Rod of Correction, and was an unambiguous condemnation of the society in which the righteous Rastafarian finds himself "captive." It addressed the lack of material wealth that causes people to be "dying for starvation" and warns that a revolution might be the result:

> Said me nah like the kind of Babylon,
> Said me nah dig them wicked men
> For I'm a righteous Rastaman,
> And I'm a dread dread one I-man
> I and I go beat down Babylon,
> I and I must whip them wicked men
> What a wicked situation,
> I and I dying for starvation
> This might cause a revolution,
> And a dangerous polution
> I and I go beat down Babylon,
> I and I go whip them wicked men

"Beat Down Babylon" was the most popular record in Jamaica during the 1971-72 period (*Star* 1/21/72). Its author was a ghetto youth and the song was his first big-seller. It had been banned by the government, but a few months before the election was allowed to be played on the radio. There were protests from some indignant Jamaicans, one of whom wrote to the *Gleaner* that "it is a disgrace that any responsible body should allow such a song on the air, or anywhere for that matter," and that it promoted "bloody revolution" (DG 1/24/72, 10).

Besides "Beat Down Babylon," other songs that were popular and that were featured in the bandwagons included two written especially for the PNP by Clancy Eccles, "The Rod of Correction" and "Power for the People," and Max Romeo's "Let the Power Fall on I," which was associated with the PNP because the word *Power* was a PNP catchword:

> *O let the power fall on I, Fari,*
> *O let the power fall on I*
> *O let the power from Zion fall on I,*
> *O let the power fall on I.*
> *O give I justice peace and love, Fari,*
> *O give I justice peace and love*
> *O let the power fall on I, Fari,*
> *O let the power fall on I.*
> *O let the wicked burn in ash, Fari,*
> *O let the wicked burn in ash.*
> *O let the power fall on I, Fari,*
> *O let the power fall on I.*

The PNP expressed its commitment not to interfere, as had the JLP, with the hit parade (DG 2/17/72, 10). In a speech in which Manley had declared himself a "sufferers' man," he discussed the songs that the audience had heard or would hear that evening:

> When a man sings "Better Must Come" he means no sedition, he means no violence. He only means that he is suffering and looking forward to a better day. "Let the Power Fall on I" means every man who can't find a job and goes and sees

others with opportunity and privilege, and who says if there is a God, "Let the Power Fall on I." It means every woman who says "me find some way to send my child to school in a way that I would like." "The Rod of Correction" says that a man looks around and realizes that graft and corruption abound and henchmen grow rich, and that if it takes a rod of correction to bring justice, then justice must come. When Junior Byles sings "Beat Down Babylon" he is not talking about the police. The police are honest people with a job to do. "Beat Down Babylon" says: remove oppression, oppression in Babylon, and let justice rise in the land. Oppression and corruption are rampant in Jamaica and I am going to beat down oppression. (DG 2/7/72, 1)

Another song that was in the top ten during the month before the election was "Dem Ha Fe Get A Beatin" by Peter Tosh, which was, according to one respondent, a deliberately partisan song (#13) and which was immediately taken to be anti-JLP (Walters 1981):

I can't stand this no longer,
The wicked get stronger
I can't stand this no longer,
The battle is getting hotter
Dem ha fe get a beaten, the wicked,
Ha fe get a beaten
Dem mus get a beaten,
The wicked ha fe get a beaten
Now that you waited,
Till your back is against the wall
One step to progress my brother and I know,
Jah will help you all.
Tell me how long,
Must the good suffer for the bad
And everytime the good open his mouth,
The bad say you musa mad
Dem ha fe get a beaten, Dem mus get a beaten
They've been reigning too long,

It has been 400 long years and
I just can't get on. Dem ha fe get a beaten.

Tosh, who had been arrested the year before in a demonstration protesting the White regime in Rhodesia (Clark,
1980), was the only reggae singer that one PNP activist
could name as definitely a supporter of the PNP (#3).

Clancy Eccles, whose songs "Rod of Correction" and
"Power for the People" were written for and used by the
PNP, organized the bandwagons and regularly addressed
crowds at PNP meetings (DG 2/20/72, 21). At one, he
hailed Haile Selassie and told the audience that Jamaicans
of African origin should respect that Black man who had
led his country successfully for so many years (DG 2/29/72,
8).

The *Gleaner's* political reporter, in a somewhat bitter
tone, summed up the "recipe" for winning elections. First,
the party emphasizes pockets of dissatisfaction. Then, it
strikes up a friendship with the "balladeers" and follows
with "an outpouring of highly hypnotic music with words of
great dissatisfaction." Because the music has a popular
beat, "the mood spreads, enveloping the whole country in a
web of dissent" (DG 3/12/72, 6). Another journalist summed up the election eight years later:

> "One Good Term Deserves Another" and "Jamai-
> cans Agree with the JLP" (were) nothing to stir
> the soul on fire, the imagination of youth and
> those who wanted social change.... It was no time
> for sweet reason. It was time to play upon the
> emotions, to paint pictures of a "New Jerusalem,"
> to embolden the spirit.... The PNP was down to
> earth with a message of change borne by a
> charismatic messenger ... "Joshua." (The JLP)
> dwelt on facts and figures, while the population,
> unused to the complexities of economics and
> impatient with the written word, danced to the
> tunes promising "Power for the People," a "Small
> Axe" to "Beat Down Babylon," and the "Rod of
> Correction" to put things right so that "Better
> Must Come." (DG 8/3/80)

Discussion

The issues of class and racial conflict were raised more
often in 1972 than in 1967, yet the object of animosity for
the masses of Jamaican people was not defined by a
consistent ideology. Claiming that he was not concerned
with "-isms," Manley did not remind the electorate at all
that the PNP was a socialist party (#5, #13). He did, of
course, promise that the poor would enjoy more material
goods under a PNP government. The commitment of a
more equitable distribution of wealth was made in the
PNP's manifesto and in advertisements; the slogan "Better
Must Come" and Manley's declaration that the PNP would
address the problems of "sufferers" echoed that promise
symbolically. Only the left-wing Trade Union Congress
referred explicitly to the "working class."

Early in the campaign, Manley and the PNP adopted
certain symbols reminiscent of Black power ideology, and
many respondents associated the campaign with Black
nationalism. There is evidence that the party studiously
avoided making a direct association between its platform
and the Black nationalists' demands, but well before the
election Manley had addressed the issues that the Rodney
affair had raised, proposing that African history be taught
in the schools and agreeing that Black power had a special
relevance for Jamaicans. However, Manley, like many
others, consistently held the position that racial conflict
expressed a class problem. In his budget speech of 1969, a
time when hotels on the north coast were regularly refusing service to Black Jamaicans, Manley said:

> Racial discrimination has virtually disapppeared
> from Jamaica.... Our problem remains a class
> problem. It remains the problem of the disinher-
> ited masses who are disqualified by their poverty
> (and) lack of training from participating in the
> economic system.... It is a tragedy of our history
> that the masses are predominantly black and the
> privileged classes predominantly fair-skinned....
> We call on Jamaicans to assault the economic
> system that perpetuates class disadvantages and
> so feeds the delusion that race is the enemy, when

poverty is the true obstacle to overcome. (Document I)

Manley had paid enough attention to the Black power
demands to win the support of some of those disgruntled
members of the middle and lower classes who had three
years before classified him as one of the "traitors among
the Negro race" (*Abeng* 2/8/69, 1). As one respondent said,
Manley defused the racial situation; he "saved the race
problem and channeled it into an ideological problem. He
identified with the aspirations of black people, Garvey and
the Rastas. When he won in 1972, he could channel those
aspirations" (#25).

The entire election campaign was characterized by a
systematic and deliberate use of reggae music, some of
which was distinctly Rastafarian, of Rastafarian language,
and of symbols particularly meaningful to Rastafarians.
The music that came from the ghettos of Trench Town and
Jones Town increasingly protested the conditions that the
poor endured, and reflected and promulgated contentious
sentiments.   The contention was directed against "the
wicked," the enslavers, the rich men, the police, and
"Babylon Shit-stem."

The JLP government's effort to ban songs was associated
by some with its repression of Black power ideology, its
persecution of Rastafarians and its desire to maintain the
status quo. Several respondents felt that the PNP's use of
Rastafarian songs was a subtle way of associating itself
with Black power (#3, #4, #7, #13, #20).

The PNP was able to hold a multiclass coalition together
through the 1972 election (see Table 4.3).   In a random
sample of polling districts classified by the economic class
of most of the residents, Stone found that support for the
PNP had increased across the board. Among the very poor
working class, the percentage voting PNP rose from 43.3 in

Table 4.3
Share of Party Vote in Sample of Urban
Polling Districts, 1972 Percentages

		PNP	JLP
Lower class	Very poor working	52.8	47.2
	Poor working	56.4	43.6
	Better off working	81.0	19.0
Middle class	Lower middle	87.3	12.7
	Middle	81.4	18.6
Upper Class	Upper Middle	75.3	24.7

Source: Stone, DG 6/8/80.

1967 to 52.8 in 1972. In the better-off section of the middle class, support for the PNP rose from 54.4 percent in 1967 to 81.4 percent in 1972. The greatest increase in support came from the upper class: in 1967, 40.0 percent; in 1972, 75.3 percent (Stone DG 6/8/80, 7).

Although many Jamaicans were still disgusted by Rastafarians and "listened in shocked disbelief" to their music, efforts by the JLP to appeal to their fears by publicizing the Henry pamphlet and caricaturing the clenched fist ultimately failed to convince a majority. Rather, many members of the middle class had found an intellectual appeal in the philosophies of Black power and Rastafari, sensed that the racial situation needed "defusing," and found Manley's dramatic use of symbols amusing at worst. Yet the coalition Manley had built did not carry him through the next election, as will be discussed in the next chapter.

The *Gleaner* had not endorsed either party before the election in 1972, but had praise for the PNP when it was victorious, writing that its projected policies were based "on sound social thinking for the good of Jamaica." It attributed the JLP's defeat in part to:

> increasing and instinctive urges for a better material way of life for the masses; partly to estrangement from citizen contact of some of the JLP's former MP's; partly to flaunted arrogance by some of the ministers of the JLP government; and partly to a loss of confidence stimulated by the massive attacks by Mr. Manley on Mr. Shearer's government as to integrity in policy and employment. (DG 3/1/72, 15)

The use of reggae music and Rastafarian symbols facilitated the PNP's presentation of itself as a party sharply different from the JLP in many of the aspects mentioned by the *Gleaner*. While JLP ministers arrogantly segregated themselves from the masses of Jamaicans by living sumptuously, "Joshua" spoke their language and appreciated their music. The JLP's claim that it had ushered Jamaica into the age of prosperity was at variance with annual salaries of $165 and the urban experience of overcrowded tenement yards. The PNP's emphasis on "people" and participation, in contrast, implied a less arrogant leadership and promised genuine relief for the "sufferers." While the JLP's bell sounded a discordant and hollow ring on Edna Manley's birthday in 1972, "Better Must Come," sung in a reggae rhythm, struck a hopeful chord.

5

The 1976 Election

The election in 1976 was the first election in Jamaica in which ideological concerns were prominent in campaign materials and constituted readily perceived differences between the two political parties. In 1972 Manley had accepted no "-isms," but in 1974 the People's National Party reaffirmed its commitment to democratic socialism as a concept integrating the social and economic programs the government had instituted. "The literate in this country," one JLP supporter said, "are educated in European ways, so they adopt European categories. It followed that if the PNP were a socialist party, the JLP must be the capitalist party" (#5).

The PNP called for a mandate for democratic socialism in 1976 and received it. The party was returned in an overwhelming victory, 13.5 points ahead of the JLP in the popular vote. The PNP won forty-seven, or 78 percent, of the seats in Parliament, to the JLP's thirteen (see Table 5.1). Even Edward Seaga called it "a very clear and decisive victory" and the selection of "one ideology over the other" (DG 12/16/76, 1).

The JLP's "Action Team" of candidates who ran in the election represented a new generation of Labourites. It was the first election in which Seaga led the party, and he had recruited individuals from the private sector's managerial class who were new to partisan politics. The election clinched the turnabout in support coalitions of the parties that had begun in 1972. The middle and upper classes that had seen Manley as a Jamaican John Kennedy

140

(#13) now worried that they had instead elected a potential Fidel Castro, and they sought alternatives in the Jamaica Labour Party.

Table 5.1
Results, 1976 General Election

Electors on roll 870,972

Ballots cast 742,149 (85.20%)

Accepted ballots 442,472

Party Share	Popular Vote	Percentage	Seats
Jamaica Labour Party	318,180	(43.23%)	13
People's National Party	417,768	(56.77%)	47

Source: Chief Electoral Officer's Report, 1972.

The election was recent enough that a wide range of pertinent materials could be collected. The *Daily Gleaner* had seventeen reports on election meetings, and these were supplemented with reports from the *Weekly Gleaner*. Both parties printed more advertisements than in 1972, with the JLP leading with 125 advertisements to the PNP's 79. Only the JLP advertised significantly for specific candidates (see Table 5.2). A two-record set of speeches and songs from the PNP's September 1976 Annual Conference was available, and provided a feeling for crowd responses to political symbols.

The more recent the election, however, the more the researcher is hindered by the lack of a good general history of modern Jamaica. The few histories that have been written end with the pre-Manley period, and the chronicles that remain are written from a decidedly partisan point of view. In that respect, the PNP retains part of its legacy as

the "intellectual party."   Michael Manley has written
several volumes in the political memoir genre (notably
1982); the JLP, ever the party of practical politicians, has
not yet found its apologist. Hence such intraparty contests
as that between Seaga and Shearer for the JLP leadership
in 1974 must be pieced together from sources of varying
reliability.

For this chapter, most of the background information
pertinent to the election campaign will be incorporated
into the appropriate sections. Only a few points need to be
made to introduce the material.

Table 5.2
Summary of 314 Election Items
Daily Gleaner - 15 November - 15 December 1976

	People's National Party	Jamaica Labour Party
Reports of Meetings	9	8
Advertisements		
General		
Full page	42	56
Less than full page	19	11
Broadcast announcements	17	18
Specific constituencies		
Western St. Andrew	1	4
E.C.St.Andrew	0	1
S.W.St.Andrew	0	4
S.St.Andrew	0	2
S.E.St.Andrew	0	15
E.St.Andrew	0	2
N.St.Andrew	0	3
Other constituencies	0	9
Total advertisements	79	125
Other Items		93

Historical Background

The PNP government of 1972-1976 was marked by important changes in domestic and foreign policy. The party delivered on several of its 1972 campaign promises. The voting age was lowered to eighteen; Minister of Home Affairs Noel Silvera quickly canceled all book-banning orders. The government gradually instituted a series of popular social programs, such as the National Literacy Programme (JAMAL), free education up to university level, a minimum wage for domestic workers (who, since the Manley years, are called "helpers" rather than "servants"), and the abolition of the Master and Servant Law, which had been the sole legal base regulating employer-employee relations. Forty-five thousand acres of land were leased to 23,000 small farmers under Project Land Lease, and sugar cooperatives were established. The Special Employment Programme, which aimed to provide work for the chronically unemployed, drew severe criticism from members of the middle class, who accused Manley of "pampering the proletariat" (DG 12/4/76, 28). To finance these programs, the government reformed the taxation system by increasing rates on certain luxury items and by changing the basis of the property tax (PNP 1976, 279). As Manley reported nine years later, "Nothing that we did in our first term caused so great an upheaval as the announcement of the property tax" (1982, 89).

The bauxite industry was totally owned by foreign companies when the Manley government came to power in 1972. A national public opinion survey conducted that year found that nearly half of skilled and unskilled laborers and small peasant farmers favored nationalization of the industry (Stone 1977, 137). Although Jamaica was the second-largest producer of bauxite/alumina, the mineral brought in less than US$30 million in government revenue annually.

One of the best known actions of the Manley government was the imposition of the bauxite levy in 1974, which increased Jamaica's bauxite income sixfold and helped the economy to cope with the oil crisis (Manley 1982, 44ff.; Stone 1977; Lewis 1981, 59ff.). The levy gave Jamaica international recognition in the Third World (Lewis 1981,

69), and enabled Manley to boast at home that his government had "put multi-national corporations under 'heavy manners'" (Manley 1976a).

After the defeat of 1972, the JLP underwent internal changes. Seaga announced that he was going to retire from active politics, and took a leave of absence from party duties (#6, #30), according to one respondent "because the party wouldn't take his advice" (#6). Apparently factional struggles within the party led to Hugh Shearer's resignation of the leadership position soon after. Seaga's return to active politics, after an absence of six months, was heralded by a mass meeting at the Bustamante statue in downtown Kingston. There, according to an respondent, "Seaga said 'Would that this cup pass from my lips,' very dramatically, quoting Jesus at the Garden of Gethsemene. He's usually quite miserly with gestures, but that night he was half down on his knees, hugging this imaginary cup to himself, as if he really did want it, it being the party leadership. Seaga decided to be the Jamaican Jesus Christ" (#6, partially corroborated by #30). At the next party conference, which, according to the respondent, "included 4000 delegates, 3900 of whom were from Tivoli Gardens, Seaga was 'coronated'" (#6). Seaga has been leader of the party since that 1974 party election, but factional disagreements continued to be a problem until late in the 1970s (#24).

The last phenomenon that needs to be addressed here is the escalating violence that was plaguing Kingston and frightening potential tourists. While the campaign of 1972 was remembered as "joyous" and "warm," "a carnival," the uglier aspects of Jamaican politics came to the fore in 1976. The period saw increasing sophistication in technique and armaments of the party gangs, ghetto youths employed by politicians who were euphemistically referred to as the "muscle" of the parties (#5) but were more commonly called "thugs" (#34; Lacey 1977). Guns were more prevalent than in 1972. Some were imported; others, called "buckies," were crude weapons of pipe and other scrap metal that were manufactured in hideaways in the ghetto communities (#13).

Nearly a hundred persons were killed in the first five months of 1976. One incident in mid-May deeply shocked the sensibilities of Jamaicans. In retaliation for the killing of a gang member by a rival gang, one gang surrounded an overcrowded tenement block and set it afire; the buildings were destroyed, leaving eleven persons dead and five hundred homeless. Reports circulated of gang members throwing escaping children back into the burning buildings (Manley 1982, 138-39).

The PNP suspected that the violence was a deliberate attempt to destabilize the country and to create an impression that the crime situation was out of the government's control. Manley wrote of the fire: "I do not believe that the Orange Lane fire was simply a case of members of a gang getting angry one night. The whole history of the escalating difficulty between the two gangs reeks of provocation. The final setting of the fire suggests not anger but the coldest calculation" (1982, 139).

Other incidents enumerated in a compendium in Manley's book (1982, appendix) do seem to point to sabotage. An unusually vicious outbreak of violence in Trench Town, in which imported weapons were used, coincided with a Kingston meeting of International Monetary Fund officials. Many foreign journalists were in Kingston to cover the meeting; they sent back stories of the violence as well. Seventeen people died from food poisoning in early 1976 from a shipment of flour that had evidently been contaminated with parathion en route to Jamaica. A number of the attacks were made against the security forces, which were in support of the government at that time (#12). The Socialist International's Bureau publicly condemned efforts to undermine the democratic socialist government in Jamaica, and said that the efforts consisted of "a systematic campaign that includes influencing international press, economic sanctions, illegal export of funds, ... industrial unrest, crime and violence" (WG 11/23/76).

In January, Manley, as PNP president, announced the formation of community defense groups called the Home Guard. The rationale was to involve people in policing their own communities so as to change the "psychological environment" in which the criminal acted (Manley 1982, 84). The move was immediately denounced by the JLP, the Jamaica Manufacturers Association, and the Chamber of Commerce (Manley 1982, 228; #24). To set an example,

Manley himself took Home Guard training, including in-
struction in the use of small firearms. The photographs of
Manley pointing a gun were used against him by the JLP in
1980.

In mid-June, a political organizer for the JLP revealed
evidence that certain members of the JLP were directly
involved in the violence. He stated upon resignation from
the party, "From my inner knowledge of the JLP I am now
satisfied that its whole strategy is based upon violence, and
the use of violence as a means of obtaining victory at the
polls" (Manley 1982, 233). He implicated Pearnel Charles,
a deputy leader of the JLP. The next day, the government
declared a state of emergency, and within a week had
detained Pearnel Charles, two other JLP candidates, and
one PNP candidate. By mid-August, 173 people in all were
in detention (see Charles 1977).

The state of emergency lasted ten months. Although
one JLP respondent named it as a factor in the withdrawal
of support from the PNP (#9), Carl Stone reported that his
survey of political attitudes conducted shortly before the
elections revealed that the state of emergency "enjoys
overwhelming support ... and has had the effect of giving
the PNP (or at least its top leadership) a clean image with
respect to the political violence" (DG 11/21/76). The PNP
advertised the state of emergency as a step in putting the
gunmen "under heavy manners," a popular phrase of the
day. For example, an advertisement read: "The best way
to stop violence is not to preach violence. Violence hurts
everyone. The Peoples National Party is unalterably
opposed to violence in any form.... *We voted to extend the
State of Emergency while the JLP voted against it.* Did
they want to let the Gunmen out? *Vote against Violence.
Vote 'Heavy Manners'.* Vote PNP" (DG 12/8/76, 15; emphasis in original. See also DG 12/9/76, 21; 12/10/76, 4;
12/11/76, 37).

Each party tried to pin blame for the violence on the
other. The PNP canvassers were instructed that the
violence began in earnest in Western Kingston in 1966, an
effort to blame Seaga (Document V). Six weeks before the
election, there was an incident in the village of York Town
in which both PNP and JLP supporters were shot, including
one candidate. Stone wrote afterwards under his pseudo-

nym "Petras": "Our politicians have been living a lie. They mouth platitudes about non-violence ... and keep arms in their party offices.... The multiple versions of what happened ... raise some serious questions of our political leaders in their desperate effort to cover up the misdeeds of their followers ..." (WG 11/16/76, 17).

The bitter antagonism between the two party leaders fanned the flames. Neither seemed to miss an opportunity to condemn bitterly the "wickedness" of the other. As one respondent said: "Eddie and Michael have set the example for what has gone wrong in this country. The supporters pick up on it. They genuinely believe that if they have the opportunity to shoot one of the opposition, Michael will love them or Eddie will love them. Passions ran high in Busta's days, but not with the same hatefulness" (#30).

The JLP's statement after the York Town incident was criticized for its provocative nature (WG 11/16/76, 17). It read in part, "The JLP cannot continue to sit idly by while its candidates, supporters and sympathisers are massacred by those who intend to swim to power in the blood of the people" (DG 11/10/76).

Seaga spoke out against the state of emergency, and one of the symbolic themes of his campaign speeches reflected his desire to call attention to the candidates in detention. The theme was "the key at midnight," that is, the key to the detention camp or, figuratively, the key to the PNP's "dirty secrets" (DG 12/4/76, 28; 12/3/76, 8). In his speech at Tivoli Sports Field, the opening of the campaign, he said: "At midnight on election night I will hold the key to the detention camp.... I am going to use the key to find out what happened to the $10 million of the Iran Sugar Deal. They don't want the key to pass, but I say it must pass" (WG 11/30/76, 6).

The PNP was more successful in presenting itself as antiviolence, as the Stone survey indicated. A campaign manager who worked for the JLP in 1980 graphically described the party's image as it was in 1976:

There were unpleasant things, exposes of JLP gunmanship. There was a case in which a man held up a Jamaican businessman for ransom, and it was traced back to the JLP. Jamaicans never

protested the JLP members being detained in the
State of Emergency; they knew they had been
involved in gun crimes. After the 1976 election,
this was the image of the JLP: violence and
negativism. The words associated with the JLP
were ones that they had used themselves: guns,
subversion, doom, confusion, fire, blood, collision,
mash-up, turn-back. (#24)

The Rastafarian perspective on politics frequently fo-
cuses on the violence that is provoked, even paid for, by
the middle-class politicians but is perpetrated in the ghettos (#2). The Rastas often express an aversion to any
violence (#18, #19; Owen 1976, 206ff.). One Rastafarian
said that he never voted because of "what politics does to
ghetto youth," and that the word *politics* itself demon-
strates that it means parasites on the people ("ticks" are
parasites). He also said that Rastas had never fought in a
war and could not be provoked to fight (#19). In Kingston's
shanty towns supporting a political party almost always in-
volves one in violence (#2).

From as early as 1966, popular music often had had
peacemaking themes, and it took on this role more seriously in the later 1970s. In "Judge Dread" by Prince Buster
(circa 1967), "Judge One Hundred Years ... from Ethiopia"
tries rude boys in his court for "shooting black people"
(Olive Blossom Records, n. d.). In the "Smile Jamaica"
concert in 1976, which will be discussed below, Bob Marley
made a point of stressing by repetition lyrics that called
for people to live together peacefully.

Several other reggae songs of the 1976 election period
share this peace theme, continuing the trend from "Judge
Dread" through songs like "Gun Fever" (discussed in chapter 3), for example, Bob Marley's song "No More Trouble,"
Burning Spear's "No More War," and the Mighty Diamonds'
"Why Me Black Brother." The last of these specifically
mentions "tribal war":

Why me black brother why
Dis robbing and killing
Why me black brother why
Dis looting and shooting...

What you gonna do when the voice say come
Remember the day of judgement
Pick up your guns and you go to town
See your black brother and you shoot dem down
That's wrong
No me black brother no
No bother with no tribal
No me black brother no
It only cost a trial

Probably the most poignant of songs on this theme is Bob Marley's lament called "Johnny Was." It alludes to the characteristic Rastafarian ambivalence about death and immortality:

Woman hold her head and cry
Cause her son had been
Shot down in the street and died,
From a stray bullet
Woman hold her head and cry
Explaining to her was a passer-by
Who saw the woman cry
Wondering how she can work it out
Now she knows that the wages of sin is death
Gift of Jah is life.
She cried Johnny was a good man
Never did a thing wrong
Woman hold here head and cry
Cause her son had been shot down
In the street and died
Just because of the system
Woman hold her head and cry
Comforting her was a passer-by
She complained, then she cried
Johnny was a good man, never did a thing wrong.
Can a woman tender care, she cried
Cease toward the child she bear?

At the same time, reggae songs did not lose their strident militancy nor did they shrink from the prediction that "heads will roll." Two songs are particularly illustrative here. The first, "War," was adapted by Marley from a speech that Haile Selassie made in California in 1968. The Rastafarian may be a peaceable individual, but racism provokes a self-righteous anger and a willingness for battle:

> Until the philosophy which hold one race superior and another inferior is finally and totally discredited and abandoned; that until there are no longer first class and second class citizen of any nation; until the colour of a man's skin is of no more significance than the colour of his eyes; that until the basic human rights are equally guaranteed to all, without regard to race; that until that day, the dream of lasting peace, world citizenship, the rule of international morality will remain but a fleeting illusion to be pursued but never attained.

> And until the ignoble and unhappy regime that hold our brothers in Angola, in Mozambique, in South Africa, in sub-human bondage, have been toppled, utterly destroyed; until that day the African continent will not know peace. We Africans will fight, we find it necessary. And we know we shall win, as we are confident in the victory of good over evil.

The second song of angry militancy is directed at the second category of oppressors: the dominant class, defined in economic rather than racial terms. Max Romeo, in his "Warning, Warning," predicts a supernatural retribution against the wealthy (the Sandy Gully referred to is a large open storm sewer running through Western Kingston):

> *And now you rich people listen to me*
> *Weep and wail over the miseries*
> *That are coming, coming up on you*
> *Your riches have rotted away*
> *And your clothes have been eaten by moth*
> *Your gold and silver is covered with rust.*
> *And this rust will be witness against you*
> *And eat up your flesh like fire*
> *You have piled up your riches in these last days.*

But heads ago roll down Sandy Gully
One of these days
Heads ago roll down Sandy Gully
That's what Marcus says
Your life here on earth have been filled
With luxury and pleasure
You have made yourself fat
For the day of slaughter
You've not paid the men that work in your fields
The cries of those that gather your crops
Have reached the ears of Jah, Jah Almighty
 Heads ago roll, etc.
Them up on Beverly Hills
A eat t-bone steak and drink cornflake
While poor people in the ghetto
A rake and scrape to get a cake
Be patient my brother be patient
As a farmer is patient
As he waits for the autumn or the spring rains
To water his crops
You also must be patient
And keep your head up high
Happy are those whose only desire
Is to do what Jah Jah require
 Heads ago roll down Sandy Gully
 One of these days
 Baldhead ago roll down Sandy Gully
 One of these days.

The 1976 Campaign

Overview

Most of the details of the campaign will be covered in the following four sections, but a few items fall into none of the specific coding categories.

In general, the PNP campaigned on its record of achievements and called upon the electorate for a mandate for democratic socialism. The JLP campaigned on the "Communist Threat" and economic mismanagement on the part of the PNP government. As the quotation in the section

above indicated, much of the JLP campaign was negative.
One of its primary slogans was "Turn Them Back." A series
of advertisements appeared with a standard format beginning with the words "The Socialists Have Failed." Other
slogans revolved around the catchword "Freedom"; Seaga
was called the "Freedom Leader" and the other candidates
were called the "Freedom Team" or "Action Team." Although "Nationalism" was the official philosophy of the
party that year, the term "Freedom Party" was more
widely known by the electorate (WG 11/30/76, 15).

The PNP's several slogans included variations on "For-
ward," such as "Forward Together" and "Forward Joshua,"
"We Know Where We're Going," and "We Are Not For Sale."
In 1972, it will be recalled, one slogan of the PNP was "It's
Time," for example, "It's Time People Live Better Than
This." In 1976, a series of advertisements began with the
words "Now! At last!" and ended with "... and this is just
the start." The party strove to demonstrate continuity
with previous leadership by repeating the words Norman
Manley spoke on his seventy-fifth birthday in relation to
the philosophy of democratic socialism: "My generation
had a distinct mission to perform. It was to create a
national spirit with which we could identify ourselves as a
people for the purpose of achieving independence on the
political plane. I am convinced, deeply convinced, that the
role of this generation is to proceed to the social and
economic reform of Jamaica" (Hearne 1976, 5; DG
12/15/76, 12-13; 11/29/76, 18).

The pattern of accusations and counteraccusations escalated sharply in this election. The PNP repeatedly warned
of the "Big Lie" with which the JLP would try to discredit
the PNP (DG 11/20/76, 9; 11/21/76, 22; 12/3/76, 18;
12/5/76, 35; and others). The JLP in turn proclaimed, "We
want no more Socialists' lies!" (DG 12/12/76, 14; 12/10/76,
32). The JLP accused the PNP of planning an elaborate
scheme for bogus voting (DG 12/12/76, 1; WG 11/30/76, 4);
the PNP claimed that the charge was another "desperate
lie" invented by "desperate politicians" (DG 12/12/76, 3) to
discredit the government, just as the PNP had predicted.
The JLP repeatedly claimed that the PNP had "secret
plans" for Jamaica. For example, one advertisement said
that the JLP had a plan for employment: "Restore confi-

dence. Revive lost jobs. Create new jobs." It then asked, "Where is the PNP plan? ... Why is the PNP silent on creating more jobs?   What is their secret plan?" (DG 12/8/76, 19).

Both parties used religious themes, but far less frequently than in 1967. Both the PNP and the JLP-affiliated Young Jamaica organization ran advertisements on election day that were prayers (DG 12/15/76). A JLP campaign manager reported that the party resisted attempts to pin a biblical nickname on Seaga (#31), but there were posters of Seaga printed with the words "Closer than a Brother," a line from an old hymn that originally continued "my Jesus is to me" (#7). Each party portrayed the other as "evil" or "wicked," especially when accusing the other of perpetrating violence (e.g. WG 12/7/76, 11).

In contrast to 1967, when references that fall into the categories under study — class, race, anticolonialism and antiimperialism — were relatively rare and somewhat peripheral to the campaign, in 1976 those four broad rubrics tell the greater part of the election story. Issues of race, class, and imperialism were overtly addressed by politicians and reggae musicians alike, were central to the campaigns and decisive in their conclusion. The first that will be discussed is the use of symbols of class and of class conflict.   As one respondent summed up the campaign, "1976 was a class thing" (#8).

The Use of Class Symbols and Class Conflict

By the time the elections were held in December 1976, Jamaica's two political parties had effected a reversal of the traditional class-party typifications.   Although the merchant class, particularly the minority groups of Syrians and Chinese, remained committed to the JLP, other groups were no longer identified with the same party that they had been ten years earlier.   The Brown middle class, notably, had increasingly come to support the Labour Party. The People's National Party, the traditional representatives of the middle classes, went to great lengths, some said too great, to demonstrate its commitment to the Black and poor masses (#5, #8, #9, #12, #13, DG 12/6/76, 14).

"Political Analyst" of the *Gleaner*, who wrote columns generally favoring the JLP, also noted this trend. He wrote that N. W. Manley's class coalition had consisted of professionals, idealists, civil servants and better-off small farmers, while Bustamante's support came from the very poor and the merchant class. "The NW coalition is split without a doubt," he wrote the day before the election. "The main reason for the middle class defection has been the Cuban connection" (DG 12/14/76, 2).

A political scientist who was pro-PNP at the time saw the middle-class defection differently. While Bustamante represented the JLP's commitment to the poor, "the party's populist tradition ... has been abandoned by the young Turks of business and managerial executives who have literally taken over the party under Seaga's guiding hand ... many of these new JLP candidates ... represent a militant and almost paranoid hostility to the social justice and poor people commitment of Manley." He went on to compare the JLP with the Jamaica Democratic Party of 1944, a planter-class party (WG 12/14/76, 17). In another column, he wrote that the JLP reflected "capitalist anxiety over socialism, middle class fears about leftism.... Paradoxically Norman Manley's son has assumed the mantle of the people champion while Bustamante's party comes across as if it were a World Bank agency" (WG 12/21/76, 13).

In the campaign, the JLP's strategy was to avoid the fray of class contention. According to two respondents, both close to the campaign, the party evaded the class issue, claiming instead to represent all classes (#12, #31). "It was not in the interest of the JLP to join the battle," one campaign manager said. "We accept the motto of Jamaica. People have to live together. In 1976 when we came under attack, we played down class" (#31). The party instead condemned the PNP for spreading "Class Hatred" (DG 11/21/76, 4; 12/4/76, 28; 12/7/76, 17; 12/14/76, 18; #12, #31). One letter to the *Gleaner* asserted that Manley "pampered urban and quasi-urban proletariates into a life of idleness and uselessness by paying them to lean on brooms and sweep dust.... (The JLP) does not emphasize class, color or race hatred, and it will be much easier for the JLP to foster social solidarity and integration after the elections" (DG 12/4/76, 28).

The PNP had instituted a number of programs to "help the needy," such as the Impact Programme to which the above letter-writer referred, and these proved to be very popular. The JLP attempted to turn those programs against the PNP, by telling taxpayers, "Your money has been wasted on projects to win support for the socialist cause" (DG 11/26/76, 24).

One of the Labour Party's major strategies was to present a picture of the PNP as incompetent managers of money who had brought hardships to the people of Jamaica (DG 11/24/76, 7; 11/27/76, 24). Unemployment, the party declared, was increasing under the PNP's policies (DG 11/29/76, 9; 12/2/76, 9, 23; 12/7/76, 17; 12/8/76, 19; 12/9/76, 22; 12/14/76, 18), as was the cost of living (DG 11/28/76, 13; 11/30/76, 2; 12/7/76, 17).

One event that was to be particularly damaging to the PNP in the 1980 election was Seaga's correct prediction of a pending devaluation of the Jamaican dollar. Two days before the election, Seaga announced that a 40 percent devaluation would occur if the PNP was returned to office (DG 12/14/76, 1). In an advertisement, the JLP warned: "Your dollar would be worth less by January! All imported items would be increased immediately and there would be no money to increase salaries. Could you survive this blow? Vote JLP" (DG 12/13/76, 20). David Coore, the PNP finance minister, immediately denied the story (DG 12/14/76, 1), calling it "irresponsible speculation," "ugly misrepresentation," and the "surest way to ruin that country's economy" (DG 12/14/76, 28). The devaluation took place in January 1977, less than a month after the election. It is conjectured by PNP supporters that the financial secretary in the PNP government leaked information about the pending devaluation to the opposition (#7, #13), but the event enhanced Seaga's image as a financial wizard among the electorate.

In an article for the "Election Forum" page of the *Gleaner*, Bobby Marsh of the JLP discussed the party's position on class. First, he paraphrased Aristotle on the advantages of a strong middle class. That class, he said, can prevent the upper class from gaining more riches "while the poor become richer. That is why the JLP pledges to build our nation by lifting the poor up — High-

Up — so that we may all dwell in a free Jamaica" (DG 12/9/76, 21).

A Young Jamaica (a JLP affiliate) advertisement illustrated the party's evasion of the realities of Jamaica's economic stratification.   It read, "Every young Jamaican looks forward to this: Good education, good jobs, your own business or farm, your own home, your own car, a happy family" (DG 11/24/76, 27). Illustrated with drawings of a suburban home and a new automobile, the advertisement blatantly ignored the fact that the overwhelming majority of Jamaicans could never hope to possess any of these accoutrements of middle class life under any system of government. It implied that imported socialism was the only barrier to a middle-class existence for the 85 percent of Jamaicans who were, relatively speaking, poor. The advertisement continued, "It's only natural. In some countries, it is not natural. Don't make us fall into the same trap with false promises and words..." (DG 11/24/76, 27).

Repeatedly, in these and other campaign materials, socialism was presented as a system in which everyone is uniformly poor. The path to lower unemployment and a lower cost of living was "No More Socialism" (DG 12/2/76, 9). The JLP promised to reinstitute "economic freedom" (DG 12/14/76, 20). Another advertisement from Young Jamaica was "Our Prayer" for election day and revolved around the "freedom" theme. It read, in part: "Through Christ in me I am set free from negative attitudes and beliefs that create adverse conditions. I am set free from feelings of lack and limitation that limit the perfect demonstration of my prosperity" (DG 12/15/76).

There were several other, less deliberate, references to class and uses of class symbols throughout the JLP material.   Rather than "manifesto," probably because the word had connotations of socialism, the JLP called its document a "People Programme," and advertised Seaga as being "High-Up with the People," accompanied by a photograph of him with individuals who were obviously of the lower class (DG 12/5/76, 39). Diverse groups were singled out in a series of JLP advertisements against the PNP government. For example, headlines of these read: "The Socialists have failed the farmer" (against the Land Lease Programme, DG 12/3/76, 7); "The Socialists have failed the Youth" (on unemployment, DG 12/6/76, 13); "The Socialists have failed the Shopkeeper" (on small business closings, DG 12/5/76, 32); and "The Socialists have failed the Worker" (on plant closings, DG 12/1/76, 18).

The PNP's use of references to class stands in sharp contrast to that of the opposition party.   respondents repeatedly said that the PNP was dedicated to improving the lives of the poor (#7, #10, #13, #20, #25). The party stated in its advertisements that "under Democratic Socialism we are committed to raising the standard of living for the most needy in our society" (DG 11/23/76, 2) and was perceived as such by many observers.

Democratic socialism, which was more widely publicized by the PNP than the philosophy of "Nationalism" was by the opposition, was, according to one respondent, "taken to heart by the masses. People were enthusiastic about it. It was the first time that an abstract slogan or concept really generated mass support" (#7). Carl Stone's research on the meanings that democratic socialism had for people showed that they identified it with improvements for the poor:

> PNP supporters attach to Democratic Socialism varying meanings including a commitment to help the small people as against the rich, social justice, and a desire to change the society in ways that will benefit the poorer classes.... In short it is interpreted in ways very close to the populist support for Bustamante's "Labourism" of the 1930's and 40's, except that it is informed by a greater sense of class enemies against the poor and a deeper feeling that social justice requires some drastic changes in the society. (DG 11/21/76)

The PNP ran a series of advertisements, each about one of the programs that had been instituted since 1972, all of which mention democratic socialism. For example, one discusses the Special Employment Programme:

> Now! At last! A chance for a better life. 30,000 more people are now at work. Through the Special Employment "Impact" Programme, they

are working on soil conservation, rice cultivation.... Between 1962 and 1972, unemployment
doubled from 12% to 24% because the economy
was organized to benefit the few. Under Democratic Socialism, the economy is managed in the
interests of the majority of our people. (DG
11/28/76, 15)

Similar advertisements highlighted equal pay for women
(DG 11/24/76, 21), better pay for sugar workers (DG
11/26/76, 2), minimum wage (DG 11/23/76, 2), and JAMAL,
the National Literacy Programme (DG 11/26/76, 7). The
song "The Message" (discussed below) enumerated these
programs and others. These reforms were quite popular
throughout the country (#7, #12, #20); in his public opinion
research, Stone reported one "remarkable" finding: the
overwhelming nonpartisan popularity of the PNP's social
and economic programs. He wrote that "in spite of party
tribalism, the people have a common sense of their class
needs" (DG 11/21/76).

As the party tried to demonstrate its commitment to the
lower class, it tried to portray the JLP as the "Big Man"
party and as the party of "capitalists" (#5, #13).   An
unofficial pamphlet released before the election said,
"'Turn them back' is the slogan of the JLP.... It means turn
them back to the day when class division was the order of
the day" (Document VI). A letter to the *Gleaner* also used
a JLP slogan, "Free Up," to make the same point: "The JLP
Action Team is clearly on the move to 'free up' the rich
people once again so that they can exploit the poor" (WG
11/23/76, 18).

A recurring theme in the PNP campaign materials is "the
clique," those persons who, according to Manley, had taken
control of the Jamaica Labour Party, replacing the leaders
of the Bustamante days who had been oriented toward
trade unions. One respondent described "the clique" as
those people whose interests were hurt by the PNP's
policies, for example, those who did not want to pay
workers the hourly fifty-cent minimum wage (#13). Manley defined "the clique" in his 1976 conference speech as
the

controllers of capital who resist change. The
clique are the beneficiaries of imperialism who
resist change. The clique are the developers who
abscond with the people's money and take up
residence abroad, skulking away like thieves in
the night, leaving citizens to suffer behind them.
Those are the clique and the ones that stole the
money of the poor people with their houses. They
lay about in Miami, loll about in Toronto, and they
dream of the day when we will be defeated so
that they can come back to scalp the people some
more. (Manley 1976a, 14-15)

Manley delineated in the same speech "the strategies of
the clique." The first was to take "final control of the
Jamaica Labour Party and the Jamaica Labour Party is
now the instrument and the yo-yo of the clique" (Manley
1976a, 16). The second was propaganda against the government; the third, gunmanship and violence. Finally, the
clique effected a "squeeze on the economy" and practiced
"economic sabotage," in reaction to the imposition of taxes
to pay for the PNP government's social and economic
programs:

We put on the taxes, not rudely, not in bad
temper; we put them on with apology, with cour-
tesy, with explanation. And every Jamaican that
cares for this land more than himself said, you are
right, and said "Right On." But the clique, oh no!
Oh no! There was a weeping and a wailing and a
gnashing of teeth. Some a dem a hollah, some a
bawl. And the clique suddenly became like a
collection of "chi-chi bud".... Even though we
gave practical, realistic incentives ... they said
no.... They said the only way we will produce is
if you turn it all back. And when you deliver the
people to us again, as we had them before, then
we will produce.... If you make us feel that we
the clique are in charge again, we will produce.
We will open the money bags. And I say to them
"the masses of Jamaica are not for sale!" (Manley
1976a, 18-19)

In one striking advertisement, not explicitly labeled PNP, the centerpiece is a photograph of a tin can whose label reads:

Seaga's nationalism
Produced and sold by the Clique
Priced High Up for the Benefit of the Few.

The advertisement continued:

Free up bauxite for foreign exploitation
Free up price controls for big profits
Free up land for land barons
Free up some developers to take big
    downpayments and never deliver houses
Free up illiteracy and turn back JAMAL
FREE UP THE HIGH-UP!
    so they can
TURN BACK the people of Jamaica!
(DG 12/2/76, 5)

Likewise, Manley said in an "Election Forum" article, "The freedom that the JLP is advocating is ... for one small clique in the society to continue its exploitation of the poor and dispossessed" (DG 11/29/76, 18).

Manley repeatedly spoke of the JLP as the capitalist party and of capitalism as the exploitation of the poor. The election would, he said, "decide whether we crawl back like a whipped dog to capitalism or go forward in socialism" (WG 11/23/76, 6). The 1962-72 period was "marked by an era of elitism and the growth of capitalism and a time during which there was economic prosperity for a few while the majority suffered" (WG 11/30/76, 11). At a third mass meeting, he told the audience that one could not look at "the history of exploitation between 1838 and 1938 without looking at the history of capitalism" (DG 12/13/76, 2).

The PNP approved of the "man with an honest business," as Manley said in defining who were not members of "the clique." One PNP candidate assured supporters that the party did not intend to "tear down the rich to bring them to the level of the poor" (DG 12/2/76, 7). An advertisement

spotlighting the construction of complexes for small industries illustrated the caution that the PNP used when
discussing local business:

> Under Democratic Socialism, we believe that
> there is a legitimate place in the society for the
> businessman who combines creativity and initia-
> tive in providing goods and services of good
> quality and at reasonable prices.... Through the
> Small Industries Complex Programme we are cre-
> ating the conditions for small businessmen to
> operate productively and efficiently. All busi-
> nessmen are expected to work within the bounds
> of the national interest and the rights of the
> people. (DG 11/20/76, 2)

Finally, the PNP used its identification with the poor as
a defense against the JLP's accusations of communist
tendencies within the PNP. The party pointed out that
Bustamante had been red-baited and had replied that
politicians who work in the interests of the poor are often
called communists (DG 12/9/76, 29).

Issues of class, in summary, were critical to the 1976
election and received a great deal of attention. When two
clergymen were called upon to comment on the election
results, both attributed the PNP victory to the party's
commitment to the interests of the lower class. The
Roman Catholic archbishop of Jamaica said the victory
meant "that the people support efforts of the government
to meet the needs of the poor and the working class" (WG
12/28/76, 11).

The Use of Race Symbols and Racial Conflict

The differences between the JLP and the PNP on the
matter of class conflicts were similar to those on the
matter of racial conflict. The JLP played down the issue
of class conflict, and it similarly and scrupulously avoided
calling racial conflict to the minds of voters. The way that
the parties used symbols of race was often quite personal;
it should be noted that in this election, for the first time, a
White man was leader of the JLP. Manley, of course, is a

Brown Jamaican, but respondents perceived that he tried to identify himself with the Black race. He reinforced this identification with his marriage to Beverly Anderson, a Black rather than Brown woman, shortly after the 1972 election (#7, #13, #20).

While several respondents said that the PNP had "made an issue of race" (#29, #30, #31), it seemed primarily to be a question of the party leaders' racial phenotypes. "The PNP made a great play of the fact that Seaga is white," said one JLP supporter. "They used colour not to turn colour against colour, but to blast Eddie for not being born here. Michael would talk about Eddie not being born here, and he'd have his mother on the platform at the same time" (#30). Manley's mother, Edna Manley, was born in England. This respondent referred here to a very popular campaign song, "The Message" composed for the PNP by Neville Martin. The song began with "My leader born yah" (yah = here), an obvious reference to the leader who had not been "born yah." The line was often interpreted as racist (#14, DG 11/18/76, 8; 11/19/76, 10), even by PNP supporters (#26). The JLP responded to the attacks on its leader by vigorously accusing the PNP of preaching "race hate" (DG 12/4/76, 28; 12/6/76, 9; 12/14/76, 18, 20). In one major speech, Seaga compared attacks on JLP supporters to Hitler's attempt to exterminate the Jews (DG 12/11/76, 2).

There was some evidence of racist rhetoric having been used by individual PNP candidates against Seaga (DG 12/13/76, 8), but such rhetoric never reached the party's official printed campaign material. Of four unofficial anti-JLP pamphlets circulated during this period, three associate the JLP solely with White or Syrian interests. For example, one read:

The JLP has announced three categories of
   candidates:
1) Syrian businessmen
2) Syrian landlords
3) One or two Jamaican-looking businessmen or lawyers who although they might look Jamaican are in fact defenders of Syrian capitalism, murder and violence. (Document VII)

A second asserted that the JLP wanted to "Turn Back":

> to slavery, to be bought and sold like cattle like
> our forefathers ... back to the days when land was
> for the privileged and poor black people could
> only occupy hillside land ... If you were white,
> everything was alright, if you were brown, you
> could stick around, if you were black, you had to
> stand back. (Document VI)

The second pamphlet echoed a not uncommon theme in
the PNP's official campaign, that is, references to slavery,
especially with regard to land distribution.   The prime
minister was historically correct when he told a mass
meeting that, during the postemancipation period, thousands of children of slaves moved into the rocky hillsides to
escape the plantation system, leaving the flat land to the
wealthy planters (DG 11/29/76, 10; see chapter 2).   He
asserted that the trend continued in the 1960s, when
farmers who were not already big landowners or JLP
supporters had to settle for "Wha' lef' land" (i.e. remnants)
and that the PNP's Land Lease Programme was reversing
this inequality for the first time (DG 12/4/76, 28).
Likewise, the National Literacy Programme was for the
first time "smashing the chains of illiteracy" (DG 11/26/76,
7).   Canvassers of the PNP were advised to familiarize
themselves with the idea that "the clique" of 1976 was
equivalent to "the clique" that had suppressed Sam Sharpe,
the Jamaican National Hero who had led a slave rebellion
(Document V).   Capitalism as a system was equated by
Manley with slavery (DG 12/13/76, 2).
In turn, the JLP equated democratic socialism with
slavery.   At one mass meeting, the JLP's Barlow Rycketts
spoke on the similarity of the PNP's policies and communism.   Then he asked if the members of the audience were
willing to go back to the slavery system in which ownership
of land was denied them, a reference to the Land Lease
Programme (DG 12/14/76, 9).   The Young Jamaica Election
Day Prayer quoted Galatians 5: "For freedom Christ has
set us free, stand fast therefore and do not submit again to
the yoke of slavery" (DG 12/15/76).   Although the JLP's
slogan "Freedom" did not originally have a connection with

emancipation from slavery, it gained that connotation by 1976. The JLP's Bobby Marsh equated the struggle for freedom from slavery with the struggles of Paul Bogle, George William Gordon, Marcus Garvey, and Bustamante (DG 12/9/76, 21).

Both parties frequently referred to the National Heroes, especially to Garvey. Manley called him "the living symbol of the awakening of Africa" (DG 11/29/76, 18) and "a martyr in the struggle to cast off the shackles of oppression" (WG 11/20/76, 6). The JLP emphasized Seaga's accomplishment of bringing the bones of Garvey back to Jamaica (DG 11/18/76, 8; 11/28/76, 9; 11/29/76, 18). Both parties referred to a continuity in Jamaica's history of struggle; for the JLP it followed the early heroes through to Bustamante, and for the PNP, to Norman Manley. The PNP had, since 1972, added Sam Sharpe, the leader of a slave revolt, and Nanny, a leader in the Maroons' fight against the British, to the official list of National Heroes (#7).

The PNP's government of 1972-76 was characterized by a continuation of the somewhat ambivalent support of Black nationalist causes that had been expressed in its 1972 campaign. Under the guidance of some party members, an African-Caribbean Institute was founded, the mission of which was to heighten Jamaicans' awareness of their African cultural roots and to provide a forum for the discussion of African history (#34). In 1972 the party had ended the ban on books written by Black nationalists, and reminded the electorate of this during the campaign (DG 12/9/76, 29; WG 11/23/76, 18). An older JLP candidate made the mistake of announcing to an audience that he would, given the opportunity, "ban books from Marx to Mao" (DG 11/18/76).

The PNP had supported the African liberation struggles in Rhodesia and other front-line states (DG 12/11/76, 9; Document IV), and accused the JLP of indifference to these struggles. Among the demands of "the clique," according to Manley, were that "we must stop fighting for Angola," "stop meddling in Southern Africa," and "forget the struggle of the poor of the world ... turn your eyes inward while our black brothers are killed and murdered in Soweto" (Manley 1976, 17, 19). Later in the same speech

he said he was "colour-blind, but I see who suffers and I
fight for whoever suffers and if a white Cuban suffers
under Batista, he is my brother. And if a black brother
suffers in Zimbabwe, he is my brother" (Manley 1976a, 19).
    An unofficial anti-JLP pamphlet accused the JLP of
ignoring the struggles in Southern Africa:

> Is Seaga's party a White Man's Party? Within
> recent times some of the most brutal crimes
> against humanity have been committed by white
> racist regimes against our Black Brothers in South
> Africa, Rhodesia, and Namibia. To this day
> neither Seaga nor the JLP has said one single
> word in condemnation of those acts. Does their
> silence mean consent? Come, Mr. Seaga, Black
> Jamaica wants to know your stand on Rhodesia,
> Soweto.... Who is against Africa cannot be for
> Jamaica. (Document VIII)

One respondent who was an instrumental organizer in the
PNP's 1976 campaign noted a decrease in Black nationalist
connotations in the party's rhetoric, and a rise in its
emphasis on class. In Jamaica, he pointed out, they
coincide:

> By 1976 it wasn't necessary for the PNP to stay
> on the black nationalist bandwagon. Through
> their social programs, people saw that the PNP
> was helping the black man. There was evidence
> that the PNP could use in the campaign to show
> that it had acted in ways that represented the
> black and poor majority: the minimum wage for
> domestic workers, the Land Lease Programme,
> the National Housing Trust — 99% of the people
> who benefitted from those programmes were
> black, and people knew that. (#20)

In contrast, the JLP deliberately downplayed the conflicts of a racially heterogeneous society. "We went after
unity," said an respondent who was a JLP candidate in that
election. "Seaga would say at meetings, 'Look out there —
white, brown, black, Chinese people.' We needed the

expertise of the ex-migrants. If you didn't identify with the whole country, it was no good. White and brown people were needed for financial support. The JLP was the less racially divisive group" (#12).

Other respondents, including a 1976 JLP campaign manager, agreed (#7, #9, #12, #30, #31). The campaign manager indicated that it was deliberate:

> Jamaica is mostly black, and the question of colour is important. In the Labour Party where the leader is not black, the question of colour must be dealt with delicately. We tried to project Seaga as colourless; he'd already proven beyond a doubt that colour of skin didn't affect colour of sight. We emphasized his work on cultural development ... and his achievements in Western Kingston. This was evidence that a black man didn't need to fear the party.... We had pictures and films of him playing skittles, reasoning with young people, and the people he'd associate with in the films were ordinary black people. Also we had to be careful to involve all ethnic groups, and not to have him on the platform with too many white people. We didn't want this to look like a South African political party. (#31).

Anticolonialism

Anti-imperialism and anticolonialism were central topics of the 1976 elections. Under this broad rubric are included diverse issues of the campaign that have as their common theme the question of foreign ownership and control of economic enterprises. The notorious "Cuban connection" and the furor around it formed a part of this debate, and is included here for two reasons. First, Cuba was a familiar and geographically close example of a revolutionary state that had rejected foreign control over its economy. Second, as a rationale for his close relationship with the government of Cuba, Manley referred repeatedly to the common experience of colonial domination. Other general issues that will be discussed in this section are the PNP's are the PNP's position on foreign capital in Jamaica, including the bauxite levy, the PNP's emphasis on Third World unity, and the question of destabilization.   The Cuban connection was by far the most intensely debated, and will be discussed first.

Jamaica had long had close connections with the neighboring island of Cuba because of frequent interisland migrations.   Many Jamaicans had migrated there to work on the sugar plantations; some had returned.   Bustamante had spent many years there.   Several prominent Jamaicans including the editor of the *Gleaner* in 1976, Hector Wynter, had been born there.   Under the JLP government of the late 1960s, Jamaica had regularized relations with Cuba, and became the first member of the Organization of American States to be allowed to join that organization while refusing to participate in efforts to isolate Cuba.

Manley had actively pursued friendly and close relations with the Castro government.   Castro had been invited to Jamaica;   Manley visited Cuba in 1975.   The Cuban government contributed materials and labor to build a school near Spanish Town, in the parish of St. Catherine, and Cuban physicians had been sent to Jamaica to work in rural health care centers.   The Cuban gift school was opened formally a few weeks before the election.   At the ceremony, Manley referred to Cuba's and Jamaica's common colonial past. He said that there was no other country "with which we have known a greater sense of principle" than Cuba, and explained in a letter to the *Gleaner* that the remark was made in a particular context: all Third World countries have shared the experience of domination, and therefore relationships among them were "marked by a strict sense of respect for sovereignty and non-interference in the internal affairs of each other" (WG 12/14/76, 18).

Manley's relationship with Cuba and the 1974 announcement of the PNP's democratic socialist orientation combined to make the "communist threat" seem a fruitful avenue for the opposition to pursue.   Manley had always professed that there were strong and clear lines of demarcation between communism and democratic socialism, and had expelled avowed communists from the PNP ranks shortly after his election in 1972 (Manley 1976b, 172-73).

In the 1976 election the PNP had the support of one Jamaican communist organization, the Workers' Liberation League (WLL) (#21), but some respondents noted that Manley had tried to made the connection as indirect as possible (#7, #13). One of the WLL's songs, "Forward March," was sung at PNP rallies, and one of its slogans, "Forward to true socialism," was seen on banners at PNP rallies (#7) but its use was discouraged by PNP officials (#13). The PNP's connection with this group was to become an issue in the 1980 election.

The PNP's sensitivity to the communist-threat issue was obvious in the campaign materials. During the campaign, Manley repeatedly assured the electorate that Jamaica would not "go communist" (DG 12/14/76, 1; WG 12/21/76, 2). A series of small advertisements were labeled "Truth, Not Propaganda." The PNP said that the JLP was using the "Big Lie Technique" with respect to the Cuban question (WG 11/23/76, 4). At the opening of the Cuban school, Manley deplored the fact that the JLP was making the "good gift" seem "sinister" (WG 12/14/76, 6). A pro-PNP columnist likened the "job being done on Jamaica's relations with Cuba" to "the futile games that were played in 1972 with the Claudius Henry pamphlets" (WG 11/30/76, 17).

When Manley was visiting Cuba in 1975, he made a stirring speech about the solidarity of Jamaicans and Cubans:

> Sometimes the road will turn, there will be obstacles but our eyes are fixed on that mountain top, and our feet are marching on the road. And I want you to know that every step you take, you do not take alone, because the feet of the Jamaican people are marching beside you. And one day together we will stand on that mountaintop and look back down the road, and we shall say together: "We have overcome." (DG 12/21/76, 7)

This quotation was used extensively by the JLP in both the 1976 and the 1980 election campaigns, and appeared in its entirety in several advertisements. In one JLP advertisement, for example, there is a photograph of Manley embracing Castro, and the words "The people of Jamaica will not walk hand in hand with communism" (DG 12/12/76, 7). This advertisement was reprinted the following day, and, in the same issue, the PNP reprinted the same Manley quotation in its own advertisement, which stressed the unity of the Third World and began with the headline "Hand in Hand: The Trade Union of the Poor" (DG 12/13/76, 34).

Another JLP advertisement began with an appeal to youth, then continued: "My name is Colin Williamson. I am a young man with a heart.... I am dedicated to save Jamaica. I don't want to walk to any mountaintop with any foreign leader. I don't want to lead no third world (sic)" (DG 12/11/76, 7). Other JLP candidates and supporters referred to the "mountain top" quotation as well (DG 12/11/76, 3; 12/14/76, 39). The advertising executive who had worked with Manley since 1969 abandoned him in 1976; he asserted that Manley had said that "he would walk with Castro to the mountain top. He never could explain what he meant by that. Manley worshipped Castro.... We told him we think you're crazy ... in July of 1976, we met with him and told him 'You are going communist and we can't promote you any longer'" (#24).

Seaga was unrelenting in his criticism of the PNP's relationship with Cuba. In a mass meeting he likened the PNP's Land Lease Programme to the Cuban system (WG 11/16/76, 11). In a radio broadcast he compared the "wide scale abuse of the information media by the PNP" to the "communist system," under which "it is perfectly in order for taxpayers' funds to be used to promote the party in power." He equated the state of emergency with Castro's powers in Cuba. He continued with a defense against the PNP's "Big Lie Technique" accusation by saying: "It is a fact that Cuban Communist Secret Police and Master Spies have been delegates to the PNP's annual conference in Jamaica. That's no lie!" (WG 12/7/76, 4). Seaga said repeatedly that if the PNP was returned to power, Jamaica would be another Cuba (DG 12/6/76, 12), and that the Cuban Communist Party would run the government (DG 9/20/76).

An eleventh-hour advertisement paid for by the "Save Jamaica Forum dedicated to the prevention of communism in Jamaica" was a parody of the PNP's advertisements. It began with "Forward," a PNP slogan. A full-page cartoon showed Manley encouraging a frightened man, labeled "Jamaica," to jump off a diving board. The man has a ball and chain labeled "Democratic Socialism" and the pool beneath him is "One Party State." An alligator labeled "communism" lurks beneath, and Manley is saying, "Ah sey jump. Man born fe hang can't drown" (DG 12/14/76, 22).

Manley was sometimes compared personally to Castro. One JLP advertisement compared Manley's change of heart about socialism between 1972 and 1974 to Castro's conversion to communism between 1959 and 1961 (DG 12/12/76, 31). A letter to the *Gleaner* from "A Red Watcher" claimed that Castro had used the term "Democratic Socialism" before 1961 (DG 12/14/76, 39).

At a public meeting a JLP candidate said the "economy is suffering from Castro-enteritis" (DG 12/14/76, 9). An advertisement from the "Jamaican Anti-Ananias League" promulgated the ultimate in campaign promises; it ran, in its entirety:"Jamaican People. Don't let the Comrades Castro-ate you. Vote JLP for Better Living, Better Loving" (DG 12/11/76, 34).

Research into the attitudes of voters before the election revealed that the JLP campaign had not succeeded in convincing the electorate of the "communist threat." The Cuban-Jamaican friendship was viewed positively by a majority of voters (Stone, DG 11/21/76). The electorate was aware of the benefits of the Cuban presence; the aid of the Cuban doctors and the new school building were tangible and welcome benefits. Indeed, the PNP did not hesitate to draw people's attention to the help from Cuba. In the campaign song, "The Message," the Cuban school was mentioned. According to one respondent, who was a campaign worker in 1976, the PNP projected this only to certain audiences, specifically, constituencies where there had been concrete Cuban assistance and in those that were poorer, urban communities (#26).

There was no direct use of Rastafarian symbols in connection with the Cuban question in any of the campaign materials reviewed. The indirect use was the fact that the Cuban school was mentioned in "The Message," which also used strongly Rastafarian language. There was a complex set of relationships operating that would have made the use of such symbols inappropriate: Emperor Selassie had been overthrown and killed two years earlier in a revolution supported by the Cubans. At least one Rastafarian respondent expressed disgust for that reason when asked about Cuba (#36).

The role of foreign capital received some attention from both parties. The JLP specified six strategies subsumed by its slogan, "Nationalism." One was "Local control of the economy:" *"Nationalism requires a minimum local participation of 51% in all enterprises...."* But quickly adds:

> The whole process will be governed by mutual arrangement and moral suasion, *not by force....*
>
> Nationalism rejects that model of society in which:
> o The State owns everything
> o The State controls everything
> o The State decides everything
> o Private property virtually does not exist. (JLP 1976, 290-91)

The PNP's manifesto also condemned majority foreign ownership of enterprises, and considered this one of Jamaica's primary economic problems (DG 12/14/76, 39). The manifesto pointed out that in 1972, the bauxite industry, all major public utilities, the municipal bus service, and the sugar and tourist industries were mostly foreign-owned; since then, the PNP had bought back for Jamaica 51 percent ownership of the bauxite operations and had brought the other industries mentioned into Jamaican control (PNP 1976, 279-80).

The PNP drew attention especially to its stance toward the bauxite companies. The state of emergency had brought JLP gunmen "under heavy manners"; the bauxite levy had done the same for foreign capital (Manley 1976a, 18). Manley mentioned the levy in the Sam Sharpe Square, Montego Bay, speech that had begun the campaign (WG 11/30/76, 6) and in advertisements (DG 11/21/76, 21; 12/2/76, 11). Although the JLP had not opposed the levy at the time of its imposition (#13), the PNP borrowed the JLP slogan "Free Up" to accuse the JLP of wanting to "free up bauxite for foreign exploitation" (DG 12/2/76, 5).

The bauxite levy was popular and was considered an assertion of national sovereignty (#20). Early in the campaign, it was presented as such by the party. In an advertisement, a photograph of Michael Manley signing the agreement between Jamaica and one aluminium company was accompanied by the headline "Forward on our Feet ... Not on our Knees!" It continued: "A Bold New Bauxite Policy for the benefit of our people. We welcome foreign private capital as long as it comes on terms consistent with our national sovereignty and national self respect" (DG 11/10/76).

The image of foreigners in control was a provocative one, and the PNP's song "The Message" conveyed the fact of Seaga's foreign birth much more directly than his racial status (#13). An unofficial pamphlet, published by the "Committee for National Unity to Defeat Imperialism and in Defense of Democracy," asserted that Seaga was plotting with "powerful capitalists in the United States ... to murder thousands of supporters of the democratically elected PNP government" (DG 11/25/76, 10). An advertising executive who worked for the JLP said that most Jamaicans would prefer Hugh Shearer to Seaga. When asked why, he replied matter of factly: "Hugh Shearer is a Jamaican" (#24). However, the PNP's official campaign materials do not reveal explicit exploitation of Seaga's foreign birth.

Another aspect of the PNP's anti-imperialist orientation was the party's emphasis on Third World unity. From the beginning of his tenure as prime minister, Manley expressed a preference for trading with Third World countries, when possible: "Every item you can buy at an equal price from Venezuela or China rather than America ... that makes you a little bit stronger as part of the third world. You ... look a little independent strength instead of everybody being Uncle Tom" (Document III).

Ground was broken shortly before the election for a "JAVEMEX" plant in Manchester, an alumina plant to be owned by Jamaica, Venezuela, and Mexico. It was hailed by the party as an "experiment in third world cooperation" (WG 11/23/76, 1), and was named as a PNP achievement in

Manley's speech at Sam Sharpe Square (WG 11/30/76, 6),
but the plant was never completed.

An advertisement mentioned earlier was symbolic of
Third World cooperation. It included a drawing of two
hands clasped across a globe. Around the globe are names
of Third World countries, such as Tanzania, Barbados,
Cuba, and Panama. These are united in "The Trade Union
of the Poor" (DG 12/13/76, 34), a phrase borrowed by
Manley from Julius Nyerere.

The PNP supported the liberation struggles in Africa
despite criticism from the Ford administration (Manley
1982, 116). The PNP's Youth Organization in particular
was actively raising funds to support the struggles in
Mozambique and elsewhere (Document IV). In an advertisement the PNP called attention to that aspect among
other aspects of itsforeign policy. Photographs showed
Manley with the heads of state of Tanzania, Venezuela,
Mexico, Cuba, and Canada. The copy read:

> A true leader. Respected for his honesty. A man
> of courage.   Together with his colleagues ...
> Jamaica has come to be known in the world for
> our principled defence of the African Liberation
> Struggles, our fight against apartheid, for racial
> equality and our struggle for a new world econo-
> mic order to liberate the poor of the world.
> Jamaicans know too and have pride at last. For-
> eign Policy. And this is just the beginning. For-
> ward with Democratic Socialism. (DG 12/11/76, 9)

Several observers of the 1976 elections perceived interference on the part of the United States in the electoral
process. Fred Landis asserted that the headlines in the
Gleaner during the election period resembled those of *El
Mercurio* in Chile during the Central Intelligence Agency's
destabilization of the Allende regime (Landis, 1980). Manley himself has expressed no doubt that the CIA played a
role (Manley 1982), and mentioned destabilization in his
budget speech of 1976 (#7). In his speech at the public
session of the 1976 convention he commented: "We watch
how certain forces abroad try to mash up our tourist trade
by writing vicious articles about us and we wonder whose

hand is manipulating the strings.... They tell me the whole thing happen by accident.... I don't believe it" (Manley 1976a, 19-20). He argues in a more recent book and in public speeches that U.S. interference began with Jamaica's decision to back Cuba in its military support of the MPLA government of Angola. At that point, U.S. aid dried up, and the embassy staff increased by seven (Manley, 1982).

The accusation of destabilization almost never reached the printed page in the campaign, but evidence of its promulgation by the PNP may be gleaned from other sources. In a column about Manley's accusing the JLP of using the "Big Lie Technique," a pro-JLP columnist asserted that Manley was guilty of the same in regard to the "JLP-Seaga-CIA" plot (WG 11/30/76, 17). "CIA OUT" was scrawled on walls throughout Kingston (#8), and Seaga acquired the nickname "C-I-A-ga" (#8). The PNP, according to the JLP, was showing films about CIA destabilization in Chile (WG 11/23/76, 4). In a song called "Rat Race" that was released during the period immediately before the election, Bob Marley sang:

> When the cat's away, the mice will play
> Political violence fill your city
> Don't involve Rasta in your say say
> Rasta don't work for no CIA

One respondent interpreted this as referring to the JLP's use of Rastafarian language in its leadership's campaign speeches (#8). Another song, "Roman Soldiers of Babylon" by Jacob Miller, ends with a phrase that at first sounds like scat singing, but on second and third hearing its meaning becomes clearer:

> See them coming in plain clothes
> Don't give up, don't give up
> The Roman soldiers of Babylon
> Are here to fight us
> Don't give up, don't give up
> The Roman soldiers of Babylon are right behind us
> Coming from the North with their pockets
> Full of ammunition

Trying to turn dreadlocks into politician
Marcus Garvey did say
Things like this would happen in this time
They're in plain clothes!
They're coming trying to fight Rastafari
But they can't but fear the wisdom of Selassie I
Rastafari, Rastafari will blow them away
Yes the C, the I, the A-oh
Yes the C, the I, the A.

In general, the PNP "preempted" anti-imperialism, as one respondent put it (#12);   however, the JLP never indicated any interest in it. The PNP referred to imperialism often in its symbols and slogans. "We are not for sale" was one anti-imperialist slogan, the full meaning of which was not evident until after the election, when it was disclosed that the PNP had been in negotiations with the International Monetary Fund and had chosen the slogan as a response to IMF demands (#13). In the PNP's notes for canvassers for the election, one of the topics with which they were required to familiarize themselves was "How does imperialism work?" (Document V). The song "Forward March," written by a member of the Workers' Liberation League, was played on the platforms of the PNP's mass meetings (#8):

Forward march against oppression forward march
Now we the youth have caught their vision
End of misery and oppression
So we fill Jamaica full with our song
Forward march against imperialism....

"Youth Week" in the election year had had as its theme "Youth for National Unity Against Imperialism," and the parliamentary secretary in the Ministry of Youth and Community Development commended the youth, saying he was "pleased to see that young people had realised the necessity for the struggle against imperialism" (WG 11/23/76, 19). Anti-imperialism was the major theme of Manley's final preelection broadcast (WG 12/21/76, 8). Even the clothing that PNP ministers were wont to wear, Kariba jackets, were perceived as "progressive" in contrast to the three-piece suits associated with the JLP, which were "symbols of imperialism" (#22).

The Use of Rastafarian Symbols and Reggae Music

By 1976, Rastafarians enjoyed a considerable improvement in social status compared with their reputation as "Blackheart men" and "Dutty Tils" (dirty tails) of the previous decade. One respondent said that they had been "accepted" by 1976. "Rasta was more fashionable, more legitimate" (#20). Another said that by 1976, "Rasta had gained acceptability and respectability — it was accepted as a part of Jamaican life. Rasta had been something of a revolution. Fifteen years ago (i.e. 1967) to be a Rasta would have made you anti-social. You were defying the social order. Now it is more accepted, more middle class. That was assisted to some extent by Manley's endorsement of it" (#31).

People perceived Rastafarians as having made a positive contribution to Jamaican culture. One middle-class respondent saw their main influence "in social attitudes about the roots of Jamaican culture. They identified with Africa; it was an assertion of African pride. There were changes in manners, away from genteel British manners, and in eating habits. There was also a change in the attitude toward the poor. The Rastas sensitised the national consciousness in attitudes toward black and poor" (#17).

Another respondent, a 1976 JLP candidate, said he let Rastas in his constituency "know that I respected the Rasta thing. They have a very proud, positive attitude toward blackness" (#12). Another respondent said Rastas had become more integrated into social institutions, and their influence had "put a little melanin into the authority structure" (#10).

One respondent saw Rasta as "almost institutionalized" by 1976, but the Rastas had formed three "streams." One was religious, exemplified by the Twelve Tribes, a group based in Kingston with a number of middle-class members and with chapters in other cities, including Brooklyn. The second was political, and these Rastas, he said, are distinctive because they accept the fact of Selassie's death. The third, and most significant for mass politics, were "those influenced by Rasta morals, dress, and manners, a much larger group that cuts across class barriers" (#8).

The PNP government, according to some respondents, made efforts "to deal with Rastas, to utilize them and appoint them. Rasta was partially assimilated into the Manley government" (#25). Manley was rumored to have met with Rastafarians and to have been instrumental in obtaining land in Ethiopia so that they could repatriate (WG 12/21/76, 17). According to a leader of a Rasta organization, PNP "thugs" tried to persuade the organization's leadership to affiliate with the party but did not succeed. "We would have had real problems," he said, "if we had done so" (#35). Others report that the police were still harassing Rastas (#12).

There are signs that the Rastas were being assimilated into certain aspects of Jamaican culture, especially the arts. Two plays produced in 1976 were called "Summer Dread" (#7) and "I-Man" (DG 11/26/76, 5); a number of painters and other visual artists wore locks; and Jamaican poets addressed Rasta themes (e.g. Morris 1977).

A ceremonial opening of a new library reported in the *Gleaner* illustrated the degree of Rasta assimilation. The building was the culmination of a two-year effort by members of the Mystic Revelation of Rastafari, a group of Rasta drummers. Rastafarian Brothers Moses Nelson and Sam Clayton spoke at the opening and expressed thankfulness that Rasta ideology was moving "from strength to strength." Also speaking were William Isaacs, the PNP MP for Eastern Kingston, and PNP Councillor Gladys Ellington (WG 12/14/76, 20). It is worth noting that the library-community center was built in a strong PNP area.

Other items in the newspapers indicated that Rasta activities were increasingly considered newsworthy. When Twelve Tribes sent a delegation to Ethiopia, the *Weekly Gleaner* reported the departure (12/21/76, 7). Another article appeared in the *Star* about two groups of Rastafarians celebrating Ethiopian Christmas (*Star* 1/5/77, 11).

Both parties used Rastafarian symbols in the 1976 election, and Rastafarian language, which some respondents considered more important than other Rasta symbols (#8), was liberally sprinkled throughout the campaign material.

The most often used Rasta phrase was the major JLP slogan for the campaign, "High-Up." "High-Up" was a Rasta greeting, and, according to one respondent, the greeting was really "I-up" but "the JLP used 'high' to make it more respectable" (#13). It was intended to imply that the JLP was "up top, above the PNP, right up there ready to take over the government" (#6). A slogan used in conjunction with "High-Up" was "We're Ready!" (DG 11/23/76, 15).

"High-Up" was used throughout the JLP campaign (e.g. DG 12/9/76, 21, 22; WG 11/30/76, 6; DG 12/14/76, 14) but was also used against the JLP by the PNP. Seaga's "nationalism," according to PNP advertisements, was "priced high-up" (DG 12/9/76, 9), and an unofficial PNP poster shows a John Crow (a common turkey vulture) with a bell around its neck and a menacing look on its face. The poster read simply "High-Up" (Document IX). This poster was noted in the *Gleaner* (DG 12/13/76, 8) and was clearly remembered by respondents (#6, #7, #13). The PNP contrasted one of its catchwords, "roots," which implied the lower classes, with the JLP's "High-Up," which implied the upper classes (#13; DG 12/13/76, 11).

The JLP used other Rastafarian words as well. Seaga's speech at Tivoli Sports Field, which officially opened the JLP campaign, is replete with Rasta references. The *Gleaner's* account read: "Seaga announced the date of elections and said 'Them going get a beating' which was greeted with loud cheers of 'high-up' and bell ringing." Seaga reportedly said the Prime Minister "looks down on the land as his kingdom. But I want him to know that Eddie is trodding creation, and the kingdom over which he rules no longer exists, because "Jah Kingdom Gone to Waste".... Youthman and daughter should know which is their party.'" (WG 11/30/76, 6).

"Youthman and daughter," "trodding creation," and, of course, "Jah Kingdom" were Rastafarian phrases. "Youth-man" was often used by the PNP Youth Organization (Document X). "Them going get a beating" was a reference to the Peter Tosh song used by the PNP in 1972 (see chapter 4) and "Jah Kingdom Gone to Waste" alluded to a more recent song by Ernie Smith used by the JLP (discussed below).

One JLP respondent said that the PNP dealt with Rasta on a deeper level than the JLP, which "just used the rhetoric. Seaga used Rasta images to communicate, to establish a common set of symbols ... he uses language that most people understand" (#5). This description is consistent with the fact that although the PNP is usually perceived by respondents as having more appeal to Rastas (#12, #20, #26, #31), the PNP materials revealed very little use of Rasta language by politicians. Manley rarely used it (#26), although he used some patois phrases, and he still used the greeting "Love," noted in chapter 4. The only other Rasta language that found its way into print was the standard headline on PNP broadcast advertisements, "A Time for Reasoning." The word *reasoning*, originally biblical, was popularized by the Rastas. The Rasta language was said to be prevalent among members of the PNP Youth Organization (#8).

One term that is also derived from Rastafarian language appeared in unofficial PNP pamphlets. Instead of "Seaga," the JLP party leader was called "Blind-aga" (Document VI). In Rasta "reasoning," "to see" has a meaning comparable to "to see the light" or to believe. Seaga clearly did not "see," hence his name must instead be "Blind-aga" (Birhan 1980).

Of other Rasta symbols used by politicians, none was more frequently mentioned than dress. Rastafarians seem to have strict dress codes, particularly for women, and have popularized certain items of clothing. The most visible was the tam or knitted cap that is worn to cover the locks. Sometimes a tam is simply convenient, for example, to hide the locks from an employer, but for some Rastas it has ritual significance. For example, in the Twelve Tribes, when the congregation sings the Ethiopian national anthem, all women must wear a tam or otherwise cover their hair, and men must remove their tams unless it is of the Ethiopian national colors, red, green, and gold.

Photographs of PNP officials during the 1976 campaign frequently showed them wearing tams (DG 12/16/76, 23) and their use of tams is noted in letters to the *Gleaner* (DG 10/28/76) and by respondents (#5, #7, #10, #17, #22, #29). The beard was another such symbol, but by 1976 was less strongly tied to Rastafari than the tam. One JLP candidate admitted to cultivating a full-face beard for the 1976 election, "to appeal to youth," and promptly shaved it off after the election (#29). Photographs of all candidates, regularly printed in the *Gleaner* before each election, showed that an increasing number of candidates sported beards. No candidate in 1967 and only two candidates in 1972 wore beards, while in 1976 sixteen candidates wore beards, and in 1980, nineteen.

Finally, PNP politicians were recognizable by their style of dress, usually a Kariba suit (a modified safari jacket) rather than the jacket and tie associated with the JLP. In a 1977 photograph of the newly elected cabinet, of twenty-eight people, only three wore jackets and ties (*Star* 1/5/77). The question of attire in politics is imbued with considerable significance. In 1981 it became the subject of debate on the floor of Parliament when the JLP MPs, then forming the government, announced that the Kariba suit was no longer proper dress for parliamentarians. Respondents frequently noted the party dress codes (#7, #10, #22, #29, #33), and said that the Western style suit was a "symbol of conformist behavior and tradition" (#7) and "a symbol of imperialism" (#22), and that while the Kariba jacket was "a symbol of cultural decolonization" (#22). In *The Politics of Change*, Manley interpreted the change in manner of dress similarly, considering the adoption of the jacket and tie the "first act of psychological surrender" in the "colonial trauma" (1974, 65-66). One JLP respondent saw the PNP's dress code as "Going overboard to convince the masses that they were for them. The predominant value was being like the masses. The PNP wanted to 'elevate' or single out the masses to get across that this set of PNP deal with you ... The policies of the PNP really changed people's behavior. Tailors couldn't sell jackets and ties. People with ties were anachronisms" (#29).

Although the Kariba suit is not a Rastafarian symbol per se, it is mentioned here because respondents frequently mentioned it in conjunction with the PNP's adoption of other, more Rastafarian, forms of dress. "Jacket and tie" is mentioned derisively in at least one Rastafarian reggae song in connection with other symbols of oppression ("Stand Firm"; discussed in chapter 6).

Several respondents were of the opinion that the PNP had a greater appeal to Rastafarians than the JLP (#12, #20, #26, #31). The PNP seemed to have created this appeal through the use of music, which will be discussed below, and of language and dress. The Rod of Correction made an encore appearance in this election campaign (DG 12/3/76, 8; WG 11/30/76, 6), but its significance had diminished considerably. The Henry pamphlet was mentioned twice in the 1976 materials, once by a PNP supporter as an illustration of the JLP's "futile games" (WG 11/30/76, 17), and once by a JLP supporter in a letter to the *Gleaner*, that pointed out that the pamphlet had evidently "angered the Almighty," resulting in Claudius Henry's church and bakery shop being "burnt down flat" soon after the 1972 election (DG 11/30/76, 5).

Besides using Rastafarian language, the JLP used other symbols of significance to Rastafarians. The party stressed Seaga's accomplishment of arranging for the return of Marcus Garvey's remains to Jamaica, and printed photographs in its advertisements of Garvey and of Seaga shaking hands with Selassie (DG 11/28/76, 8-9). Yet the JLP also stressed Seaga's "transformation" of Back-o'-Wall that had displaced so many Rastafarians (DG 11/28/76, 8; 12/4/76, 28; 12/7/76, 10).

A JLP campaign manager explained that there was a deliberate use of Rasta symbols, by politicians of both parties:

> Rasta is a religious movement with clear tenets, objects of worship and rituals. It also has a language and a code of behavior that has a wider cultural context. Any movement which must seek mass support must address that culture. Political campaigners use its colours, language, in a special appeal to that culture, in recognition that its values are widely held and intimate to people. It's targeted to different audiences; not to the middle class, who don't respond to it and who feel they are being talked down to. It's projected mostly to the lower class. (#31)

Similarly, a PNP respondent who was close to the campaign said that some politicians did not identify strongly with Rastafarians or reggae but "they had to be realistic and give the crowd what it wanted" (#26). Another respondent, a Rastafarian musician, summed it up when he said of politicians, "If them no use Rasta, no go" (#36).

The campaign manager for the JLP added, however, that it was difficult for Seaga to use those symbols, even though his constituency is "the birthplace of Rasta." It would have been seen as patronizing (#31). That is the probable source of the ambivalence some PNP supporters detected in the JLP's use of Rasta symbols. One, for example, said: "The JLP has a difficult time truly identifying with Rasta. It isn't consistent with their Big People/brown skin approach. The PNP's socially conscious approach was more easily identified with Rasta" (#20).

One of the primary ways of appealing to Rasta culture was through the use of reggae music. As the JLP campaign manager said, "Reggae invariably has social commentary. The majority of the songs seek to address social problems. Many are protest songs, and these are perfect for opposition parties" (#31).

Music

When one respondent was asked who in Jamaica listened to and enjoyed reggae music, he quickly said, "Everybody!" After a pause he added, "Well, everybody except the middle class and the upper class" (#4). Although reggae remained "little people music" (#20), it was gaining popularity among the Jamaican middle class, especially youth. In the *Gleaner* and the *Star*, regular columns about reggae music had been instituted, and in the materials that were issued during the month before the election, nearly one hundred songs were mentioned, compared with the handful alluded to in the 1972 materials. To some extent, national cultural institutions began to accept the popular music form. In 1973, Rita Marley, a Rastafarian, won the annual Festival award for best singer, and she performed in the 1976 Pantomime, an annual official cultural presentation (WG 11/30/76, 12).

Although the North Coast hotels catering to the tourist trade still showed a reluctance to hire reggae bands for poolside entertainment, North American concert promoters saw the music's growing popularity outside Jamaica and took advantage of it. In the months before the election seven of the major bands had toured abroad; these entertainers performed live more frequently in North America and Europe than in Jamaica, where the "sound system" (see chapter 3) still prevailed (*Star* 1/7/77). Several bands signed contracts with British and American record companies, and gained a modicum of financial success.

Reggae continued to be Rasta music. Many of the most popular artists were dreadlocked and espoused Rastafari in their lyrics. Some of the song titles mentioned in the *Gleaner* and the *Star* are illustrative: "So Jah Say," "Dread out deh," "Satta Amassagana," "Rastaman Chant," and "Natty Dread a Conqueror."

The use of the Rastafarians' symbols by politicians did not escape the notice of reggae musicians. Two songs commented on the phenomenon. In Bob Marley's "Rat Race," mentioned earlier, he asked that politicians not "involve Rasta in their say say." Likewise in the song quoted above, Jacob Miller's "Roman Soldiers of Babylon," also released in 1976, was a reference to the "Roman Soldiers"

> *Coming from the North*
> *With their pockets full of ammunition*
> *Try to turn dreadlocks into politician*

The "North" probably refers to rumors that the JLP was importing weapons from the United States.

Since the 1972 election, it was not unusual to find reggae music mixing with politics. Just after the PNP's victory, the new government declared an amnesty on possession of illegal guns. A reggae song was produced and played in broadcast advertisements encouraging individuals to turn in the illegal weapons:

> *Bring in the gun*
> *The rachet and the bomb*

Bring them in one by one
Bring them in for the word is love. (#7)

Two songs that were specifically critical of the PNP were produced around 1974. One was "Promises, Promises" by the Ethiopians, which charged the government with "leading the children to the land of make believe." The song was not particularly popular but, significantly, it was not banned (Walters 1981). A second was "No, Joshua, No" by Max Romeo. The song was a friendly warning to Manley:

Since you my friend, I think you should know
Rasta is watching and blaming you.
Since you my friend, I think you should know
They say you must forward and start anew.
(Walters 1981).

This song was very popular and several respondents remembered it (#11, #13, #20). One recalled that it had not been banned (#11) and another, who was a PNP official, said the song was "taken very seriously" by the PNP (#20). A PNP supporter said that Max Romeo was "a genuine protest singer who had become disenchanted with the party. The PNP started to redeem itself in 1974, and Romeo remade the same music then, in a song called 'Yes, Joshua, Yes.' It was a song about the Bauxite Levy" (#13). Although the respondent said that the second song was as popular as the first, the research revealed no other mention of it.

Also in 1974, Pearnel Charles, a JLP senator, made a record called "Jump and Shout" (Walters 1981). The song is replete with Labour Party slogans, including "Turn Them Back," "Ring the Bell," and "The Time Has Come," and was played over the public address systems at rallies during the 1976 campaign (#31).

Other songs that commented directly on the political situation were Pluto Shervington's "I-man born yah," a pro-PNP commentary on emigration, and Lord Larro's "Foreign Press." The latter is a calypso about the way the North American and European press did not report the positive things about Jamaican life, but "Shanty town and a woman in a ragged dress / Bet you life it making headline in the foreign press" (quoted in Walters 1981).

In 1976 each political party was associated with a particular song, and both songs used Rastafarian dialect. The JLP used Ernie Smith's song "Jah Kingdom Gone to Waste." In contrast to the PNP's confident slogan, "We know where we are going," this song said "we the people" want to know where the nation is going, and where the government stands; it stressed violence and crime:

And as we fight one another
For the power and the glory
The kingdom goes to waste
We the people want fi know just where we going
Right now we hands are tied, tied behind we back
While certain people if-and-but'ing
Where do we stand?
We have too far to go, not to really know
Just how we getting there (oh Jah)
And if we getting anywhere (oh Jah)
We have too much to change,
Not to know the range
Of possibility and changeability
Violence and crime is commonplace
In these said times, no man walk free
Prophecy come closer to fulfillment
In these dread times. Why should this be?
And as we fight one another
Fi the power and the glory
Jah Kingdom go to waste
And every drop of blood we taste
A fi we owndisgrace
Can't build no foundation 'pon a if-and-but
Are we building a nation or are we building a hut?
And everytime you ask for some old friend
You hear say just last night,
He meet a sad, sad end
And if you talk too loud and if you walk too proud
Watch where you lay your head
For out dey dread, well dread
Can't build no dreams 'pon a fuss and fight
We no care who a do it Jah say that no right...

Ernie Smith was a singer of middle-class origins (#7) and was a balladeer rather than a reggae musician. Two years before the election he had produced a song called "Rebel Music" that expressed his frustration about not having success with his ballads because "sufferer don't want no pretty music" (Walters 1981). "Jah Kingdom" was in a ballad rather than a reggae style. As noted earlier, Seaga used the title words of this song in his speech opening the campaign (WG 11/30/76, 6). He also frequently used the words "Jah say that nah right" in speeches (#7).

The primary song used by the PNP was "The Message" by Neville Martin. Composed for the 1976 election, the song is in a *mento* or folk-song style, a form characteristic of the peasantry, from which Martin had come (#13), but it also used more up-dated reggae rhythms. Its lyrics enumerated the achievements of the PNP government in patois and used a popular slang phrase of the time, "jook them," meaning impress them, or hit them:

> *My Father born yah, my grandmother born yah*
> *I and I born yah, my leader born yah*
> *That's why I nah lef' yah*
> *He gave I a message, to all those people*
> *Who nah love progress*
> *He said you jook them with Land Lease*
> *Then you jook them with the Pioneer Corps*
> *Jook them with JAMAL*
> *Then you jook them with free education*
> *Equal pay for women*
> *Jook them with the minimum wage*
> *My leader born yah, so I nah lef' yah*
> *Me a satta with discipline*
> *Under heavy heavy manners*
> *Me ina the struggle too*
> *No bastard no dey again, everyone a full*
> *Jook them with the Cuban schools*
> *Then you jook them with the microdams*
> *Jook them with the basic schools*
> *Socialists a no fool, jook them with housing*
> *Then you jook them with the Impact Programme*
> *We have them under manners,*
> *Heavy, heavy manners*

I-man a satta with discipline
We have them under manners.

"No bastard no dey again" is standard patois and referred
to the PNP government's passage of the Status of Children
Act, which gave all children full legal rights regardless of
whether their parents were married. The lyrics are liberally sprinkled with Rastafarian words and phrases, such as "I
and I," and "I-Man a satta with discipline" (meaning, I wait,
I am patient). "The Message" was recognized as a very
Rastafarian song (#20). The song's conclusion was a
repetition of the patois phrase made popular by the PNP
government: "heavy manners," meaning discipline or control.

Many respondents referred to this song (#7, #13, #14,
#20, #25, #26), and it was said to be one of the most
popular songs of the year (Walters 1981). One informant
said that "a lot of Labourites bought the record after the
election" (#7). It was first sung at the Sam Sharpe Square
meeting, at which the PNP launched its campaign (#13),
and was a "rallying point" in the Manley campaign (#26).
As mentioned earlier, the phrase "My leader born yah" was
interpreted as a reference to Seaga's status as White and
foreign born. That line gave rise to other, unofficial
slogans that took the same form. For example, Seaga is
not known as "an ebullient, effervescent people-person. He
doesn't smile a lot" (#31; corroborated, #9). An unofficial
PNP slogan was "My leader smiles. Sorry about yours"
(#13).

One incident that received a lot of attention in the
campaign was a free concert given by Bob Marley under
the aegis of the prime minister's cultural office shortly
before the election. Marley was one of the handful of
reggae singers who had achieved financial success. He had
grown up in the slums of Trench Town and began singing
professionally in the mid-1960s. He was one of the first to
tour abroad, and by 1974 had signed a contract with Island
Records, an international recording company owned by a
White Jamaican that was based in London. He moved
uptown, figuratively and literally, to a large residence on
Hope Road, one of St. Andrew's major thoroughfares, to
the dismay of his middle-class neighbors. He had been

dreadlocked since the early 1970s and espoused Rasta doctrines in his music. When the news hit Jamaica that Selassie was dead, Marley produced a song called "Jah Live," which was reportedly the best selling record in Jamaica up to that time (#2).

Marley was highly revered in Jamaica and his music was often the only reggae known to members of the middle class (#11, #14). He was named "Man of the Year" by reggae columnists in 1976 (*Star* 12/31/76). One PNP official said that with Marley, Rasta influence reached its highest point (#34), and a leader of a well known Rasta organization said Rastafari would never be the same with "Marley and Selassie no longer on the scene" (#35). One respondent said of him, "He was really a part of the people; he reflected their ideas rather than trying to direct them, like Tosh did. Marley always summed up public opinion" (#13). A JLP-oriented *Gleaner* columnist expressed his opinion of Marley's influence when he wrote about the fact that the government did not prevent Cindy Breakspeare, a Jamaican beauty queen, from participating in a Miss World Contest in which a South African candidate was also competing. He attributed it to the fact that Breakspeare was Marley's girlfriend, and said: "Our leaders are willing to risk the odium of the Third World, (who, when all is said and done, won't have the slightest effect on our electorate) but know full well that a pop star like Marley could bring 'em down with a statement!" (DG 11/22/76, 10).

The concert in which Marley performed before the election was dubbed "Smile Jamaica," and was planned for a Sunday evening at the National Heroes Park in downtown Kingston. Admission was free; the costs of the production were paid by the Cultural Section of the prime minister's office. The concert was attacked by critics of the government as opportunistic exploitation of the musician's crowd appeal (DG 12/5/76, 8).

The Friday evening before the concert, a number of gunmen invaded Marley's Hope Road residence, shooting and wounding Marley, his wife, and his manager; only the last was seriously injured. The perpetrators were never apprehended. The concert took place as scheduled, after a brief delay "apparently caused by the reluctance of Marley to appear on the show after being shot" (DG 12/7/76. 4).

His regular musicians refused to go onstage at all, and he had to be backed up by another band.   Marley left the island shortly thereafter, and never again lived for an extended period in Jamaica.

The concert had several political features, according to the *Gleaner* report.   Marley said on stage that the had always wanted to do a free show and did not want politics to be involved.   Yet Prime Minister Manley, who watched the show, rushed on stage after Marley's arrival to shake his hand.   Marley sang, among other songs, "So Jah Say," and, according to the *Gleaner*, repeated one line many times: "Puss and dog can get together, so why can't we, my brothers?" (DG 12/7/76, 4).   The song combines social consciousness with the peace theme discussed earlier:

So Jah say
Not one of my seed shall sit on your sidewalk
And beg bread
And verily verily, I'm saying unto the-I
I-nite thyself and love I-manity
Cause puss and dog they get together
What's wrong with you my brother
So Jah say
Ye are the sheep of my pastures
So verily, thou shall be very well
So Jah say
And down here in the ghetto
And down here we suffer
I and I, a hang on in there
I and I, I nah leggo
For so Jah say
I'm going to prepare a place
That where I am, thou shall abide
So Jah say
Fear not for mighty dread
Cause I'll be there at your side
So Jah say.

Whether or not the Marley shooting was politically motivated is still a matter of debate.   A PNP official said he doubted that it was political.   "Bob was a ghetto youth, and he was mixed up in any number of things.   Horse-racing was more likely" (#8). One *Weekly Gleaner* columnist reported that "new indications are that the incident was not political" (WG 12/28/76, 12). The opinion that it was political was more frequently expressed, and two respondents said that most people, including themselves, thought it was political (#7, #20). Carl Stone called it "another stage in the political war we in this country describe as an election" (DG 12/7/76, 12). One music columnist condemned the attack and expressed the opinion that it was the Labour Party that had arranged it (WG 12/21/76, 12), and five years later, during Marley's funeral, several people expressed the opinion that the JLP, then underwriting an expensive state funeral for Marley, had tried to kill him in 1976. Marley for his part was commended by another columnist for his "show-must-go-on" attitude (WG 12/21/76, 12).

The PNP treated the shooting as political. In an "Election Forum" article called "The Choice: Violence or Heavy Manners," the PNP attributed the new wave of violence on the new clique in the JLP; "The Labour Party of Busta" would not have been responsible for such deeds. Then it mentioned the Marley shooting, saying 50,000 people who came out to hear Marley "bear witness to (his) courage and the resistance of terrorism in Jamaica" (DG 12/9/76, 21). A PNP advertisement asked: "Who stands to gain from violence?.... When Bob Marley, well known for his songs against imperialism, was attacked on the eve of his FREE public concert to all Jamaica, WHO STOOD TO GAIN?" (DG 12/10/76, 14).

An Agency for Public Information advertisement paid tribute to Marley for his courage. Under a photo of him, it read:

> Bob Marley
> All Jamaica salutes your courage! By defying the threats against your life you have shown that a people's determination cannot be set back by violence or intimidation. By your example you have made us stronger in the face of violent threats. May your courage be an inspiration to us all! —From all Jamaicans who despise violence. (DG 12/11/76, 21).

Finally, in Vivian Blake's planned broadcast on "The Fascist Threat," portions of which were printed in the *Gleaner* after the radio station had declared it too inflamatory to broadcast, he discussed the "shooting of Bob Marley, who was to give a free concert under the patronage of the Prime Minister for the struggling masses from whom he sprang" (DG 12/12/76, 6).

Other uses of music by political parties are less dramatic than this but indicate that music was utilized deliberately and systematically.   Advertisements and news reports indicated that live music was used at rallies by the PNP (DG 12/10/76, 30; 11/17/76, 7, 13) and by the JLP (WG 11/30/76, 6). A JLP campaign manager said that the party stressed Seaga's involvement in culture, partly to counterbalance his non-Black status (#31), and advertisements reminded the electorate that Seaga had produced and promoted Jamaican popular music (DG 11/28/76, 8-9) and had initiated the Jamaica Festival, an annual cultural event (DG 11/29/76, 18).

The PNP's use of music generally had a higher visibility than the JLP's. An respondent said that it was still used to mobilize crowds and helped to get across the PNP's commitment to the poor: "Reggae was definitely 'little people music.' In the mid-70's it was an overall popular thing. A lot of people knew about it, but the middle class didn't really indulge in it. In 1976 the PNP was still in the midst of helping the small man, and reggae was still appropriate. 'The Message' was serious, fundamental mobilizing music" (#25).

One former PNP supporter said that he began to become "suspicious" of the PNP when he "heard certain songs" (#24). The JLP's affiliate, Young Jamaica, ran an advertisement that mocked the PNP's association with music. It was dominated by a full-page cartoon picture of Manley with a straw hat, tap shoes, and a rod. The ad read:

The Same Old Song and Dance
The PNP Top Ten:
  1. Worker's Bank Skank
  2. Cement Plant Funky
  3. Luana Swan Song
  4. Chat Chat Rockers

     5. Iran Sugar Deal Reggae
     6. Cost of Living Hustle
     7. Mash Potatoes Policies
     8. Socialist Twist
     9. Pioneer Corps Classic
    10. Cuban Love Song
   This just can't go on any longer! Vote JLP. (DG
   12/11/76, 17)

Besides "The Message," reggae songs used by the PNP included the Pluto Shervington song about emigration mentioned above (#7, #13). This song was so well known and popular that Jamaica's ambassador to the United States quoted it for the amusement of his audience when he returned to Jamaica (WG 11/16/76, 6). Another song, "The Clique," written by Neville Martin, was not as popular as his "Message" (#13). A pro-PNP letter to the *Gleaner* used a reggae song by Third World, a band with close ties to the party and one that had performed at the "Smile Jamaica" concert:

> There is a popular song which asks "Who put the hammer and the hoe in the hands of the poor?" The song then goes on to suggest that the poor people of this country have never been free. The JLP has been using as their campaign theme "Freedom" but Jamaicans must be careful and read behind this quest for freedom. We must ask "Freedom for whom?" ... The JLP Action Team is clearly on the move to "free up" the rich people once again so that they can exploit the poor. (WG 11/23/76, 18)

The song referred to is "Freedom Song," which exemplifies the idea that musical production *is* social action:

Who put the hammer and the hoe
In the hands of the poor
Why must the rich man
Be craving for more
Because some of us ain't got no freedom
Beelzebub keeps riding on

Oh can't you hear those people
How they weep and moan?
When will they leave us alone?
That's why we're singing
Freedom song.

Another song by Pluto Shervington was reportedly inspired by a PNP speech (#13) and contains the PNP slogan
"Heavy Manners." "Dis Yah Hard Time" was a warning
directed against the wave of emigration of middle-class
Jamaicans who wanted to evade the socialists' policies
("catch foot" = gain foothold):

One yard with furniture and a wheels fi sale
Owner leaving island fi good
It make you really wonder where did we fail
Draw your brakes and wait a minute,
We down but we not quite dead
Where there's smoke there must be fire
Salvation instead
So, who a leave, gone already
Who a stay better sit down steady
Cause tide is rising fast
Dis yah hard time can't last
Cause when is time to reap
Only them that share the sour
A them a go share the sweet
Some long years afterwards
When we catch we foot
Through hard determination and will
The prodigals will realize where them pot a cook
Heavy Manners

The JLP's affiliate, Young Jamaica, used the line "Dis yah
hard time can't last" in one of its advertisements as well
(DG 12/14/76, 46).

Reggae songs used by the JLP included "Dem ha fi get a
beatin'," which had been a PNP song in 1972, and was
quoted by Seaga in his speech opening the campaign at
Tivoli Sports Field (WG 11/30/76, 6). One respondent who
was part of the JLP's "Action Team" of candidates that
year remembered reggae's being used on the platforms at

mass meetings but did not remember specific songs except the Pearnel Charles record "Jump and Shout." He did say that all the speakers on the platform would dance (#12).

Both parties used music that was folk or religious music as well as reggae or other popular music. One respondent rode a bus through Tivoli Gardens during the 1976 campaign, and by the time the bus left the neighborhood, it was covered with posters that bore Seaga's picture and the slogan "Closer than a brother." Seaga, according to the respondent, "tried to pose as Jesus Christ. That slogan came from a hymn, a Sankey, that goes 'Closer than a brother, my Jesus is to me'" (#7).

Religious music was frequently used by both parties. In a recording of the PNP's September 1976 conference, a soloist sings "I Must Have the Savior with Me," reportedly Manley's favorite hymn. Its lyrics may have served to reassure Protestant voters that the party leader did indeed follow God, but they may have further inspired confidence that Manley himself was the individual who should be followed "without a murmur":

> I must have the Saviour with me
> For I dare not walk alone
> I must feel His presence near me
> And His arms around me thrown
> Then my soul shall fear no ill
> Let Him lead me where He will
> I will go without a murmur
> And His footsteps follow still.

Other songs on the recording are simple verses created from slogans, such as "We're moving forward with socialism" and "We are not for sale"; patriotic hymns such as "Jamaica Arise"; a British Labour Party song that figured highly in the next election, "The Red Flag"; and songs adapted from Sankeys, such as "When Joshua Get Ready," "Press Along, Joshua," and "You Wrong fi Trouble Joshua." These short verses almost always refer to Manley as "Joshua" and express confidence in his leadership. For example:

Them got to run, Lord them got to run
When Joshua get ready, them got to run
Lord them got to run.

Press along Joshua, press along, in God's own way
Tribulations you must bear,
Trials and crosses in your way
For the hotter the battle
The sweeter the victory.

You wrong fi trouble Joshua, you wrong
For Joshua is a lion and lion will devour you
You wrong fi trouble Joshua, you wrong.

These songs have a reggae flavor, but the style in which they are sung is reminiscent of the older *mento* or folk songs, and occasionally African call-and-response form is used.

Discussion

Although the incumbent party was reelected in 1976, the election was "critical" (Key 1955) in the sense that the people who reelected the PNP represented a new coalition of forces. The stereotypes of party supporters prevalent from the founding of the parties in the late 1930s and early 1940s were, as of this election, completely undermined. The JLP no longer was the "Quashi" party, the champions of the grass roots man fighting undefined enemies. The PNP emerged as the party representing not the "little man" but the victims of exploitative, uncontrolled capitalism, not only in Jamaica but globally. For the first time more or less coherent ideologies of class were systematically expressed in the election arena.

The Manley administration succeeded in fusing the issues of race and class conflict. The major achievements of his first term in office were programs designed to help not just the lower class but the poorest sections of that class: the chronically unemployed, the landless sugar workers, the domestic workers. Although Manley's philosophy did not dictate fundamental changes in the class structure, the PNP and democratic socialism came to be strongly identi fied with improvement in the lives of the poor, and with making the lives of the well-to-do more difficult with higher taxes.

Data from the Corporate Area show that the middle and upper classes had, for the first time since 1944, abandoned the PNP (Stone DG 6/8/80, 7). In 1967, 40 percent of the upper class had voted PNP; in 1972 the class demonstrated its enthusiasm for the new PNP leader by delivering more than three-quarters of its vote to him. But in 1976, only 27 percent of that class voted PNP. The trend for the better-off section of the middle class is similar; support dropped from 81.4 percent in 1972 to 40.2 percent in 1976. But the very poor section of the lower class likewise abandoned the JLP; only 28.4 percent of that group voted Labour in 1976, compared with 56.7 percent in 1967 (see Table 5.3).

The PNP highlighted conflict among classes while the JLP stressed unity. The PNP claimed that if the electorate voted JLP, it was "crawling like a whipped dog back to capitalism." The Labour Party could not defend its position effectively while simultaneously treating the electorate as a unified nation uninterested in ideologies of class and class conflict.

The PNP managed to fuse issues of class with issues of race in 1976. The overwhelmingly popular social programs of the PNP had undeniably benefited Black Jamaicans; the taxes had been levied against the primarily Brown, White, and other minority Jamaicans who could afford to pay them. Seaga's race and place of birth became a symbol of the dominant class that had ruled Jamaica since the days of slavery.

The PNP acted on the electorate's new interest in Africa and took decisive stands on politics there that cost the government U.S. aid and goodwill. The JLP, ever the practical politicians, concentrated on the domestic scene and courted the financial support of Brown, White and minority businessmen.

Rastafarians enjoyed a new status in 1976; both parties recognized the extent to which lower- and now middle-class Jamaicans who were not strictly Rastafarians nonetheless sympathized with their values. Their philosophy had become a permanent part of the Jamaican social landscape. The hostility toward Rastafari on the part of the middle class turned to an uncomfortable ambiguity. One's child returned from the university with dreadlocks; Bob Marley became a rich man and moved next door; musicians who could not find work in Montego Bay were entertaining packed concert halls in New York City; and the intelligentsia was speaking Rasta language. It seemed only natural to respondents that politicians would as well.

Reggae musicians were more aware after 1972 of their role as influential commentators, and their lyrics showed a more self-conscious effort to convey messages to those in power. Protest songs were still the order of the day, and both parties were able to make use of them. The JLP recognized that protest songs, such as Ernie Smith's, were ideal for parties in the opposition, and used them with some effectiveness in 1976. The party found another role for reggae music as well. In emphasizing the unity of all Jamaicans, regardless of class or race, reggae for the Labour Party became a symbol of Jamaica as a whole, a truly Jamaican cultural product. Seaga's involvement in promoting reggae music and other aspects of Jamaican culture was one of his best defenses against the fact that he was not a "born yah" Jamaican.

Table 5.3
Share of Party Vote in Sample of Urban
Polling Districts, 1976 Percentages

		PNP	JLP
Lower Class	Very Poor Working	71.6	28.4
	Poor Working	60.6	39.4
	Better Off Working	64.5	35.5
Middle Class	Lower Middle	63.1	36.9
	Middle	40.2	59.8
Upper Class	Upper Middle	27.0	73.0

Source: Stone, DG 6/8/80.

The PNP, consistent with its perspective of Jamaican society as one plagued with inequalities and contradictions, could still use protest music effectively even though it formed the government. In the process of "going overboard to convince the masses" that it was committed to their interests and not the interests of the middle and upper classes, the contentious stance of some reggae music could be used as a symbol of that commitment.

The reputation that the JLP had for fostering violence, coupled with the overwhelming popularity of Bob Marley, made the shooting incident in Marley's home a damaging blow to the JLP's campaign. Whether or not the shooting was politically motivated, the incident fell into the PNP's lap and could not but have hurt the JLP's reputation. It also had the effect of making some musicians highly reluctant to associate themselves with political parties in the 1980 election, as will be seen in chapter 6.

6

The 1980 Election

Of the elections under study here, the election in October 1980 exhibited the greatest partisan polarization. Its distinguishing feature was violence; what many respondents remembered most was the sound of gunfire "all night, every night" (#4). Seven hundred fifty people, including one candidate, were killed between the February announcement that the election would be held and the election itself. The violence masked other aspects of the election; "The most potent symbol of 1980," said one respondent, "was the M-16" (#6).

On election day, the streets of Kingston were nearly deserted (#7). A few ballot boxes were burned, six polling stations never opened, and there is some evidence of overvoting by both parties. In the most extreme case of overvoting, one polling station in South East St. Andrew had 227 registered voters; of these, 956 voted JLP (Director of Elections 1980, 102).

The Jamaica Labour Party won a landslide victory. Its 58.34 percent of the popular vote (see Table 6.1) was a higher proportion of the vote than either party had ever won before. The JLP won fifty-one, or 85 percent of the seats in Parliament, compared with the PNP's nine. Seventeen of the JLP's seats represented constituencies that had been PNP since at least the 1959 election; some had never before been won by the JLP (Stone DG 10/7/80, 3)

The political situation in 1980 created obstacles to gathering data that are strictly comparable to the elections before it. The JLP's campaign against the PNP was partly waged in the pages of the *Daily Gleaner*, and not only in its advertising pages. The *Gleaner* increased the space allotted to opinion columnists, who hammered away daily at every weak spot in the PNP government's record. The PNP chose not to advertise in the paper as a matter of principle, and so advertised only in the *Daily News*, a less widely read paper. For this research, then, that newspaper was also reviewed for four weeks before the election.

Table 6.1
Results, General Election 1980

Electors on roll......990,367

Ballots cast......860,746 (86.91%)

Accepted Ballots.....852,706

Party Share	Popular Vote	Percentage	Seats
Jamaica Labour Party	502,115	(58.34%)	51
People's National Party	350,064	(40.67%)	9

Source: Director of Elections Report, 1980.

Table 6.2 illustrates the number of advertisements that each party ran in the two newspapers. Although there were two fewer run by the JLP, that party spent more on print advertising; its advertisements were more expensively produced (#20, #28) and appeared in a larger newspaper with a higher circulation. The *Daily News*, which was shut down in April 1983, was a tabloid with a circulation of about 15,000 (#7), compared with the *Gleaner's* 50,000.

Respondents, of course, remembered the events of the 1980 campaign better than those of any other election. More documents, such as campaign literature, leaflets, and posters were available, and even some of the graffiti on the walls of Kingston were legible two years later.

Table 6-2
Summary of 256 Items in the *Daily News*
and the *Daily Gleaner* October 1980

Daily Gleaner	*Daily News*
Advertisements	
JLP – 37	JLP – 0
PNP – 0	PNP – 39
Young Jamaica – 4	
	PNPYO – 5
	WPJ – 3
Meeting Reports	
JLP – 8	JLP – 1
PNP – 2	PNP – 9
WPJ – 0	WPJ – 1
Columns*	
Anti-PNP – 60	
Neutral – 28	
Pro-PNP – 3	
Letters*	
Anti-PNP – 48	
Neutral – 7	
Pro-PNP – 4	

---

*in 18 issues of the *Daily Gleaner* only, including all Sundays and Wednesdays between 10/1/80 and 10/30/80.

Background

The PNP government suffered a number of setbacks in the years preceding the election. The first and foremost were in the economy. Even at the time of the 1976 election, the economy was in serious trouble. Imported oil, upon which Jamaica depends heavily, had jumped in price from $11.00 to $36.00 a barrel in five years; agricultural production had declined, partly because of the shortage of foreign exchange necessary to purchase spare parts for farm machinery, and an estimated US$300 million had left the country illegally (Manley 1982, 151). Seaga's prediction that the dollar would be devalued was fulfilled within a month after the 1976 election. In April 1977, facing a severe foreign exchange crisis and the prospect of hundreds of factories closing for want of imported raw materials and machine parts, Manley and the PNP chose to try to obtain the "seal of approval" from the International Monetary Fund that, in addition to loans and credits, would in theory open the doors to loans and lines of credit from commercial banks. The IMF program is designed to encourage exports but does this in a way that is costly for the domestic economy. The receiving government is usually obliged to cut public spending, eliminate food subsidies, and take measures that "harden" the local market, driving the cost of goods out of the reach of most consumers, and forcing manufacturers to turn to foreign markets to sell their goods.

By July of 1977, negotiations with the IMF were completed, and the bitter medicine of austerity was tasted by all Jamaicans. Pensions and wages were controlled while price controls were removed. The PNP officially estimated that there was a 40 percent cutback in the standard of living (Duncan 1980). The PNP government was heavily criticized from without and was divided within. As one PNP staff member said of the IMF agreement of 1977: "You can mark the decline of the PNP from that summer. It was viewed by many as our most fundamental mistake. We missed the opportunity for change without revolution. It caused a great upheaval in the party. We're still feeling the effects" (#8).

An IMF agreement stipulates that an economy must meet certain quarterly requirements; if it does not and thereby "fails the test," a new agreement must be negotiated. At the end of 1977, the IMF suspended the July agreement because there were J$9.6 million more in circulation than allowed. The year 1978 brought further cutbacks and attendant hardships. Manley described the negotiation process as "harrowing" and "ghastly" (1982, 159, 161), while graffiti artists suggested that "IMF" stood for "Is Manley Fault."

By March 1980, the economy was probably in worse shape than before the IMF had been approached. Three hundred thousand people, or 30% of the labor force, were out of work, and the foreign exchange deficit was greater than in 1977. The economic growth that the IMF program was designed to produce had not materialized.

In February 1980, Manley announced that elections would be held by October of that year, as soon as the newly renovated election machinery was in place. Some possible election dates were generated, and, according to D. K. Duncan, the IMF began to set dates for future tests of foreign exchange assets that coincided with possible election dates (1980). Finally, in March 1980, the PNP decided to break permanently with the IMF. Alternatives to the IMF plan were hastily pursued, and loans were sought from Sweden, Algeria, Kuwait, OPEC, Libya, and Germany.

The IMF debacle had serious ramifications within the People's National Party itself, as the staff member's words above indicate. Some members of the party, referred to by respondents as the "PNP Left," were against the IMF's involvement from the very beginning. Others, referred to as the "PNP Right," favored pursuing IMF agreements. These two factions tended from 1977 on to be on opposite sides on other issues as well, such as the government's stance toward the *Gleaner*, that will be discussed below. The PNP's Left was often younger members, more enthusiastic about the party's democratic socialism. They included several former members of Abeng, notably Duncan, a Brown dentist, who served as the PNP's general secretary and was known as a first-rate organizer with an orientation toward grass roots mobilization. The PNP Right included

many of the older party members, some of whom were MPs
in Norman Manley's time, including Florizel Glasspole, now
governor general, former Finance Minister Eric Bell, and
others. Michael Manley tried diplomatically to balance the
forces so as to present a united front.

Other forces of the Left had also regrouped during this
period. The Workers' Liberation League (WLL), a pro-
Soviet political education group, had been formed in 1974
and under the leadership of Trevor Munroe — a lecturer in
political science at the University of the West Indies and a
graduate of Oxford — had supported the PNP in 1976 (see
chapter 5). In 1978, the WLL became a full-fledged
Marxist-Leninist political party, the Workers Party of
Jamaica (WPJ). The WPJ had good relations with the
PNP's Left, and, according to one respondent, the PNP
solicited the aid of the WPJ in the 1980 elections (#21).
The WPJ supported the PNP's Left on several substantive
issues, including urging a break from the IMF (Manley 1982,
153).

Another of the PNP government's second-term difficulties was its relations with the Security Forces (the Jamaica
Constabulary Force -- JCF; the Jamaica Defence Force --
JDF). Keble Munn, appointed minister of national security
in 1976, had, according to one respondent, handled the
police with political insensitivity (#26). Dudley Thompson
was appointed to succeed Munn, but his tenure was marred
from the beginning by what came to be known as the Green
Bay incident. A number of JLP supporters who were
allegedly gunmen were approached by army personnel and
told that they had an opportunity to be given guns and
money for their services. They were brought to an army
camp, the day after Thompson became minister, and am-
bushed. Five died, but seven lived to testify to the
deception. Thompson denied any involvement, but made
what one respondent called an "unfortunate statement"
(#26), often quoted in JLP advertisements (e.g. DG
10/24/80, 16), that "no angels died at Green Bay." At least
two reggae songs were composed and released about the
incident (#13).

A significant minority of the security forces was overtly
anti-PNP (Manley 1982, 209). Two respondents speculated
that the U.S. Central Intelligence Agency was active in

the police force (#8, #26). One reported in detail two incidents that illustrated the tenuousness of the PNP's control over the security forces. One was a 1979 PNP demonstration against the *Gleaner*, during which PNP supporters met and clashed with JLP demonstrators who were protesting the presence of Cubans in Jamaica.

> In the melee, the police were defending the JLP attackers, who were throwing stones and bottles. The police didn't do much to quell it. D. K. (Duncan) ran for his life, and he was running from the police as much as from the Labourites. There was a panic because no one knew where D. K. was. Dudley Thompson was there, and at one point he ordered the police inspector to quell the disturbance, and the police just didn't move to the orders.... People were beginning to realise what control of the streets the JLP had. The police had done nothing to help us. (#26)

The second incident was a PNP election rally a few weeks before the election. The meeting was disrupted and finally broken up when shots were fired toward the speakers' platform. It seemed to the respondent and others at the meeting that the shots were fired by a group of uniformed soldiers standing on the outskirts of the rally (#26).

The 1980 Election Campaigns

Overview

The JLP's campaign for the 1980 election began in earnest in the spring of 1978. According to one respondent centrally placed in that campaign, the party regrouped early that year and its executive committed itself to presenting a united front under the uncontested leadership of Edward Seaga (#28). A newspaper advertisement series was executed around the theme "Equal Rights and Justice." It presented the JLP as the primary advocate of human rights in Jamaica, and, by implication, the PNP as responsible for the alleged abrogation of those rights. It is

worthwhile noting that U.S. President Carter was emphasizing human rights during the same period.

The first advertisement in the series was a picture of the
bell tower of a country church. The same respondent
explained:

> The bell that had been broken by the rod in 1972
> was back together again. It symbolizes the fact
> that the party was united again, back in place, at
> peace. "Equal Rights and Justice" did it, put the
> bell right again. The copy reads, "Jamaica be-
> longs to all of us.... Your political rights have
> been abused in electoral matters," that was refer-
> ring to the corruption in the 1976 election, "your
> economic rights have been abused through mis-
> management.... The JLP is spearheading the
> campaign to protect your rights." (#28)

Each advertisement in the campaign thereafter focused on
one particular right, such as electoral rights and freedom
of the press.

There was another side to the campaign, which the same
respondent called the "underground" campaign in contrast
to the "legitimate" one. The underground campaign consisted of fliers and posters that were not identified as
official JLP material and contained statements that "the
media would consider borderline" (#28), although early in
the campaign some found their way into the *Daily Gleaner*
(Kopkind 1980, 47; see below). The posters were primarily
anti-PNP rather than pro-JLP and focused on the presence
of large numbers of Cubans, most of whom were actually
anti-Castro Cubans in transit between the United States
and Cuba during the period when the Cuban government
was encouraging emigres to visit their homeland and the
most convenient route was via Kingston (#7). They focused
also on the alleged presence of Soviet spies, on the security
forces issue, and on Manley himself. In these leaflets
"Joshua" became "Judas." A sample of headlines illustrates
the nature of these posters: "Cubans get work and Jamaicans starve"; "Are the Cubans here to spy or are they
soldiers in disguise?"; "KGB in Jamaica"; "Communists
capture the PNP"; "Judas -- Mek Up Yu Mind -- Stand

Firm or Step. Stand Firm in Poverty. Step into Communism"; "Judas is thy name, Lying is thy game"; "The Cuban
Butcher"; and "Cuban Feces Found on Ship" (#28). Capital
Cs as in "Cuban" were often formed with the hammer and
sickle symbol (e.g. DG 10/17/80).

One poster significant in retrospect asserted that there
was a PNP "Doomsday Plot," a plan to kill a PNP member
and blame it on the JLP. The pamphlet, according to the
respondent, was released well before nomination day, 15
October 1980. Early on the morning of nomination day,
Roy McGann, the PNP's candidate for the constituency of
East Rural St. Andrew, and his bodyguard Errol Whyte were
shot and killed in a clash with JLP supporters after a rally
in the constituency. The JLP tried to insinuate that the
PNP itself had had McGann killed. The day before the
election the JLP ran a full-page advertisement in red block
letters that seemed to have bullet holes in them. Drawings
of bullets were strewn about the page. The copy read, in
its entirety:

WHO KILLED ROY McGANN?
STOP LYING!
STOP COVERING UP!
TELL THE NATION THE TRUTH
THE NATION WANTS TO KNOW
NOW.   Paid by JLP" (DG 10/29/80, 16)

The other advertisements in the JLP's "legitimate" cam-
paign carried the slogans "Deliverance is Near," "Equal
Rights and Justice," "You have a Right to a Better Life,"
"A Brighter Day is Coming," and "This Time Make Sure."
Besides the customary promises of increased and improved
utility services, health care, and transportation, the advertisements warned of "PNP Plots to Smear the JLP," that
included the "Kill-Your-Friends-Blame-The-Enemy Plot"
(DG 10/23/80, 13), and blamed political violence on the
PNP (DG 10/26/80, 19). Above all, the advertisements
accused the PNP of being communists. "We highlighted
that part tremendously," said the respondent central to the
campaign (#28). For example, one full page advertisement
the day before the election had a red stop sign and the
following text:

> Red means danger. Stop. Don't move. Stand
> Firm. The "Reds" have captured the PNP. They
> have run the country recklessly and dangerously
> and now even the economy is deep in the red.
> Everything is at a standstill or, as they would say,
> standing firm.... The next move can only be to
> even sink deeper into red -- total communism.
> (DG 10/29/80, 12)

The Labour Party received support for their red-baiting
campaign from three crucial sources: the *Gleaner*, the
Evangelicals, and the foreign press. The *Gleaners* of this
period have more pages devoted to opinion columns than in
other election periods, and in the month before the election there were virtually no columns that were pro-PNP.
John Hearne, a White journalist who had once been a strong
supporter of the PNP and who had been head of the government information agency under Manley, had become one of
Manley's harshest critics. If the people of Jamaica reelect
the PNP, he wrote a few weeks before the election,

> they will never again have a chance to vote a
> governing party out of power, and their children
> will never know what it is like to live under laws
> made by the elected parliament.... Our earnings
> will be controlled.... Our homes may be taken....
> Our children will get the best scholarships (only if
> their parents) belong to the highest ranks of the
> ruling party.... Communism is the harshest, most
> rigid aristocracy that has ever been imposed ...
> tyranny more certain and more efficient that that
> of the slave-master in plantation days — because
> the PNP will always be subsidized by very rich
> Communist foreigners. (DG 10/5/80, 10)

"Listening Post," a daily gossip column written, according to one respondent (#7), by *Gleaner* editor Hector
Wynter, a former chairman of the Jamaica Labour Party,
never let up in its criticism of the PNP and its accusation
that the party was communist.

The *Gleaner* published far more letters in support of the JLP than of the PNP. On the day before the election, fifteen letters to the editor were printed on three pages; one was pro-PNP, fourteen were anti-PNP. Also published were a favorable poem about Seaga entitled "The Harvard Scholar" and a cartoon drawing of Manley and Castro riding donkeys along a mountain road with a sign reading "To Mt. Barren" (DG 10/29/80, 6, 18, 19). Yet in a videotape about the election made by the JLP, the current minister of information complained that under the PNP government, the then-opposition party could not find an outlet for its views (JLP 1982).

The PNP railed against the *Gleaner;* the minister of finance referred to the "dread alliance between the Daily Trash" — holding up a copy of the *Gleaner* — "and the JLP" (DG 10/8/80, 2). A year before the election the party had organized a demonstration against the Gleaner Company after the paper had printed a series of articles against the Cuban ambassador to Jamaica, Ulises Estrada, an article about North Shore resorts being swamped with cancellations because of Manley's "anti-American" speech at a summit of the movement of non-aligned countries, and a full-page advertisement signed by a spurious organization that read, in giant block letters: "JUDAS sold out Jamaica to the Cubans for less than 30 pieces of silver!" (Kopkind 1980, 47). At the demonstration, Trevor Munroe of the WPJ urged the government to shut the *Gleaner* down. Manley refused, but threatened ambiguously, "Next time ... next time" (#26) while supporters at the demonstration chanted "Freedom of the press, yes, but no more lies" (DG 9/25/79). The party did not take any strong steps against the *Gleaner,* but Manley sued one columnist for libel. As of this writing, the suit is still pending.

The Evangelicals were a second source of strong support for the Labour Party's anticommunism. One respondent who worked at the Jamaica Broadcasting Corporation, the state-owned broadcasting station, said that there were specified times on Sunday evenings set aside for religious broadcasts, and continued: "We tried to get them not to use the time for political broadcasts, but they had explicitly political programs, saying Manley is a communist and communism is evil and atheistic. When we banned a broadcast as not religious, they would come back and say the devil had banned them" (#8).

Letters to the *Gleaner* concerning the incompatibility of communism and Christianity were not infrequent (e.g. DG 10/3/80, 6; 10/14/80, 11; 10/22/80, 5), and Billy Hall, the *Gleaner's* resident Evangelical columnist, wrote two articles about how Evangelicals would vote in the upcoming election. His prediction: "A certain moral issue is in the election pot and that is Communism, founded on Scientific Atheism as its philosophical base.... Increasingly, there is a conviction among Evangelicals that a vote for the JLP ... would be seen as a vote against Communism, the politics of the devil" (DG 10/19/80, 8). His next article asserted that Evangelicals simply want to do God's will:

> God's will could be to bring into power the worst party possible, so that world events might move more swiftly to their climactic end in Jesus taking control of world politics.... On the other hand, it could be God's will, because of the special way in which He loves Jamaica, ... that He does not desire a godless political ascendance and so will definitely keep out a particular party. (DG 10/26/80, 8)

A letter to the *Gleaner* from "Ten Concerned Christians" claimed that "Evangelicals should not enter directly into ... politics," but every minister should "arouse his people to make a united stand against the forces of communism" (DG 10/14/80, 11). It is interesting that one Evangelical, Owen Tibby, ran as an independent in 1980 in D. K. Duncan's constituency. His advertisements promised that, if elected, he would "inform the nation on matters of spiritual, social and political importance ... call the nation back to God and encourage Christian morality among parliamentarians" (DG 10/19/80, 13). Although Evangelical symbols proved to be potent in the 1980 election, this candidate failed rather miserably, receiving only 77 votes of 18,635 cast (Director of Elections 1980, 81).

The JLP's advertisements used language that meshed well with that of the Evangelicals. They referred to the PNP as "this wicked government" that commits "evil

deeds" (DG 10/14/80, 6-7; 10/24/80, 16). McGann's funeral
was presented as sacrilegious (DG 10/26/80, 10).   PNP
respondents expressed the opinion that the Evangelical
churches, especially those headquartered in the United
States, also had CIA links (#20, #26).

The U.S. press at times also supported Seaga's allegations that the PNP was "going Communist." The writer of
a *Wall Street Journal* article reprinted in the *Gleaner* said
that Manley was responsible for the "world's most impressive record of official ineptitude," and incorrectly claimed
that Manley had expropriated private property. The article
went on to blame violence on the PNP government's "public
vituperation aimed at anyone who so much as owned a car
or a house. (Manley) thus encouraged the baser elements
of Jamaican society to feel justified in inflicting whatever
violence they might choose on their 'oppressors'" (reprinted
DG 10/26/80, 25). Similar articles appeared in the *Miami
Herald* ("Jamaica Aims Gun at Free Press," 10/7/79) and
the *Washington Star* ("Manley's Soviet Love-Fest: Is Jamaica the Next Cuba?" 10/8/79).

Unlike 1976, when Carl Stone reported that most voters
did not believe the JLP's allegations of PNP communism,
the JLP's campaign in 1980 was successful for a number of
reasons. First, the communist Left was better organized
than it had been in 1976. It now formed a full-fledged
political party, the Workers Party of Jamaica (WPJ), and
its affiliation with the PNP had a higher visibility. Trevor
Munroe, leader of the WPJ, had been seen alongside PNP
officials on public occasions, such as the demonstration
against the *Gleaner* in 1979. Informants noted that WPJ
banners were seen at PNP campaign rallies. At a rally for
the PNP in Savannah-La-Mar, "the only banner in the
crowd was the WPJ banner, and that hurt the PNP's
campaign" (#11). Second, the PNP's abrupt break with the
IMF was seen as Manley's giving in to the demands of the
Left. The WPJ as well as the PNP Left had long pressured
the government to abandon the IMF. Finally, the barrage
of propaganda from the JLP, with the cooperation of the
Gleaner, was aimed at convincing the voters that Manley
was firmly linked with communism.

"In 1980," said one respondent, "lots of people thought
that if the PNP won, Trevor Munroe would be in charge"

(#7). Manley had consistently denied being a communist, but others then implied that his days as party leader would be numbered if the PNP won. One column in the *Gleaner* suggested that if the PNP won, Jamaica would be "controlled by the Kremlin's politburo" (DG 10/26/80, 15). A cartoon published by Young Jamaica, the JLP affiliate, showed Manley being driven toward "Moscow Avenue," with the Kremlin's spires in the background, by D. K. Duncan, who is threatening Manley with a rod. The legend read "Joshua lose him Rod of Correction" (DG 10/28/80, 10-11). An "Election Forum" column, "Dilemma of a Frightened Prime Minister," portrayed Manley as "terrorized" by the leftists in his party (DG 10/26/80, 15).

One indication of the success of the JLP's anti-Cuba campaign can be found in the report of a survey of Jamaican fifteen-year-olds conducted in 1980. Morrissey asked 105 respondents to rank forty countries according to preference as a place to live. The youngsters ranked Cuba fortieth, and the USSR thirty-ninth. The survey indicated that the young Jamaicans would prefer to live in South Africa and in Iran rather than the neighboring island of Cuba (Morrissey, DG 3/20/83). These results can be explained only as an effect of the barrage of propaganda against Cuba from the JLP and from the Gleaner Company newspapers that overshadowed information about other parts of the world.

Aside from pejorative statements about the PNP government, the JLP strove to present Seaga as "a financial wizard" (#28). His prediction of the 1977 devaluation was advertised (#28); as one *Gleaner* columnist put it, Seaga is "a brilliant economist and orator with a charming record of accurately forecasting Jamaica's economic misfortunes" (DG 10/12/80, 9). "Charming" is a word not often used in connection with Seaga — even his supporters acknowledge his lack of magnetism and the infrequency of his smiles (DG 10/5/80, 15) — but his seriousness fit the stereotypical hard-nosed economist. Another columnist contrasted the PNP's "millenarianism" with the "coldly realistic" JLP (DG 10/12/80, 7). Given the economic situation in Jamaica, there was not much to smile about, and Manley was criticized for smiling too much (DG 10/3/80, 6).

Each party presented the other as antidemocratic. As the campaign against the alleged communism of the PNP escalated, the PNP retaliated by calling its opponents fascists. At McGann's funeral, D. K. Duncan, speaking of McGann as a "true revolutionary," said that he had been killed by "fascist terror" (DN 10/23/80, 1). The PNP's Youth Organization published lists of incidents of "JLP violence" and said that a minority "clique of fascist mercenaries" within the security forces was getting more "vicious" (DN 10/26/80, 31). The Jamaica branch of the American Association of Jurists issued a statement about the "anti-democratic nature of the JLP" (DN 10/21/80, 3), and PNP Finance Minister Hugh Small predicted that if the JLP returned to power, it would mean an end to democracy in Jamaica (DG 10/8/80, 2). Respondents and *Gleaner* articles intimated that the American television series "Holocaust" was shown on government-controlled JBC-TV just to project the idea that the JLP was a fascist party (#5; DG 10/3/80, 6; 10/7/80, 6).

The PNP's campaign used three slogans, "Stand Firm for the Third Term," "Stepping," and "Foundations for the Future." The contradiction between the first two did not escape the opponents' notice, and it was often mocked by JLP supporters. The advertisements in the *Daily News* were not as dramatic as the JLP's *Gleaner* advertisements nor those of the PNP's previous campaigns. For example, the PNP's 1980 advertisements were not alarmist, and they used drawings rather than photographs. Some JLP advertisements effectively incorporated photographs of alleged JLP supporters who had been killed.

One respondent close to the PNP's campaign described the problem as "financial: the ads were put together by volunteers" (#25). Each advertisement began with the words "Foundations for the Future," then specified a group such as workers, women, or youth, and then described the achievements of the government for that particular group. For workers, minimum wage, redundancy payments, trade union rights, and worker participation were listed (DN 10/9/80, 4). The advertisements all ended with "Progress, Pride, Dignity." One that appeared during National Heroes Week focused on the seven National Heroes, including Bustamante (DN 10/16/80 Supp.).

The *Daily Gleaner* supplied little information about the PNP's campaign. When PNP news was reported, it seemed that the intention was more to provide grist for the anti-PNP mill than balanced reporting. For example, it was mentioned on the front page that Dudley Thompson had returned from Cuba, where he had received medical attention for a heart condition (DG 10/2/80, 1). Thompson's visits to Cuba had been interpreted by the *Gleaner* columnists as illicit business trips to arrange for the importation of weapons to use against JLP supporters (#11). Hugh Small, the former Young Socialist who was minister of finance in 1980, was reported by the *Gleaner* as telling audiences that it was time to "take revolutionary steps" (DG 10/15/80, 10), and that the PNP planned to "'take power' in the third term" (DG 10/6/80, 1).

Just as the JLP warned voters to "Beware of PNP Plots," the PNP repeated a theme that its advertisements carried over all four elections: "Beware of Lies!" (DN 10/23/80, 13). The WPJ ran several advertisements supporting the PNP in the *Daily News* that had as their theme the connections among the IMF, the JLP, and the "big private sector" (DN 10/24/80, 9).

Although the *Gleaner* obviously favored the Labour Party, the PNP, as the government, was in control of the television station and one of the two radio stations. It tried to use them to the party's advantage (#5, #7, #9) but did not use them effectively, as will be shown below. Because of the increasing violence, the number of mass meetings declined, especially in the urban areas, and the broadcast media became especially important. Both parties advertised heavily on television and radio; one writer estimated that the parties spent about $4000 a day in the final weeks of the campaign (DG 12/7/80, Supp.). But it was the impression that the government was "controlling the news" that hurt the party's campaign. A JLP councillor who had worked at JBC said:

> The system was really manipulated by the PNP.... They held the newsroom; key people were stationed there. Nothing went on the air that wasn't pro-PNP. It shocked me that a child like K---, who was six at the time, and a television fan,

nightly got features on anti-imperialism and the ugly side of America. He saw "Roots." On the plane to New York he said that he didn't want to go to a country where they killed Martin Luther King and Bobby Kennedy. He was very antagonistic. (#9)

John Hearne wrote in his column that the WPJ was getting free advertising under the guise of news (DG 10/4/80, 6). A British expatriate wrote a *Gleaner* article about the KGB, intended to counteract JBC-TV's "squirting a stream of propaganda against the American CIA" (DG 10/15/80, 11). Another columnist wrote after the election that

> JBC-TV was consistent in giving the general -- and most untrue -- impression that most of the political violence being experienced was from JLP activists. Any violence that could be attributed to the JLP received full coverage.... Another abuse of the electronic media by the JBC was the constant propaganda that appeared in news reports, Sunday Report, and documentaries about alleged and utterly unproven CIA destabilization in Jamaica both prior to the 1976 election and even during 1980. (DG 12/7/80, Supp.)

The JLP went further, implying that the PNP set up the violence that was reported on television and tried to blame it on the JLP. One JLP advertisement said: "Their sinister and desperate Plan to Increase Violence is on.... Nowadays as though by a plan their cameras and reporters seem to be standing by, ready whenever there is terrorism and violence to set up their interviews and stories to try to blame it on the JLP" (DG 10/26/80, 19).

Throughout the campaign the hostility between some elements of the PNP and some elements of the security forces was overt. The PNPYO accused the Police Information Center of issuing "half-truths" (DN 10/26/80, 31). D. K. Duncan claimed that the police had a list of prominent PNP officials, including himself, who were slated for assassination (DN 10/16/80, 1). Meanwhile, the Private

Sector Organisation of Jamaica (PSOJ) advertised for public cooperation with the Security Forces (DN 10/15/80, 9).

The JLP accused the PNP, JBC, and "the Communists" of conspiring against the security forces. Two weeks before the election, a JLP advertisement read:

> Every day there is a chorus of abuse directed at the Army and the Police by the PNP, the communists and the JBC. They want the people to turn against the Security Forces.... Why? The PNP and the communists want a breakdown in law and order, so that peaceful and fair elections cannot be held to put them out of office. (DG 10/17/80, 18)

The PNP was said to be campaigning against the security forces so that it could confine them to barracks and the Home Guard could take over security and prevent Labourites from voting (DG 10/5/80, 5; 10/26/80, 13; #28). A photograph of Manley aiming a gun, taken while he was training for the Home Guard in 1976, was used in a JLP poster (#28), with the obvious implication that Manley was willing to resort to force to retain power.

The Use of Class Symbols and Class Conflict

The major thrust of the PNP campaign's references to social class was not much different from that of the 1976 campaign. The PNP emphasized international solidarity among poor Third World countries vis-a-vis international capitalism, and the social programs of its two administrations that had brought the poor some measure of relief. In Manley's speech announcing the date of the election, he called for the poor "to stand firm together in the struggle to build a new kind of world." The JLP, he said, wanted Jamaica to "slip up beside those with money," and he called the *Gleaner* "a rag that talks for the existing world economic system" (DN 10/6/80, 1).

The PNP advertisements, as in 1976, highlighted programs such as Land Lease (DN 10/20/80, 4), JAMAL (the National Literacy Programme) (DN 10/17/80, 9), and Youth

Programmes (DN 10/16/80, 4), as well as the legislation providing a national minimum wage, trade union rights (DN 10/9/80, 4), and maternity leave (DN 10/15/80, 4). In a special advertisement for National Heroes Week, the PNP emphasized the National Heroes' struggles for economic rights. For example, Paul Bogle "fought for justice for the poor," and Norman Manley worked for "all adults regardless of their economic status to have the right to vote." The advertisement ended with an assertion that the PNP government was a continuation of these efforts: "The PNP's mission today is to stand firm, and to pursue with increased vigour and determination the programmes which our heroes started and which the PNP upholds" (DN 10/16/80, Supp.).

The 1980 Manifesto of the PNP promised consolidation and expansion of the programs already instituted, and emphasized job creation to reduce the unemployment rate. Among the party's "major aims" was a commitment to "provide the basic necessities of food, shelter, jobs, education and health care for all" (PNP 1980, 2). Ironically, the JLP Manifesto also promised a consolidation and expansion of some of the PNP's programs, such as the Maternity Leave Law and the Trade Union Representational Rights sections of the Industrial Relations Act (JLP 1980, 21).

A JLP respondent readily admitted that after the 1976 election, the Labour Party's "public image was one of rapacious capitalists trying to be government" (#28). The PNP and its supporters tried in 1980 to foster this image. The WPJ ran advertisements with photographs of JLP leadership with IMF officials. One headline read, "Seaga is bringing back the IMF on top of us. He knows we can't take it" (DN 10/25/80, 13). An advertisement paid by a coalition of youth organizations, including the PNPYO, featured a cartoon of youths standing on a bit of land, while approaching through the water are four thugs in dark glasses, all carrying guns. One is labeled "CIA," another is in a military uniform, and a third is labeled "PSOJ" (Private Sector Organisation of Jamaica) and is carrying a bag of dollars (DN 10/11/80, 19).

One JLP leader who was relatively free of the capitalist image was Hugh Shearer. As a trade unionist and as Bustamante's protege, Shearer was often contrasted with Seaga, who was not identified with the working class (DN

10/16/80, 7).   A letter to the *Gleaner* shortly before the election urged that Shearer take over the JLP leadership because the current JLP leadership did not have enough "grass roots thinking and action" (DG 10/5/80, 15).   Carl Stone's opinion polls have never shown Seaga as "most popular leader"; usually that honor went to Manley, but in the period before the 1980 election it was Shearer who emerged as most popular and Seaga as "most equipped to manage the affairs of the country" (DG 10/12/80, 6). Shearer's campaign speeches differed markedly from the JLP's national campaign material in several ways. Rather than join in the anti-Cuba rhetoric, Shearer pointed out at a mass meeting that it was the JLP that had supported Cuba in the 1960s and had begun Jamaica's participation in the movement of non-aligned countries, two episodes of JLP history that were not alluded to by Seaga (DG 10/8/80, 13).

In the same speech, Shearer departed from the JLP projection of all classes as having identical interests. While expressing an anticommunism reminiscent of Busta-mante, he assured voters that "on behalf of the labour movement I am in a position to say that working class interests shall be projected and promoted under the banner of the JLP.... There is a commitment to back working class interests" (DG 10/8/80, 13).

The general position of the Labour Party on class was somewhat different. First, the JLP said it would foster the interest of all classes, and it was infrequent that a promise was made to any one particular group. Second, the party argued that the PNP was indifferent to the suffering of the poor, and had caused the poor more suffering as a result of its policies. A JLP slogan appearing as graffiti was "The Poor Can't Take No More"; photographs of these words scrawled on filthy Kingston walls were a favorite of foreign journalists.

The first part of the position was no different from the party's 1976 campaign position. "In 1980 as in 1976," said a JLP campaign manager, "we played down class and co-lour... one of the major assaults was that we were the Big Man party. We had to respond to that, so we sought to define as clearly as possible what we stood for. We said that we were in favor of free enterprise, and how it could benefit the mass of the people" (#31). A JLP advertisement warranted that "Jamaica has the human capacity and the God-given resources for economic recovery, social harmony, and the achievement of the aspirations of all Jamaicans, regardless of class, creed, and political persuasion" (DG 10/6/80, 6-7).

Although JLP supporter John Hearne argued in his column that "neither side has raised too many hopes of material benefits to come if it is elected," the JLP did imply that the hardships suffered under the PNP government would end. The lower class was told that "money would jingle in your pockets" (DN 10/15/80, 8; #7, #22); the JLP's rhetoric to the upper class "made them feel that the licensing system would be completely freed up." The slogan "Deliverance is Near" and the party song that highlighted the slogan raised material expectations as well (#22).

Material expectations were elevated partly because JLP propaganda laid so much of the blame for economic difficulties at the PNP's doorstep. While the PNP blamed Jamaica's problems on the crisis in the world economy and the machinations of OPEC and the IMF, the JLP cited only "mismanagement." As in 1976, communism and democratic socialism were equated with poverty and suffering by Seaga (DG 10/8/80, 10) and others (DG 10/3/80, 6). One letter said democratic socialism "has turned into democratic sufferism" (DG 10/12/80, 11). A Young Jamaica (JLP) advertisement featured a photograph of rubble in Kingston, and read, "The ravages of government mismanagement, incompetence and neglect (have) turned Kingston into a city of Death and Decay" (DG 10/27/80, 14). In a similar advertisement by the Labor Party itself, a drawing of a huge pothole is superimposed on a photograph of a road. Inside the drawing are photographs of the faces of Manley, D. K. Duncan, Trevor Munroe, and others. The text read:

THIS POTHOLE GOVERNMENT MUST GO! The PNP government has taken Jamaica down the road to chaos and economic ruin. Everything is in a shambles. Factories are closed —you can't get work. The country is broke -- we can't get food. We don't pay our debts -- so we can't get credit. Young people are idle having nothing to do. Equip-

ment and machinery lie in waste -- we have no
spare parts. Hospitals are closed -- sick people
suffer. Tourism is in a mess -- education is in a
mess — housing is in a mess. Transportation is
slowly coming to a halt. Roads are falling apart
as the potholes get deeper and wider, each day
this government remains in office. VOTE THEM
OUT! (DG 10/22/80, 14)

One incident that the JLP utilized to deepen the impression that the PNP's policies hurt the poor concerned a
shipment of rice -- a gift from organized JLP support-
groups in the United States -- that was imported into Jamaica bypassing certain customs regulations. The PNP
government turned down the JLP's request to distribute the
rice. The incident inspired a couple of letters in support of
the PNP's decision that were printed in the *Daily News*.
One, for example, pointed out that the JLP-affiliated
Women's Freedom Movement had said in an advertisement
that

"the rice is free, it is a gift to those in need"....
Must we believe that this rice, brought in illegally, was to be distributed on a non-partisan basis?
God forbid! No Jamaican with a sense of pride,
common sense or moral judgement believes one
word of this Judas organization. (DN 10/13/80, 7)

But the bulk of the letters, and all of those in the *Gleaner*,
condemned the decision. One, curiously, revived the line
from a song used in the 1967 election (see chapter 3):

Oh Lord how long shall the wicked reign over my
people? ... While the JLP would have given out
the rice to the poor and starving, the government
wants to make money out of the misery of the
people. Are we now like Cuba in that we can't
get free gifts from abroad? (DG 10/3/80, 6)

Another, printed the day before the election, read:

Mr Seaga is trying to feed the hungry nation while
Manley is starving us. Mr. Seaga is like Moses; he
is going to lead us into deliverance.... Deliverance is Near! Eddie gone clear! (DG 10/29/80,
18).

Seaga told a crowd at South Parade that Manley had said
"that rice must stand firm on the wharf" (DG 10/8/80, 10).

The incident was especially meaningful to Jamaicans,
given the severe food shortages they had undergone in the
months before the election (#13, #27). The shortage of
food was the subject of the reggae song that had the most
impact upon the election ("Crucial"; see below). Two
respondents said that the PNP was blamed for the food
shortages (#13, #27), but Carl Stone, in an article based on
opinion polls, reported that the issue had lost its impact by
election time; the blame had shifted to supermarket managers who were accused of hoarding (DG 10/12/80, 6).

One of the few letters to the *Gleaner* in support of the
PNP called the Jamaican Association of Higglers (a street-
sellers' affiliate of the JLP) "an active and vocal stooge of
Seaga's JLP" that was conspiring with merchants "to sabotage the government by playing politics with the people's
food" (DG 10/15/80, 10).

The JLP did use the issue in its campaign, most memora-
bly in the variations on the slogan "Stand Firm." The
original song from which the slogan is derived reads "Stand
firm or go feed worm," meaning, "stand firm or die." The
JLP changed it to "Stand firm and nyam worm" (#13), or its
equivalent in near-standard English, "Stand firm and eat
worm" (DG 10/9/80, 3).

Another way in which the JLP implied that the PNP had
neglected the poor was by suggesting that the PNP paid too
much attention to foreign policy. It was in that field that
Manley had taken the most decisive stands and had developed a considerable reputation for leadership within international organizations such as the movement of non-
aligned countries, the International Bauxite Association,
and a trade negotiation alliance called the African, Caribbean and Pacific Group (ACP). The basis of the PNP's
anti–IMF campaign was a global class-struggle or depen-

dency theory model. Hugh Small, in a speech on the IMF, condemned "the way in which the poor developing countries are forced to bear the main burden of adjusting to the deep world economic crisis" (DN 10/3/80, 1).

But these successful foreign policy ventures lost their meaning in the face of the domestic economic crisis. One respondent said Manley's "major blunder" was "gavotting around the third world" (#30). The idea that Manley's attentions to foreign policy were contributing to Jamaica's domestic problems was summed up in a striking cartoon printed as a full page advertisement by Young Jamaica a few days before the election. It showed Manley offering a bundle to a White-looking, well-fed and -dressed youngster labeled "Third World." Behind Manley is another child, a thin, Black, barefooted girl dressed in rags and labeled "Jamaica." The legend read, "You have turned your back on me" (DG 10/25/80, 12).

The programs that the PNP had instituted that had benefited thousands of lower-class Blacks were, at times, mocked by the JLP. For example, Seaga said that the PNP manifesto looked like it was prepared by a National Litera-cy Programme class (DG 10/8/80, 10; 10/12/80, 11). The PNP was also presented as patronizing toward the poor, or "talking down to the people" (DG 10/10/80, 6). One incident recalled by respondents (#5, #29) seemed to be especially damaging. A German firm had built a center to train youth in automotive repairs. The school was located in a lower-class area, and D. K. Duncan, at its opening ceremony, "said that the place looked too clean, that it should be demystified, desanitized. It was too orderly to have psychological access to the constituency. That is a middle class perception, and a mindless one too" (#5).

The JLP coupled its presentation of the PNP as indiffer-ent to the plight of the lower class with some statements on the Labour Party commitment to meet the needs of the poor. A past president of Young Jamaica, in an article called "The Political Thinking of the JLP," wrote that the party was committed to free enterprise and opportunity for the poor. The party would create employment opportuni-ties by encouraging foreign investment, as in the "Puerto Rican model" (DG 10/12/80, 11). The advertisements, as discussed above, usually avoided classifying Jamaicans in economic terms, but they did direct certain advertisements to the rural voter. The JLP would help farmers attain "a decent standard of living" (DG 10/18/80, 20), and bring "the long neglected rural areas ... into the mainstream of national development" (DG 10/16/80, 9).

In terms of actual party support, the PNP had lost ground among the middle and upper classes by 1976, and did not regain it in 1980 (#13, #14). The party had shown in 1976 that these groups, forming a minority of the electorate, were not necessary for electoral success. But by 1980, the PNP may have lost the support of the better-off section of the lower class, a group on which it had always counted. Many of the antigovernment demonstrations between 1978 and 1980 had been spearheaded by the middle class and often took place in its neighborhoods (#7, #26). Notable among these were the demonstrations about the price of gasoline, an issue relevant mainly to the minority of Jamaicans wealthy enough to own automobiles (#26).

While the JLP deplored the PNP's fostering of "class hatred," the Labour Party may have simply drawn the line of polarization farther down in the class structure, identifying the PNP with the poorest section of the lower class. The PNP government, it said, had created a "beggar nation" (DG 10/2/80, 7; 10/12/80, 11), supported "outrageous ... gutter behavior" (DG 10/10/80, 6), and wanted to "desanitize" the nation with a plan written by illiterates (DG 10/8/80, 10).

The Use of Race Symbols and Racial Conflict

By the JLP and the *Gleaner*, the PNP was presented alternately as anti-White and as not acting in the best interest of Blacks. As in 1976, the JLP played down the color of its leader (#31), but used black nationalism to bolster its cause where possible. Although several respondents said that race was not a factor in the campaign (#14, #25, #29), references to Africa, to Marcus Garvey and other Black nationalists, to slavery, and to the color of the candidates standing election were not uncommon.

Rastafarians' and reggae musicians' interests had expanded from Ethiopia to the entire African continent as their status and personal power increased. Some reggae musicians toured Africa and had been received with enthusiasm. The Rastafarians who had settled in Ethiopia in the early seventies remained there after the revolution (#36). After an extended tour of Africa, Bob Marley produced an album with a number of songs relating to the current politics of Africa, including one called "Zimbabwe," that identified Rastafari with the struggles of the liberation forces there and is rich in Garvey language:

> Every man got a right to decide his own destiny
> And in this judgement there's no partiality
> So arm in arm, with arms,
> We'll fight this little struggle
> Cause that's the only way
> To overcome our little trouble.
> Brother you're right, you're right
> We gonna fight, fight for our rights.
> Natty dread it ina Zimbabwe,
> Set it up ina Zimbabwe
> Mash it up ina Zimbabwe,
> Africans a liberate Zimbabwe
> No more internal power struggle
> Soon we find out who is the real revolutionaries
> Cause I don't want my people to be contrary
> To divide and rule would only tear us apart
> In every man chest, there beat a heart
> Soon we find out who is the real revolutionaries
> I don't want my people
> To be tricked by mercenaries....

Marley was invited by the Mugabe government to perform at the commemoration of the first anniversary of the victory of those forces, an honor that deeply impressed him. He claimed that Africa was reggae music's biggest audience (#36).

The PNP expressed support for the liberation movements that were bringing majority rule to Africa, supported Cuba's decision to sent troops to Angola, and highlighted its opposition to apartheid in its manifesto (PNP 1980). The only strong statement on Africa by the JLP in the materials reviewed came from Hugh Shearer, who told a

large audience at the rally that began the campaign:
"When they speak about friendship with Africa, under
which party did Haile Selassie, Kaunda, Siaka Stevens and
William Tubman visit Jamaica?   ... Our relationship was
built up with the entire bloc of African nations. We always
maintained ethnic connections...." He went on to say that
the JLP supported Mozambique, Angola, and Namibia and
defied South Africa (DG 10/8/80, 13). Africa was mentioned in the JLP manifesto only to point out that Jamaica
"is sentimentally bound to its African roots." The manifesto asserted that the JLP supports "liberation movements
against racism, oppression, and colonialism," except where
"nationals freely vote," and that the JLP does not support
"expansionist movements operating under the guise of
liberation movements; and we condemn all the disguised
attempts to infiltrate and exploit any country" (JLP 1980,
36).

Both parties continued to allude to Marcus Garvey and to
present their platforms as consistent with his ideals (#25).
Both used the anniversary of Garvey's birth to associate
themselves with him.   Two White *Gleaner* columnists,
Morris Cargill and Jane Patmos, condemned the parties for
it. Cargill wrote: "the ripe silly season began with the
unseemly contest over the remains of Marcus Garvey.
Each party tugged him to and fro, claiming him to be their
true prophet, with the kind of insistence and vulgarity of
which only Jamaica is capable" (DG 10/16/80, 7). Patmos
agreed, when she wrote that "both political parties deteri-
orated the Ninety-third Anniversary ... into a squabble with
each other claiming to be the indisputable heir of Garvey's
ideals" (DG 10/16/80, 7). A man identifying himself as a
Muslim expressed cynicism about Garvey's name being
bandied about during election campaigns. "If it was not
power time," he wrote to the *Daily News*, "you would never
hear the name of this noble brother so much" (DN
10/17/80, 7).

For the PNP's part, Arnold Bertram, former Abeng
member and then minister of state for information and
culture, delivered the keynote address honoring Garvey at
the National Heroes Week celebrations (DN 10/21/80, 2),
and in the party's special National Heroes advertisement,
Garvey was mentioned first, as one "who fought for respect

to be given the poor and oppressed black people of the world and their right to choose their own destiny" (DN 10/16/80, Supp.).

The JLP also paid tribute to Garvey, but stressed especially his anticommunism.   C. Roy Reynolds, now information officer for Jamaica's consulate in New York, wrote a long article for the *Gleaner* about Garvey and his followers' clashing with communists in Harlem in the 1920s and 1930s. He quoted Garvey as calling communists "dangerous, cold-blooded, and wicked" (DG 10/19/80, 21).   Another columnist, in "The Communist Threat to Jamaica," also used Garvey's words to bolster his argument (DG 10/29/80, 6). The JLP slogan "Deliverance" was introduced in February 1980 during a "Garvey Anti-Communist Rally" (#28) that was held in Garvey's home parish.

Another resurrection of Black nationalism to support the JLP's program appeared in another Patmos column.   She cited the Black Panther Party of the United States, a group that had actually disbanded many years before, asking, "Is Cuba a cancer in Jamaica? ... Is our cancer now so acute that Jamaicans who are mainly black people fail to consider the U.S.A. Black Panthers' charge that Cuba's military intervention in Angola, Mozambique and ... Ethiopia are less for liberating oppressed natives than for exporting Cuban blacks from Cuba to Africa?" (DG 10/19/80, 11). The PNP was often accused by the JLP and the *Gleaner* of being racially divisive and anti-White, but the use of Black nationalism to support the JLP's program was a relatively new phenomenon.

The PNP had long been associated with Black nationalism and that association was still evident in this election. One letter to the *Daily News* discussed issues "related to us whether we be Christians, Rastas.... issues that affect 85 - 95% of the Jamaican people.... The majority of people who benefitted from ... the minimum wage (and other programs) are members of the black family.... The black majority must control Jamaica — the PNP is the stepping stone" (DN 10/16/80, 7).   The PNP in 1980 actually did have more Black candidates than ever before, as will be discussed later.   Its youth and left wing occasionally engaged in Black nationalist rhetoric (#7); on the evening of election day, D. K. Duncan was moved to ask, during a radio broadcast in what a respondent called a "ranting stream of consciousness" (#7), "What happened to the black people's vote?" The PNP had gained a favorable reputation with Black Americans, and had received support from influential American Blacks such as Ossie Davis, Paul Robeson, Jr., Julian Bond, and Andrew Young (DG 10/8/80, 2).

Uses of emotionally loaded words and phrases, such as variations on the word "slavery," were also bipartisan. The PNPYO ran an advertisement requesting contributions with the headline "We must pay for our freedom — others are paying to enslave us" (DN 10/3/80, 8). A JLP columnist wrote that a minority group of PNP politicians sought to "enslave us with communism" (DG 10/29/80, 6). And John Hearne saw a PNP third term as "tyranny more certain and more efficient than that of the slave-master in plantation days" (DG 10/5/80, 10).

The JLP and the *Gleaner* railed against the PNP as racially divisive. *Gleaner* columnists described the party as racist (DG 10/3/80, 6; 10/4/80, 6; 10/7/80, 6; 10/13/80, 6; 10/19/80, 10, 11) and as preachers of "barefaced hatred" (DG 10/29/80, 18). The PNP's use of the song "The Message" brought a flurry of similar accusations from JLP supporters who considered the song an attack on Seaga because of his color.

Respondents most often mentioned Seaga's color as the major race issue of 1980 (#7, #11, #14, #26). As the JLP took a low-key stance on race, the party's supporters came to Seaga's defense. In a long "Election Forum" article about a JLP mass rally, the author quoted an American newspaper: "'An unlikely looking Deliverer for a country that is 96% black,' sneers the *Wall Street Journal*, ignorant of the fact that Seaga broke the racial barriers long ago in Tivoli, to the extent of becoming a consecrated Shepherd of a Revivalist church" (DG 10/5/80, 15).

In a postelection article by the *"Gleaner* News Desk" entitled "Why the PNP lost the election," Seaga became a Brown man:

Did the PNP stop to think how naturalised Jamaicans, as well as those white and almost white 'born ya' Jamaicans felt about the racial attacks and talk about "My leader born ya?" Such talk made these people uncomfortable and most of them must have voted JLP. And there were thousands of them. Besides, the majority of Jamaican people, who are black, regard Mr. Manley and Mr. Seaga as "brown" men; and since they had nothing against Mr. Manley because he is a "brown" man they saw no reason why they should not like Mr. Seaga merely because he too is a "brown" man. The PNP by its acts and utterances alienated so many people that it would require a miracle for them to win. (DG 12/7/80 Supp.)

The Use of Rastafarian Symbols and Reggae Music

Respondents perceived that by the 1980 campaign, Rastafarian symbols had waned in importance (#8, #10, #17, #21, #22, #34, #35). Three reasons were most frequently cited. First, Rastafarian doctrine became less cohesive; there was little consensus among Rastas as a group about central issues such as the reported death of Selassie, which some still denied, and the question of repatriation. The more politically oriented Rastafarians expressed the idea of repatriation as a figurative idea; the desired goal was to bring Jamaica as a nation "out of Babylon." Others took repatriation more literally, which demanded that the Rasta withdraw from Jamaican politics and passively await Selassie's call, or, if possible, migrate to Ethiopia. As a result, the movement "split up into 1001 little movements" (#8). Second, the Evangelical or fundamentalist sects, such as Church of God, were competing with the Rastafarians in attracting converts from the poorest section of the lower class. "People that might have become Rasta a decade before" (#10) were turning to these groups for spiritual guidance. A third reason for the decline in the use of Rasta symbols was that the campaign was characterized by a higher degree of orientation to concrete issues, such as the IMF and Jamaica's relations with Cuba (#22).

There was some evidence that Rastafarians had withdrawn from partisan political questions. Some feared retributive violence from supporters of the party they did not support. The Marley shooting put a damper on political statements from some reggae artists and other Rastafarians. Marley said in London in 1977 that he would not return to Jamaica "to set myself up as a target again, for the Government, the Opposition, or anyone else" (Clarke 1980, 110). Ernie Smith and Pluto Shervington, who had produced songs important to the 1976 election, had left Jamaica after receiving threats on their lives (DN 10/24/80, 7). Michigan and Smiley were threatened when a song they had produced was interpreted as an endorsement of the PNP government (DN 10/26/80, 18). Those singers who had not yet met financial success still lived in slum com-munities that were engulfed in political warfare. At the same time, however, some reggae musicians did endorse the parties at partisan musical festivals, described below.

One respondent said that many Rastafarians had withdrawn from the materialistic to the spiritual side of their doctrine (#8). Rather than "reasoning" about politics, the role of Jamaican blacks or the oppression of the poor, they became more concerned with ganja, "ital" cooking, and "trodding Jah creation" in the countryside. An apolitical *Gleaner* columnist described a bearded locksman in the countryside of St. Ann's Parish whose name was Sobers. When asked whom he would be voting for in the upcoming election, Sobers said "I am not into that. If I do that, I spoil everything." The columnist commented: "I think he means that voting is too ordinary, too defiling an activity for a man of his stature.... All these selfish people who support political parties are making me wish I had the courage of the otherworldly Sobers" (DG 10/19/80, 5).

Another indication of Rastafarian pursuits outside the realm of partisan politics was the sustained and unsuccessful efforts of one group, the "Royal Ethiopian Judah Coptic Church — Theocracy Government," to attract serious attention from the British authorities. When Parliament is dissolved before an election, the crown, represented by the governor general, is responsible for the state. In the period before the 1980 elections, the group cabled the queen requesting that she use her authority to "delay no further the granting of a Bill of Repatriation for I and I those descendants of the emancipated slaves so desirous" (DN

10/19/80, 3). They visited the offices of the British High Commission numerous times with the same request (DN 10/23/80, 7).

Apart from statements made in the form of reggae songs, one of the only issues raised by Rastafarians in the preelection materials was discrimination against them in Jamaican schools. One secondary school denied two dread-locked youngsters admission but rescinded the decision later (DN 10/17/80, 7). A letter to the *Daily News* called attention to the fact that Rastafarians could become university students and lecturers more easily than young-sters with dreadlocks could become primary and high school pupils (DN 10/11/80, 7).

Despite respondents perceptions of the waning use of Rasta symbols, there is evidence that both parties con-tinued to use them to some extent. Members of the PNP, especially the younger members and the left wing (#26), continued to use Rasta words and phrases and dress. D. K. Duncan characteristically began speeches with the Rasta greeting "One Love" (#7, #13; Duncan 1980). Hugh Small, also of the left wing of the party, said in an interview that people were under the illusion that "North America is an escape from Babylon" (DN 10/13/80, 3). Dudley Thompson continued to wear a tam and sprinkled his mass meeting speeches with Rasta terms like "I-and-I" (#11; DG 10/15/80, 11). A satirical article about Manley suggested that his speeches were delivered in "I-and-I-man-ese" (DG 10/12/80, 9). In one PNP "Foundations for the Future" advertisement, a silhouette drawing of nine work-ers includes a figure with dreadlocks and a guitar.

The JLP abandoned the slogan "High-Up" and adopted "Deliverance" instead. "Deliverance" does have meaning for the Rasta -- deliverance from Babylon -- but it is more often used in other lower class religions, especially the Afro-syncretic cults of Pocomania and Revival (#13).

Most of the Rastafarian symbols of the 1980 campaign were expressed through music. The PNP had begun to make use of the "dub poets" in the cultural segments of their mass rallies and conference public sessions (#7). Dub poetry is a hybrid of reggae and spoken poetry. Usually in patois and often using Rastafarian dialect, the dub poem is spoken in a definite reggae rhythm, sometimes with drum accompaniment. Several of the more successful dub poets are Rastafarians (DG 3/27/80).

The two trends in reggae music noted in the previous chapter continued until 1978. The violence of the 1976 campaign had caused a great deal of suffering among lower class people, and many reggae musicians turned to music to convey messages of peace. One duo, Althea and Donna, made songs called "No More Fighting" and "Make a Truce"; Big Youth sang "Love We A Deal Wid"; Max Romeo produced "Let's Live Together," "Reconstruction," and "War Rock." All these were songs against "tribal warfare," that is, clashes between armed supporters of the two parties, and were released in 1977 and 1978. In the same period, however, Peter Tosh, one of the most influential reggae musicians and a former member of the Wailers band, made a song called "Equal Rights and Justice," an angry song in which the singer says that he wants "no peace," only "equal rights and justice," and only when those are procured will there be "no crime... no criminals":

> *Everyone is crying out for peace, yes*
> *None is crying out for justice*
> *I don't want no peace,*
> *I need equal rights and justice*
> *Everybody want to go to heaven*
> *But nobody want to die*
> *I don't want no peace,*
> *I want equal rights and justice*
> *I-man need equal rights and justice*
> *Just give me my share*
> *What is due to Caesar,*
> *You better give it on to Caesar*
> *And what belong to I-and-I*
> *You better you better give it up, to I...*
> *I don't want no peace,*
> *I need equal rights and justice.*
> *Everybody is talking about crime*
> *Tell me who are the criminals*
> *I really don't see it*
> *I don't want no peace,*
> *I need equal rights and justice*
> *And there'll be no crime, Equal rights and justice*

And there'll be no criminals
Everyone is fighting for equal rights and justice
Palestinians fighting for equal rights and justice
Down in Angola...
Down in Botswana...
Down in Zimbabwe...
Down in Rhodesia...
Right here in Jamaica
Equal rights and justice.

The desire among Rastafarian musicians for an end to tribal warfare in the slums was demonstrated in the Peace Concert of 1978. The gunmen-leaders of two lower-class neighborhoods -- Claudie Massop, a JLP supporter from Tivoli Gardens, and Bucky Marshall, a PNP supporter from Arnett Gardens — that had long been involved in politically motivated violence jointly agreed to a peace truce. The truce was celebrated with a six-hour musical show held at the National Arena and organized by Massop, Marshall, and Bob Marley (Clarke 1980, 111). Bob Marley, Big Youth, the Mighty Diamonds, Peter Tosh, and Jacob Miller were among the performers. At one point, Marley called Seaga and Manley onto the stage and had them join hands over his head (#13, #17, #26, #27; Boot and Goldman 1982). Rastafarians were prominent in the audience, and smoked ganja freely in the vicinity of the minister of national security and the police (#26).

All the performers called on youths to abandon their guns and violent ways, except Peter Tosh, who delivered a highly critical speech about police brutality and violence against the poor. He said the violence of the youths in Kingston was a by-product of the violence upon which the colony was founded in the first place:

> I don't want no peace, we all need equal rights and justice — right here in Jamaica.... This colonial shitstem a rule the underprivileged. I am one of them who happen to be in the underprivileged sector.... Right now Mr. Manley, me wan talk to you personal cause me and you is friends, so you say.... Right now as a man of power and a ruler of this little country, not you alone Mr. Seaga too, we would like the Members of Parliament must

come together to deal with the poor people and
the suffering class and the police to know that
they brutalize poor people and fi what?   A little
draw of herb ... me go through the lowest degradation, humility and discrimination and brutality....   I no seh that my brother is a criminal.
Cause when Columbus, dem pirate and put them
in a reading book and give us all observation that
we must look up and live the life of and the
principle of pirates.   So the youth dem know fi
fire dem guns like Henry Morgan same way.... Is
just a shitstem lay down to belittle the poor.
Poor people go to jail every time. Is pure poor
poor people me see in there. (Clarke 1980, 112)

Tosh's speech indicates that the streak of belligerence
among Rastafarians was still expressed.   Despite the
lower-class orientation of the PNP government, suffering
among the lower class was increasing.   The IMF agreement's imposition of austerity had brought more want and
fewer jobs to the lower class, and youths were not reluctant to turn to crime or political tribalism to gain a small
reward.   Thus reggae musicians were sympathetic with the
victims of the Green Bay killing.   One, Big Youth, referred
like Tosh to Henry Morgan and Christopher Columbus, in a
highly critical song about the incident:

You know the same way
Them take we people out a Africa
And bring we down here...
Them take we on Columbus trip
With the one Captain Bligh, Sir Francis Drake
And another one called Henry Morgan
It's the same way them take we
Them bring us down here in a chain
And have us to slave and cutting sugar cane
Then them teach we how to
Fight against one another
Them just call them poor youth them
And tell them promising and promising
To give them work
And then a knowing that he was gonna take them

On the range and shoot them down...
This time we won't forgive them
For the Green Bay Killing...
A whole heap of one who love Jah
And love the people and
Know say people is people
Most feel the Green Bay murder
It coulda happen to him
The Green Bay Killing..."

The truce was short-lived. Massop was shot by police a few weeks later, and Marshall was dead before the 1980 election period. One respondent said that both parties may have been motivated to have the truce broken because it would have meant the unity of the lower class; divided, the lower class was more susceptible to control by politicians than a united one would have been (#26).

Peter Tosh's song was echoed in the anthem that the JLP adopted in 1978, "Stand Up Jamaicans":

Equal rights and justice is our everlasting song
Unity and progress will make our nation strong
   Stand up for your rights
   When you hear the bell
   Stand up for justice
   Hear the freedom bell
   Remember Bustamante
   He served you well
   Stand up Jamaicans, when you hear the bell.
Stand to build our nation -- opportunity for youth
Prosperity for our nation, out of many one,
   Stand up...
Stand up sons and daughters,
Your only hope is the bell
God will guide our progress
And make our nation strong.
   Stand up...

"Stand up for your rights," a phrase from the well-known and often re-recorded Marley song "Get Up Stand Up," was a recurring phrase in the JLP campaign (DG 10/8/80, 10; 10/23/80, 13). An advertising executive who worked with the party in this period readily admitted the source of the phrases, replying that it demonstrated that the party was "on the same wavelength, a collision of ideas. The reggae people were expressing it, but they didn't really know what rights they meant. These ads spelled out individual rights, like freedom of the press and electoral rights" (#28). The phrase "equal rights and justice," he said, was useful in its "simplicity. We wanted to ensure that the party philosophy was understood by the masses of the people" (#28).

It is noteworthy that Tosh is a supporter of the PNP, if any party (#8), and that the song "Equal Rights and Justice" has an international focus, naming countries around the world in which liberation movements were active, that fits the PNP's campaign far better than the JLP's. "Get Up Stand Up" is also alien in its content to the JLP's other projected images of itself. It is one of the best statements of Rastafarian's views against organized Christianity (see chapter 1). The JLP accused the PNP of being anti-Christian in 1980, whereas the JLP were "Jesus Loving People."

Two traits that the two songs have in common and that may have made them attractive to the JLP campaign managers were their popularity and the fact that both are fighting, contentious, and belligerent. A mood of opposition to the government was a desirable goal for the Labour Party, but the lines from the songs were presented in isolation from their original contexts and there is no evidence of these songs being played in JLP rallies.

Later in the campaign, the JLP's repertoire expanded beyond reggae music. An American disco song, "Ain't No Stopping Us Now," became associated with the Labour Party and was played on sound systems at party rallies (DG 12/7/80 Supp.). An employee of the independent radio station said that another American disco song, "Ring My Bell," was taken off the station's play list because of what could be construed as its partisan content (#23).

The JLP also revived older songs, including "Everything Crash," which had been used so effectively before 1972 by the PNP (#29). The party held music festivals in at least three areas in the two weeks before the election. These were billed as "Jamaica's Golden Years Show Extravaganza," and for the most part featured music from the 1960s.

An eyewitness reported that the stage was decorated with a huge "Deliverance" banner and jingling bells mingled with the applause after each song.   At one point, Seaga was introduced and "gave a very concise history of Jamaican music and its stages of development." The concerts were free and "thousands" reportedly   attended (*Star* 10/24/80, 6). Byron Lee and the Dragonnaires, by now long associated with Seaga and based in his constituency, were a part of these shows and other major JLP meetings (DG 10/5/80, 15; 10/26/80, 5).

Several songs were written and sometimes recorded to highlight Labour Party slogans.   One was a commissioned song, "This Time Make Sure," that implied, according to one Labourite, "that 1976 was all wrong, that most people didn't mean for the PNP to get re-elected" (#31). Another was "J-O-Y," (DG 10/8/80, 10), a *mento* or folk tune based on a Revivalist hymn by Ira Sankey (DN 10/17/80, 7). The original verse went as follows:

> J-O-Y, J-O-Y,
> *Joy not shame nor sorrow*
> *Take it to J-E-S-U-S*
> *And J-O-Y will follow. (#7)*

The partisan version ended with the lines:

> *Take your vote to the J-L-P*
> *And J-O-Y will follow.*

An advertisement revised the verse further:

> *Put your X beside the bell*
> *And J-O-Y will follow"* (DG 10/7/80, 14)

A third such song contained a specifically Rastafarian reference: "Brother Eddie is our leader / Our conscious leader / A leader who know Jah-Jah" (DG 10/8/80, 10; #4, #7, #17).   Another included a line that referred to the Rastafarian meaning of the word *deliverance*:   "For God has sent us a deliverer / Who is going to deliver us out of this wicked Babylon" (DG 12/7/80, 4).

By far the most popular song produced by the JLP for
1980 was "Deliverance is Near." Sung by the Tivoli Garden
Singers and written by an advertising executive, G. Grind-
ley, the song departed from the use of reggae rhythms, and
represented a "return to old-fashioned folk songs ... Mento
and non-conformist or Evangelical" (#17). It was identified
specifically as Revivalist by some informants (#7, #8, #9,
#13, #20). The lyrics referred to the mountaintop to which
Manley promised that Jamaicans would climb alongside
Cubans. The song is distinctly millenarian. It referred to
joblessness, starvation, and fear, but promised deliverance
from all those conditions shortly:

> We all are wayward travelers
> In tattered garments clad
> Struggling up a mountain
> That makes us seem so sad
> Our backs are laden heavy,
> Our strength is almost done
> We're shouting as we journey
> "Deliverance is near,"
> > Palms of victory, bells of freedom
> > Palms of victory, deliverance is near
> We've seen our children starve,
> With nothing left to wear
> Most of us are jobless, and many live in fear
> Our burdens we must bear,
> Yet we will show no fear
> For in our hearts we're singing,
> "Deliverance is near,"
> > Palms of victory....

This song was used as a voice-over for an advertisement,
described as quite effective by some respondents, in which
poor rural Jamaicans were seen climbing wearily up a steep
mountainside, until the cameras switched to a crowd
joyfully singing the song (DG 10/4/80, 6).

One popular reggae song, "Crucial," also expressed the
economic desolation of the poor, and this was the most
frequently used popular song in the campaign. The singer
was a Rastafarian who is generally regarded as progressive
but who may have given the JLP permission to use his song

on radio advertisements (#25). "The Rock" is sometimes used to refer to Jamaica, and "squall" is a rumbling storm:

Dis yah system, a crucial i' crucial
In yah dis yah rhythm, a crucial i' crucial
I'm out on the rock now,
With no clothes on my back now
No shoes on my feet now,
I've got nothing to eat now.
Not even lickle flour a crucial i' crucial
To mix lickle dumpling a crucial i' crucial
Said no rice on the shelf a crucial i' crucial
To make little Sunday rice and peas
A crucial i'crucial
Good gosh, di crucial!
Whoy, di crucial!
Dis yah pressure a crucial i' crucial
It's getting dreader and dreader a crucial i' crucial
My back on the wall now,
My belly fill with white squall now
Got no job to get paid now,
Not even borrows to spend now
Not even little sugar a crucial i' crucial
To mix lickle wash, my gosh! a crucial i' crucial
No bread nor butter a crucial i' crucial
Can't even make little supper a crucial i' crucial
Dis yah system a crucial i' crucial...

The lyrics, as PNP supporters readily admitted, were based on the realities most Jamaicans were actually facing (#8, #27). The use of the song had a tremendous effect (#8, #13; Walters 1981) and the word *Crucial* became a catchword during election time. As one respondent said, it was "more of a feeling than a description. Because of our oral tradition, words take on condensed meaning, more profound connotations" (#8). The word was associated with the Labour Party (DG 10/5/80, 15).

Two songs that were used by both parties were "Coming in from the Cold" and "Bad Card," both by Bob Marley (#4, #7, #20, #25, #26). Reportedly, the JLP asked Marley for permission to use "Bad Card" but Marley refused (#11). Two respondents said that while both parties used the songs, they stressed different sections. In "Bad Card," for example, "Manley was saying, 'You can't get we out of the race,' and Seaga came back with, 'You draw bad card'" (#25). D. K. Duncan told a youth rally shortly before the election, "Tell everyone out dey. 'Dem ago tired fi see mi face'" (DN 10/13/80, 1). "Bad Card" is not an intrinsically political song; one respondent said it was probably written by Marley about his middle-class neighbors on Hope Road in St. Andrew, who never quite became accustomed to dreadlocks in the neighborhood (#39):

> You ago tired fi see me face
> Can't get me out a the race
> Oh man, you said I'm in your place
> And then you draw bad card
> Propaganda spreading over my name
> Say you want to bring another life to shame
> Oh man, you just a playing a game
> And then you draw bad card
> A make you draw bad card
> I want to disturb my neighbor
> Cause I'm feeling so right
> I want to turn up my disco
> Blow them to full watts tonight
> Ina rub-a-dub style.
> Cause we guarding the palace so majestic
> Guarding the palace so realistic
> Them a go tired fi see we face, yeah
> Them can't get we out a the race
> Oh man, it's just a big disgrace
> The way you draw bad card.

"Coming in from the Cold" is a song against violence among "brothers" and has a millenarian flavor to it. The JLP considered it an appropriate theme for a party that wants to become the government after ten years in the "cold" of the opposition benches; the PNP thought its use legitimate for itself because the PNP was behind in the polls (#8):

> In this life, in this life, in this oh sweet life
> We're coming in from the cold

It's you, it's you, it's you I'm talking to
Why do you look so sad and forsaken
When one door is closed, don't you know
Another one is open
Would you let the system
Make you kill your brotherman
No dread no
Would you let the system
Make you kill your brotherman
No Jah no.
Would you let the system get on top your head
No Jah no.
The biggest man you ever did see
Was once a baby.

Two respondents (#8, #13) pointed out that the cover of the record album that contained both songs was distinctly PNP. On the back and front are pictures of rising suns, a major PNP symbol, and in the drawing on the front, Marley has both fists clenched.

The PNP's campaign included some new selections and some from the 1976 election. One respondent said ruefully that there were songs from 1976 that couldn't be used in 1980: "We didn't dare try to use 'We Know Where We're Going,' because we didn't know where we were going" (#13). "The Message" (see chapter 5), however, was used again and received strong criticism from JLP supporters, as it had in 1976, because it pointed out by inference that Seaga was not born in Jamaica. One letter called it "that disgusting song ... the most despicable, racist and blatant attack against the leader of the opposition" (DG 10/2/80, 7). Others agreed (#14), calling it "revolting" (DG 10/4/80, 4), "contemptible" (DG 10/4/80, 6), "Hitler-like" (DG 10/5/80, 11), "distasteful" (DG 10/29/80) and "disgraceful" (DN 10/27/80, 7). It was played at PNP rallies and the party used one line, "No Bastard No Deh Again," as a headline in an advertisement about the Status of Children Act (DN 10/26/80, 23).

As mentioned earlier, "Stand Firm" or "Stand Firm for a Third Term" was the PNP's main slogan for 1980. Neville Martin, songwriter of "The Message," wrote a song highlighting this and another PNP slogan, "Stepping." Both these slogans came originally from other reggae songs (#13). "Stand Firm" was originally a Rasta phrase (#38) and was the title of two well-known songs, one by Jacob Miller and one, a condemnation of Christianity, by Peter Tosh:

Wan bald hed tell me say
Dis ya bald hed a tell me say
Put on me cloze and come wid im
A mek we go to church Sunday
Soul Seekers, Soul Seekers I say

Jakit an tie, come tell me say
Clean cloze, come tell me say
Mi fi come wid im
An go to church dis Sunday
Soul Seekers, Soul Seekers, I say

All you got to do
Live clean, let your works be seen, my brothers,
Stand firm, or you gonna feed worm.

Dis a one come tell I say
Another one come tell I say
If you want to be saved son
You got to go in your grave son
Pack of bull shit, that is bull shit I say

The other one come tell I say
If you want to be in the light son
You got to love Jesas Crise son
Dat is fantasy
A whole pack of ignorancy I say

All you got to do
Live clean, let your works be seen, my sisters
Stand firm, or you gonna feed worm.

Neither version of "Stand Firm" is particularly germane to the election. Martin's version, commissioned by the PNP, asserted that the PNP was fighting colonialism and imperialism and made reference to sabotage and propaganda. It is a melancholy song with a melody in a minor key.

"Stepping" came originally from Marcia Griffith's song "Steppin' Out A Babylon." The PNP requested permission to use the original, but Griffiths refused. "I think she was sympathetic," said a PNP campaigner, "but she was fearful for her career" (#20). Martin's song combined the two catchwords in one song:

> Stand firm, we are fighting for a cause
> Stand firm, our country they're trying to sabotage
> In slavery days my poor brothers couldn't rest
> Our pregnant mothers they tied them in ants nest
> Stand firm, we are one family
> Stand firm, stand firm against our enemies
> Them spreading propaganda,
> They only want to destroy us
> Their only intention is to separate us
> Stand firm, against colonialists
> Stand firm, against imperialists
> We are stepping, we are stepping
> Stepping into progress
> We are stepping, we are stepping
> So let's join our hands together
> We are stepping, we are stepping
> Against foreign influence
> We are stepping, we are stepping
> Against all violence
> Marcus Garvey he fight dem for the same cause
> Paul Bogle, he fight dem for the same cause
> Old Nanny, she fight dem to the finish
> Old Cudjoe, he ring the abeng for freedom
> We are stepping, we are stepping,...

A letter to the *Gleaner* from a JLP activist pointed out the difficulties inherent in the incumbent party's using belligerent reggae music:

> "Babylon" to the man in the street and especially the Rastafari, used to denote "police".... The word has now come to mean an oppressive system of government. It is this word that the PNP in their frightened anxiety to appeal to whom they call "the masses" have been exploiting in their elec-

tion campaign with a slogan which runs "Stepping out a Babylon." Now if Jamaica is experiencing oppressive government at this stage in our history, who is responsible? Certainly not the Opposition ... we will have truly stepped "Out a Babylon" when we vote this government "out a" power. (DG 8/31/80)

Martin's other song for the campaign was called "No, Mr. IMF, No." Written to justify the PNP's break with the International Monetary Fund, the song asks Jamaicans to unite and "stand up on our feet." This song was also written in a minor key:

> *Oh No Mr. IMF no*
> *Your mountains we will not climb*
> *Oh no Mr. IMF no*
> *Everyone can see even the blind*
> *Your terms it's a shame I must say*
> *Jamaicans won't continue this way*
> *It ain't no shame that we fail your test*
> *Our Lord knows we tried our best*
> > *Oh no Mr. IMF no...*
> *We must seek alternatives*
> *Ways that are true and more productive*
> *Oh no we ain't making a new start*
> *We only taking a new part*
> > *Oh no Mr. IMF no...*
> *Every step Jamaicans step forward*
> *There are ways that are pushing us backward*
> *Oh no we won't go on no further*
> *They give us basket to carry water*
> > *Oh no Mr. IMF no*
> > *Your rivers we will not cross*
> > *Oh no Mr.IMF no*
> > *Our pride and dignity we don't lost*
> *Every road that Jamaicans grow forward*
> *There are ways that are pushing us backward*
> *They won't cooperate so we must separate*
> *We're gonna show them Jamaicans are great.*
> > *Oh no Mr. IMF no...*
> *Let us stand up now on our feet*

Let us show them Jamaicans no weak
All that we need now is unity
And by God we will build this country
Oh no Mr. IMF no...

The importance of the choice of music to use in the campaign and the divisions within the PNP are illustrated by the lack of decisiveness about music within the party. One campaign manager said of the song "Coming in from the Cold": "We had a big argument about that. Manley wanted to use it a lot, but we thought the JLP already had a hold on it. We used it some, but the JLP used it more" (#20). Another said of "Bad Card": "I tried to get them to play it, but they didn't use it until too late in the campaign. And 'No, Mr.IMF' wasn't used as effectively as it could have been" (#13).

A number of reggae musicians openly supported the PNP, despite the fear of many musicians to support any party. The government organized a concert in Kingston to celebrate National Heroes Day. A *Daily News* report of the concert read:

> The general mood of the presentations marked a departure from the normally reserved attitude of entertainers, especially Dreadlocks, in making their political views known. No less than a dozen reggae artists used the stage ... to lobby for the party of their choice.... Sammy Dread ... set the precedent by announcing "Special dedication to all socialists...." Johnny Osbourne shouted amidst cheering "Let everyone stand for Comrade Roy McGann. If one can stand up for so much of I-and-I, why can't I-and-I stand up for him?" Everyone did.... Louis Lepkey, the D.J., said "If you want progress you better vote fi the Head," then he sang "Dem kill Docta Rodney." (DN 10/22/80, 3)

The most controversial of the PNP songs was not a reggae song but "The Red Flag," the party song of the British Labour Party, and of the Social Democratic parties of Germany and Holland. It had long been a part of the

PNP repertoire, and was especially appropriate on occasions marking the death of a comrade. Criticism of this song began before Roy McGann's death, when a letter from "Ten Concerned Christians" expounded the evils of communism and mentioned that PNP members "openly sing 'The Red Flag' at their meetings" (DG 10/14/80, 11). During McGann's funeral, D. K. Duncan led the congregation in singing the hymn, and the event provoked a spate of criticism. The Jamaican Association of Evangelicals, in a first-page *Gleaner* story, called it an "international Communist hymn" (DG 10/25/80, 1) and the *Gleaner's* religion columnist, Billy Hall, wrote that Manley had promised in 1972 "a moral and spiritual rebirth" but had delivered an immoral and political rebirth: "The immoral aspect is charged in the way the glory of socialism has been exalted over the glory of God ... even the 'Red Flag' is sung in an Anglican church" (DG 10/26/80, 8). Similarly, a letter to the *Gleaner* criticized the Jamaica Council of Churches for its silence over the incident. "Perhaps the JCC will remain mute," the letter continued, "even after the substitution of the hammer and sickle for the crucifix at the altar" (DG 10/29/80, 19).

Within two days after the criticism began, the PNP issued a press release stating that the party "has always tried to maintain the highest Christian principles and respect for the church," and explained that the song was sung by European Labour and Social Democratic parties. The release was printed by the *Gleaner*, five days after the PNP lost the election (DG 11/5/80, 11).

Discussion

The JLP won a landslide victory in 1980 after a bloody campaign in which nearly eight hundred people were killed, many of them, exactly what proportion is unknown, in election related violence. To win the election, the task of the Labour Party was to gain the support of the lower-class and Black majority. With a White, Boston-born Syrian-Jamaican with no trade union background as party leader, the JLP faced an uphill battle. The party owed its victory to good fortune and skillful campaigning that included deft manipulation of symbols.

The JLP's good fortune was Jamaica's bad luck: the state of the economy. Lower-class Jamaicans had suffered a severe drop in standard of living despite, and because of, PNP efforts to regain economic viability in the midst of a world economic crisis. The JLP was able to convince the voters that their economic misfortunes were solely attributable to PNP mismanagement. The party appealed to voters' desire both for millennial relief and the immediate amelioration of their condition: "Deliverance."

As in 1976, the JLP played down the question of socioeconomic classes in Jamaica. It presented Jamaicans as a unified whole that would benefit uniformly from free enterprise and that had been set back by the PNP's fostering of "class hatred."

The PNP's campaign touched the class issue, as in 1976, by identifying the JLP as the capitalist party, and by trying to internationalize the issue and present Jamaica as part of a bloc of poor nations victimized by the vagaries of world capitalism. The party may have overestimated the electorate's grasp of dependency theory. As one respondent pointed out, the PNP's anti-American stance did not penetrate the opinions of many Jamaicans whose friends and relatives had migrated to the United States and were doing well there financially (#14).

As with class, the JLP stressed racial unity but was able to appeal to the Black nationalism of some Jamaicans by claiming Garvey as the Labour Party's own. The party stressed Garvey's anticommunism and implied that were Garvey alive, he would vote Labour. Seaga's work in Tivoli, his interest and achievements in the cultural fields, and his consecration as a Revivalist shepherd were cited as evidence that he had "broken the racial barrier."

Seaga and the JLP tied the party to the interests of the lower class by using non-Rastafarian symbols of this group. Rastafarian symbols were partly replaced in JLP propaganda with Revivalist and Evangelical symbols. The Rasta symbols that the party did use were usually parts of songs. Rather than tied to specific issues, these were millenarian (e.g. "deliver us out of this wicked Babylon") or ephemeral ("a leader who know Jah-Jah"). Much earlier in the campaign the party made use of the titles of two of the most belligerent reggae songs, and tied these to the issue of human rights.   The party adopted a new anthem that borrowed liberally from those songs.

The PNP's use of Rastafarian symbols and songs was not tied to issues.   The party used a somewhat millenarian song and slogan, "Stepping out a Babylon," but found it difficult as an incumbent party to use protest music effectively. The party was suffering from internal dissent on substantive issues that manifested itself also in controversy about which music to play at rallies.

By 1980 Rastafarian symbols may have lost their effectiveness in associating the PNP with the interests of the lower class for two reasons.   First, there were several very visible, very wealthy Rastafarians, and many middle class youth had become Rastas in the 1970s.   Second, the Rastafarians and reggae singers who remained close to, and expressed the experiences of, the lower class were critical of the government.   The Green Bay incident was condemned as murder; both parties' employment of poor youths as party thugs was deplored; songs like Bunny Wailer's "Crucial" still conveyed the utter hopelessness of the very poor.

At the end of 1980 the PNP was demoralized and in disarray.   The JLP, buoyed to victory by economic depression, anticommunist rhetoric, and Revivalist choruses, stepped into power determined to place Jamaica squarely in the camp of free enterprise and pro-Americanism.   Like the PNP in 1972 the JLP offered hope and salvation.   There is an ironic twist to its zealous efforts to convince the electorate that only the JLP stood for two-party democracy; by 1983 those efforts resulted in a single-party government.

7

The 1983 Election

The 1983 election was in some ways an amalgam of features found in previous elections; in other ways, an unprecedented partisan confrontation. It brings to mind the "snap" election of 1967 and Norman Manley's condemnation of that three-week campaign as a "rape of democracy." Five years before, in 1978, Michael Manley was struggling with "Is Manley Fault" and Edward Seaga was presenting himself as champion of voting rights. Nineteen eighty-three found Seaga complaining of the rigidity of the IMF and Manley accusing the JLP of subverting electoral democracy. It was the only election studied that campaigners failed to bill as "the most important" in Jamaica's history; yet history might prove that it actually was. At its end all sixty seats in Parliament were in the hands of one party.

In this chapter, the 1983 election will be examined as a culmination of the trends evident in the earlier campaigns, and a return to the relatively marginal roles of Rasta and reggae that had characterized the first election discussed in this book. First, the JLP administration will be explored, particularly the two aspects that had an impact on the timing and outcome of the election: foreign policy and economy. Changes in the parties' leadership were minor on the part of the JLP but constituted one of the PNP's primary activities during its first term as opposition, and will be detailed next. Third, the developments in the areas of Rastafari and reggae will be described. Finally, the short campaign and its prizes, won in the field of public opinion rather than state power, will be discussed.

Two sources not previously mentioned were especially helpful for this chapter. *Everybody's* is a Caribbean magazine that reprints speeches, statements and other items that can be considered "primary" source material. Dispatches from the Jamaica Bureau of the Spanish News Agency, EFE, were used to provide backgound details. Many of the EFE reports are based on *Gleaner* articles.

The Jamaica Labour Party Administration, 1980 – 83

Never before in Jamaica's history had a prime minister had as close and harmonious a relationship with an American president as did Seaga with Ronald Reagan.   Even before the latter's inauguration, Seaga visited Washington for talks with the transition team, in particular to discuss Seaga's call for a "Marshall Plan" for aid to Central America and the Caribbean (DG 12/4/80).   The JLP's anticommunism, free-market economic policy, and foreign policy meshed well with the objectives of the new Republican administration.

The Reagan administration provided the Seaga administration with a number of types of support, symbolic and material.   Seaga was the first foreign head of government to pay an official visit to the new president, just eight days after the latter's inauguration.   Reagan returned the favor in 1982, when he was the first U.S. president in office to visit the English-speaking Caribbean since 1934. Despite Reagan's public welcome, in which he called Seaga's election "a new direction for the Mediterranean," the point was made that the Caribbean was a region of high interest to the new U.S. administration.

Seaga won publicity in the United States when he offered free vacations to Jamaica for the U.S. embassy personnel who had been held hostage in Iran.   He was later awarded the American Friendship Medal by Reagan for his "furtherance of democratic institutions and a free market economy and for his courageous leadership in the cause of freedom" (*Everybody's*, March 1983). The White House ceremony was attended by President Reagan, Vice-President Bush, and a dozen or so other highly placed officials of the Jamaican and U.S. governments.

The Reagan administration also helped the JLP government materially. In February 1981, after Seaga's visit to the White House, it was announced that David Rockefeller, chairman of Chase Manhattan Bank, would preside over the newly formed U.S. Business Committee on Jamaica that would, according to a White House statement, "contribute substantially" in the effort to increase private-sector investment for Jamaican economic recovery (*Everybody's*, April 1981, 28). Other notables on the committee included the chief executive officers of Alcoa, Exxon, Eastern Airlines, United Brands, Reynolds Metals, and Hilton International. Seaga designated Carlton Alexander, chief executive officer of the Grace Kennedy group and one of the wealthiest of Jamaican businessmen, and Oliver Clarke, publisher of the *Gleaner*, among others, to serve on a Jamaican counterpart committee. The goal of the committees was to increase foreign investment in Jamaica.

At a luncheon of the Jamaica-U.S. Business Committee, then Presidential Advisor for National Security William Clark told the group, according the a Jamaican Consulate press release, that "democracy had taken strong root under Prime Minister Seaga," as if to imply that the two-party system was a relatively new idea there. He said that the U.S. "government's experiences in contributing to a brighter future for Jamaica had inspired the administration to develop a comprehensive approach to revitalize the economies of the whole Caribbean region. Hence the CBI" (Jamaican Consulate Release 2/25/83).

During the first year and a half of the JLP government, the United States provided more than $100 million to bolster Jamaican operations of American aluminum companies (*New York Times*, 4/28/82). The Federal Emergency Management Agency rearranged its priorities and waived federal laws to purchase Jamaican bauxite for the military stockpile. The purchase was, according to officials of the General Services Administration, the first purchase directly specified by presidential order for the stockpile in over twenty years. The U.S. embassy reported that Jamaica would receive about $150 million in aid during 1982 (EFE 10/1/81). It is surmised that the U.S. stamp of approval on

Jamaican developments enabled Seaga to strike a more palatable deal with the IMF than had been possible in the Manley administration.

Most importantly, the president and the prime minister worked closely in the development and promotion of the Caribbean Basin Initiative (CBI), an aid package that grew out of Seaga's call for a Caribbean "Marshall Plan." The CBI underwent many transformations before the passage of one version in 1982, a package composed of economic support funds, the formation of free trade zones, and tax credits to American corporations to encourage investment in the region.

The CBI's $350 million in economic support funds is used at the recipient governments' discretion, for debt financing, purchase of military equipment, or other purposes. One analyst estimated in 1982, when the Reagan administration was lobbying hard for the bill, that the total of these funds would meet only 9 percent of the region's debt financing needs (Youngers 1982). The free trade zones likewise appeared to offer more than they could deliver; CBI would increase regional exports only about 1 percent in three years (Youngers 1982). As the CBI was originally drafted, Jamaica was to have received the third-highest grant, $50 million; El Salvador with $128 million and Costa Rica with $70 million were to have received the highest and second-highest grants (U.S. Department of State, March 1982). Thus, these three countries were to have received almost three-fourths of the total.

The Reagan administration presented the CBI as a weapon against the "communist threat" in the region. What Reagan called the "international communist movement" would, he reasoned, take advantage of depressed economic conditions in other Caribbean countries as it had in Grenada, Nicaragua, and Cuba. Outlining plans for the CBI before a meeting of the Organization of American States in February 1982, Reagan used foreboding language:

> The dark future is foreshadowed by the poverty and repression of Castro's Cuba, the tightening grip of the totalitarian left in Grenada and Nicaragua, and the expansion of Soviet-backed,

> Cuban-managed support for violent revolution in
> Central America.
> Nowhere in its whole sordid history have the
> promises of communism been redeemed.   Every-
> where it has exploited and aggravated temporary
> economic suffering. (*Everybody's*, March, 1982).

CBI funds were to be concentrated where the perceived
threat was greatest and where issues of visibility and
mutual respect were concerned — Jamaica was also to
receive a disproportionate share of the goods.   Cuba,
Nicaragua and Grenada were, of course, excluded from the
list of beneficiaries.

Anticommunism was successfully tied to the CBI effort
in Jamaica. Testing the reaction to an early version of the
CBI, Carl Stone conducted a poll with a seemingly loaded
question: "Is it positive or negative that Ronald Reagan
promised to provide aid to Jamaica as part of his anti-
Communist struggle?"   Seventy-eight percent of the respondents said that they believed it was a positive development; 81 percent said that Jamaica should accept the aid
(EFE 8/25/81).

The U.S. Congress made a number of changes in the CBI
bill before passing it; most importantly, it set a ceiling of
$75 million on payments to any single country, thus slash-
ing El Salvador's share from $128 to $75 million.   Ironically, the bill was vetoed by Reagan because of his disagreement with other sections of the appropriations bill in which
it was included.   Congress overrode the veto in the fall of
1982.

The CBI was welcomed by most of the leaders of the
beneficiary countries.   Seaga praised it as "bold and
historic."   Its exclusion of certain countries, especially
Grenada, which was otherwise closely linked economically
with its neighbors through the Caribbean Community (CA-
RICOM), was criticized widely.   The move was seen by
some as a form of interference because countries whose
political and economic structures did not meet Reagan's
approval were isolated and refused aid.   Opposition leader
Manley joined those criticizing CBI on those grounds:
"There is no room for pluralism.   There is no room for
people who might have a slightly different view of econo-

mic strategy. Only if you will bow at altar of free marketeering is there a place in the kingdom" (*Everybody's,* March 1982, 36). The CBI figured significantly in the JLP's 1983 campaign and is referred to again below.

If the United States helped the JLP government in terms of economic support, it was more than repaid by Seaga's cooperation in the field of foreign policy. Immediately after Seaga's inaugural visit with Reagan, the U.S. embassy in Kingston announced that Caribbean "security" would be high on the Republican administration's agenda, including stopping "Cuban and Soviet aggression" and "promoting democracy" (EFE 1/28/81). The JLP had won the 1980 election with a similar public goal. Because it had worked so assiduously to establish linkages in voters' minds between the PNP and the Cubans and other left-wing governments, the Seaga government's continuing to pursue such a course had the double purpose of strengthening ties with the Reagan administration and maintaining suspicion and hostility toward the opposition party at home.

This dual advantage can be seen most clearly in the events leading up to Jamaica's breaking diplomatic ties with Cuba. Toward the end of September 1981, Minister of National Security Winston Spaulding announced that the government had evidence that terrorists were trying to disturb plans for Jamaica's economic security. Spaulding further claimed that in connection with the plots the government had discovered literature from the Soviet Union and manuals of tactics for guerrilla warfare. The PNP and the WPJ responded that the JLP was simply trying to divert people's attention from the failure of Seaga's economic policies (EFE 9/25/81).

Within a few days of Spaulding's announcement, the chair of the PNP Youth Organization, Paul Burke, was detained by police and held for four hours of questioning about terrorism in Jamaica and in Grenada, according to the government (EFE 9/28/81). The government claimed that police had found in Burke's possession a tape-recorded message from one of Jamaica's most wanted gunmen. The latter was, according to the government, living in Cuba and the message was intended for his girlfriend in Jamaica. Although the tape was never produced for opposition members or journalists to hear, a transcript was distributed. Burke, his attorneys, and the PNP claimed that neither of the two tapes in his possession, one containing a speech by P. J. Patterson, the other blank, could fit this description.

On 29 October Seaga announced, "with much regret," that Jamaica was breaking diplomatic ties with Cuba. He said in his address to Parliament that relations could not "be maintained in accordance with the basic principles of non-interference and mutual respect" (*Everybody's*, December 1981). Cuba, the government claimed, was harboring and refusing to extradite three criminals wanted in Jamaica, including the one whose alleged recording had fallen into police hands. Seaga also claimed that the Cubans were training terrorists (EFE 10/29/81).

The PNP reacted immediately by accusing Seaga of breaking ties to tighten relations between the United States and Jamaican governments or under direct instructions from Reagan; both allegations were denied. Manley sent a delegation to Cuba headed by then PNP Vice-president P. J. Patterson to thank the Cuban people for their years of assistance to Jamaica (*Everybody's*, December 1981). Public opinion polls indicated that by then, the fear of communism that had been inspired by the JLP's 1980 campaign had dissipated. Seaga's break with Cuba did not have the support of a majority of Jamaicans (Stone 1983, 32).

Grenada

By far the most important area of United States-Jamaican cooperation and collaboration was the isolation, harassment, and finally invasion of Grenada by the United States and six Caribbean allies. It is difficult to name a more decisive factor in the timing and outcome of the 1983 campaign than the invasion. It was then, according to *Gleaner* editor-in-chief and former JLP Chairman Hector Wynter, that Jamaica "passed from the age of innocence into the real world" in that it was ready to "sacrifice young people" to the anticommunist cause (WG 10/21/83, 7).

When Maurice Bishop's New Jewel Movement came to power by coup d'etat in the tiny island of Grenada in 1979, Jamaicans embraced the controversy as one of their own and proceeded to fight it out among themselves. Though few were sympathetic to ousted Prime Minister Eric Gairy, the parties quickly fell into ranks for and against Bishop. The *Gleaner* lost few opportunities to publicize allegations that human rights were abused in Grenada, and Bishop's friendship with Fidel Castro of Cuba condemned his government by association. The JLP and its leader were in the forefront of regional criticism of Grenada (Stone 1983, 31).

The PNP, in contrast, found a comrade in the young Grenadian leader. Bishop had a British education, a radical chic, and a wardrobe reminiscent of many a former PNP minister. Members of the party maintained good relations with the government of Grenada, reiterating the party's support for that government along with that of Nicaragua and the rebels of El Salvador at its annual party conferences. PNP members were recruited by Grenada to provide technical and administrative assistance (Stone 1983, 31).

Reagan frequently used his cooperative relations with the Jamaican and other Caribbean governments as a platform from which to castigate the Bishop government. His visit to Jamaica and Barbados in April 1982, was such an occasion. Besides remarks against Grenada, the president also made a number of partisan references, including mentioning Bustamante not as Jamaica's first prime minister but rather as the founder of the JLP. He stirred considerable controversy when he said that Seaga's victory in 1980 had saved Jamaica from "communism." The PNP objected vehemently to this statement, and later opinion polls demonstrated that a majority of Jamaicans agreed that the statements were too strongly worded (*Star* 6/7/82).

Reagan's whirlwind trip, on which he was accompanied by over four hundred staff and security personnel, centered primarily in Barbados. There he met with the leaders of four of the Eastern Caribbean countries that later called for and joined American forces in the Grenada invasion. Although Reagan said that Prime Minister Tom Adams of Barbados had arranged the meeting, American taxpayers underwrote the leaders' working vacations and Premier Kennedy Simmonds of St. Kitts told a reporter that the invitation came from the U.S. State Department (*Everybody's*, May 1982). According to the *Everybody's* report, Grenada was high on the agenda in the talks, and Reagan particularly wanted to know if the leaders thought that Bishop would win, should elections be held in Grenada. Following the meeting in a public address, Reagan told the audience that "all of us are concerned with the overturn of Westminster parliamentary democracy in Grenada. That country now bears the Soviet and Cuban trademark, which means that it will attempt to spread the virus among its neighbors" (*Everybody's*, May 1982, 36).

Seaga showed his concern in a confrontation the next November, during the Caribbean Community (CARICOM) summit in Ocho Rios. On the eve of the summit, Seaga joined Prime Minister Adams of Barbados in introducing an amendment to the organization's charter requiring the holding of elections as a condition of CARICOM membership. It was an obvious move to expel Grenada from the economic organization (*Caribbean Contact*, October 1982). Grenada objected strongly to the motion, which was defeated with the help of Guyana's President Forbes Burnham and Trinidad and Tobago's Prime Minister George Chambers, leaders of two countries that did not join U.S. forces in the invasion of Grenada the next year.

A brief review of the events leading to the invasion and the invasion itself is in order here before the question of its implications for Jamaican politics is addressed. Tensions in Bishop's New Jewel Movement had been reported since the fall of 1982, when Deputy Prime Minister Bernard Coard resigned from its Central Committee, and when it was reported that a plenary meeting of that committee had been critical of Bishop's leadership. Relations with the United States were growing increasingly hostile, with Reagan asserting in March 1983 that the international airport under construction in Grenada could pose a military threat to the United States. Bishop visited the United States in May of that year in an effort to ease hostility, but Reagan refused to see him. In several public appearances, Bishop denied Reagan's charges that the airport's purpose was military.

By September, Central Committee meetings were becoming more and more critical of Bishop. In September it suggested that Bishop share leadership with Deputy Prime Minister Coard, with the latter assuming responsibility for economic policy. On 12 October, the Central Committee accused Bishop of spreading the rumor that Coard was plotting to murder him. Bishop first denied starting the rumers, and later, according to some reports, admitted doing so. The committee had Bishop placed under house arrest the next day; Bishop supporters in the cabinet resigned.

Negotiations to release Bishop over the next four days failed. On 19 October, thousands of Bishop supporters released him and marched with him through the streets to Fort Rupert. Soldiers at Bishop's house and en route did not fire on the crowd. At the fort, under circumstances still not clear, Bishop, three cabinet members, and two labor leaders were killed.   General Hudson Austin announced the next day that the sixteen-member Revolutionary Military Council would take charge in Grenada temporarily. A curfew was imposed.

Two days after Bishop's death, the Organization of Eastern Caribbean States (OECS) met with Seaga and Tom Adams in Barbados. The members voted unanimously to request the United States to invade. Reagan had a letter drafted so as to have a written request; the letter was then sent from Washington to the region to be signed by the OECS members.

U.S. forces landed at Point Salines and at Pearls Airport in Grenada on 25 October. A few hours later, Reagan and Dominica's Prime Minister Eugenia Charles announced the invasion in a White House press conference, calling it a "rescue operation" and stating that the United States participated at the invitation of the OECS countries, Jamaica, and Barbados.

Interest in Grenada soared among Jamaicans. Whereas earlier polls had indicated that almost 80 percent of the respondents had no opinion on, for example, the human rights issue in Grenada, in an October 1983 poll only 15 percent had no opinion about the murder of Bishop -- it was overwhelmingly condemned by the remainder. The actual course of events in Grenada bore a strong resemblance to scenarios promulgated by the JLP before the 1980 election to defuse the personal popularity of Manley. If Manley were returned to power, JLP supporters had claimed, his days would be numbered. The left wing of the PNP, represented by D. K. Duncan among others, or the Workers Party of Jamaica itself, would wrest power from Manley (see chapter 6). Even voters who respected Manley personally were thus persuaded to support the JLP.

A Stone poll was conducted in which citizens were asked if the events of Grenada could have happened in Jamaica had the PNP been victorious in 1980 (Stone 1983, 60); about 40 percent of those reached thought that the events could have happened. The responses were almost the same regardless of party affiliation. Forty-three percent believed that Cuba played a direct role in the removal of Bishop; 35 percent, that the Soviet Union had such a role. In the case of suspected Cuban involvement, partisan loyalties made a difference. Sixty-two percent of JLP supporters and 27 percent of PNP supporters saw a direct Cuban role. It must be pointed out, as Manley did in a speech in October (WG 10/21/83, 7), that Fidel Castro's speech forthrightly condemning the killers of Bishop was not reported in the *Gleaner*.

Most important, the same October 1983 poll demonstrated that the events in Grenada had bolstered JLP support. The party's popular support had slipped below that of the PNP in October 1982, and remained so by three to five percentage points until the events in Grenada. Stone reported that 38 percent of his sample supported the PNP compared to 43 percent for the JLP (1983, 60) and that almost half said that their views of the major parties had been influenced by what had happened in Grenada. This issue, as will be seen below, also figured in the 1983 election campaign.

Economy

In its November 1980 report about the Jamaican elections, *The Economist* printed a photograph of Seaga at his swearing-in, with a solemn expression on his face and his hand resting on a Bible. The caption read: "I swear to borrow as much as I can." Despite or as a result of his efforts, the state of the economy over the three-year term of the JLP government proved to be a major issue. The drop in support of the JLP detailed above was primarily due to the erosion in the domestic economy (Stone *Gleaner Annual*, December, 1982).

One of the major economic problems Jamaica faced was the sharp decline in the bauxite market; as mentioned before, bauxite production is Jamaica's primary foreign exchange earner. In 1980, 12 million tons were produced; in 1983, 7.3 million (Seaga, 1983). Shortly after the 1983 election, Reynolds, one of the biggest producers, announced that it was pulling out of Jamaica altogether. Tourism, another source of foreign exchange, increased but not enough to make up for the decline in bauxite.

Seaga came to power with a reputation as a financial wizard. He looked to the economic development programs in Singapore, Puerto Rico, and Hong Kong for models on which to base his own strategy of recovery (Seaga, DG 2/6/83). His plans encompassed three components. First, the government used its influence in the United States and on the U.S. Business Committee on Jamaica to encourage proposals for new foreign investments. After a hundred days in office, an optimistic Seaga announced that he had received 140 proposals with a value of $101 million. A *New York Times* article a year later revealed that only 18 of these proposals had been implemented, their value was $10 million and they created at most a thousand new jobs (28 April, 1982).

Second, Seaga planned to use funds borrowed through the IMF and other sources to spur the domestic economy, especially export manufacturing. Seeking IMF approval, of course, meant subjecting the Jamaican economy to stringent controls and, later, currency devaluations. Late in 1982, a two-tier devaluation was instituted, the existing rate of J$1.78 to the U.S. dollar was kept for basic imports and travel allowances, but for other purposes the currency was allowed to float. This system was later abandoned in an outright devaluation. The Jamaican dollar, which was worth $.56 in 1980, is worth $.26 as this book goes to press.

The loans received by the JLP government, because they must be repaid in foreign currency, are dependent on expanding overseas markets for Jamaican products. According the the PNP, during the eight and a half years of its administration, it borrowed a total of $800 million. The

JLP's economic plan called for borrowing $3.3 billion in five years. In 1981, it borrowed $513 million; in 1982, $642 million, and in 1983, a projected $601 million (*Rising Sun*, August, 1982, 11).

Third, Seaga's economic policies opened up the import market. As Stone explains it, the floating exchange rate resulted in merchants outbidding manufacturers for scarce U.S. dollars. Instead of purchasing raw materials for manufacturing new products, the foreign exchange purchased luxury imports (Stone, *Gleaner Annual*, December, 1982). In the long years of the Manley administration, those who could afford luxury goods complained about their scarcity. Under Seaga, automobiles, video recorders, and the product that had become a symbol of imported luxuries — corn flakes — were readily available to those who could afford them. This particular policy drove many small farmers and small manufacturers into the red because they were not capable of competing with the prices of foreign products. Manufacturers "panicked in reaction to the challenge of having to face competition from imported goods" (Stone, *Gleaner Annual*, 12/82).

The results of the economic policy were mixed. Despite the reduction in bauxite production and some parts of the agricultural sector, the economy experienced a small growth and inflation decreased. Affluence in the upper-middle class increased conspicuously. Luxury houses and apartment buildings were built in record numbers. At the same time, the level of unemployment remained above 25 percent, the cost of living rose over 18 percent in 1983 alone, and public-sector, bauxite, and sugar workers experienced layoffs. The JLP government, in accordance with the IMF agreement, cut back social expenditures and implemented austerity programs.

By November 1983, negotiations for a new IMF agreement were completed. It was necessary once again for the Jamaican dollar to be devalued, and a new wave of hardship was anticipated. Once its effects were fully felt, popular support for the government would no doubt have eroded, so it was not surprising that Seaga dissolved Parliament and called for elections before the implications of the devaluation could be realized.

The PNP in Opposition

When the People's National Party lost the 1980 election, its ranks were divided. Its decision not to contest the elections in 1983 probably demonstrated a far greater consensus than it had shown on any issue since 1978.

The defeat of 1980 had precipitated a leadership crisis. In February 1981, Manley offered his resignation to the National Executive Council of the party and it was rejected 54 to 4, with 25 abstentions (EFE 2/11/81). Manley was dissatisfied with the vote; another was held in May, which reconfirmed him as party leader.

In the reports to the 1981 PNP conference, the defeat of the year before was discussed and analyzed. It was attributed, among other factors, to the economic crisis and to the allegations that the PNP was a communist or near-communist party. The former problem now faced the JLP, but the latter remained a source of disunity among PNP members. Manley said that the PNP needed to distinguish itself from the Workers Party of Jamaica, but not to the point of "vulgar anti-communism" (EFE 5/81). Some party members wanted to maintain a friendly alliance with the WPJ and welcomed its critical support; others felt that this alliance was the primary cause of the 1980 defeat. A Stone survey shortly after those elections showed that 76 percent of those polled thought that the PNP should dissociate itself from the WPJ (EFE 2/26/81).

The 1982 conference provided a forum for the intraparty differences. According to a *Sunday Sun* (the Sunday edition of the *Daily News*) report, "pandemonium" broke out when a vendor selling the WPJ's paper, *Struggle*, was accosted at the entrance of the Arena where the conference was being held. PNP Youth Organization chair Paul Burke invited the vendor to leave. The *Sun's* account went on:

> Following this interplay, a delegate got up in the conference and accused Mr. Burke of inviting communists to the confab. Another delegate rose to the microphone, inside sources said, and charged that communists were in the PNP executive.

> The Party president who "nearly lost his temper"
> ordered the delegate to drop his claims, if names
> could not be furnished. A heated debate ensued
> with charges and counter-charges....
> The moderates are strongly against Dr. Duncan
> holding the post of general secretary. (September
> 12, 1982)

Michael Manley and many PNP members clearly respect
Fidel Castro's charismatic leadership and are unwilling to
disavow their admiration of the gains made in Castro's
Cuba. Combining these open alliances with support for
Nicaragua, the New Jewel Movement, and the rebels in El
Salvador makes the party's task of convincing the elector-
ate that it is not a communist party all the more difficult.
Two resignations seemed to have been initiated as part of
the effort.

In early 1983, D. K. Duncan resigned his office as general secretary and Beverly Manley resigned as head of the
PNP women's movement. Both were leaders of the PNP
Left. Duncan in particular came under heavy fire in the
JLP's 1980 campaign to portray the PNP as a communist-
front organization. In a letter to the *Gleaner,* he acknow-
ledged that his resignation was a "retreat" if not "defeat"
of the PNP left wing:

> There are many in the ruling circles ... who
> believe that my impending resignation ... means
> that the "left" in the country has been delivered a
> death-blow. Those who believe this are living in
> an illusionary world. In every war and struggle
> between class forces, there are moments of re-
> treat.... But retreat does not mean defeat, and
> even if I am never again involved in active
> politics, I am confident that others will take up
> the sword and shield of the Jamaican people's
> struggle and that sooner or later, the forces of
> victory will overcome. (DG 1/9/83, 17).

Although the party repeatedly renewed its commitment
to be "more active" in the opposition, it was one of the
most inactive in Jamaica's history (Stone 1983). A June

1981 Stone poll showed that most Jamaicans thought the PNP was not doing a good job as opposition; some of the responses were that it was silent, too inactive, divided, and leaderless and that it had not yet recovered from the 1980 defeat (EFE 6/17/81). The party leader accepted a number of lecture appearances at universities in the United States and was often criticized for his frequent absences from Parliament (e.g. WG 12/12/83, 11).

The issues around which the PNP tried to mobilize included electoral reform, layoffs and other aspects of economic policy, and freedom of the press, which the party said was violated when thirteen PNP supporters were fired from the newsroom of the Jamaica Broadcasting Company (*Rising Sun*, various issues).

Rastafari and Reggae

One of the most important developments of the post-1980 period was the untimely death in 1981 of reggae's most popular Rastafarian, Bob Marley. The funeral that the JLP government arranged will be discussed below.

The "d.j." style, in which a singer "dubs in" lyrics over recorded music, enjoyed immense success in the early 1980s, although the form dates to the earliest days of reggae. Sound systems, as described earlier in this book, were still the center of entertainment for dances. The d.j.'s working with a sound system would sing or chant — into a microphone — often improvised lyrics over recorded music that was not much more than drum and bass guitar.

The d.j.'s developed a specialized presentation. First, they made the most of performing live, ad libbing songs about members of the audience, other d.j.'s in the show, or the venue itself. Second, they often conveyed an image that has been called "badmanism." The "toughest" possible posture was part of the intense competitiveness among themselves. Interspersed with expert scat singing were catchwords that formed a special d.j. argot. During a dance at Skateland in Halfway Tree Square in early 1982 (Panton 1982), an exceptional performance was applauded as "Murder!" "Posse" was used to refer to any group. In singing the praises of the sound system, in this case Gemini HiFi, one d.j. called them "the roughest," "the General

sound," and said that "Gemini control." The names of the
d.j.'s present included several with militaristic pseudonyms:
Brigadier Jerry, General Plough, and General Buroo among
them.

The most popular d.j. was Winston Foster, an albino
known as Yellowman. He recorded an unprecedented
eleven albums in 1982 alone, and sold out shows throughout
Jamaica, including a Labour Day concert attended by
60,000 in Kingston (*Gleaner Annual*, 1982). His specialty is
sexual lyrics, and he is noted for his boastfulness. In the
same Skateland dance, "the yellowest man around" began
his turn at the microphone by calling himself the "sexy d.j.
... that the girls them love the most" and continued to
delineate very specific reasons why they do so. Such a
song could certainly never have been played on the radio,
and several of Yellowman's records were banned.

Although most d.j. lyrics were not political, they occasionally dealt with issues like police violence. In the song
"Pain," delivered at the same dance, Brigadier Jerry sang
about the pains inflicted by "Babylon" that "Rastafari
know." Some songs of the pre-1967 period were revived by
d.j.'s, notably "Bam Bam," which was rerecorded by both
Sister Nancy and Yellowman.

The Festival Song winner of 1982, "Mek We Jam" by the
Astronauts, provoked considerable controversy over the
precise meaning of the verb "to jam." The artists con-
tended that it meant "to dance." For some months, letters
suggesting other possible meanings appeared in the pages
of the *Gleaner* nearly every day. Even the *Gleaner's*
reggae music writer considered standards "lowered by this
year's festival song" (Barnes, DG 1/9/83). In an article
about the song, White Jamaican columnist Morris Cargill
expressed himself so clearly on the subject that he deserves to be quoted at length:

> I find the whole scene of what is called reggae
> remarkably unpleasant. The words and the music
> are illiterate, the performers mostly inept, unable
> to sing, and for the most part hideous, and the
> performances an almost classical example of
> mindlessness. That the whole awful business is so
> immensely popular is proof, if proof were needed,

of the vulgarity and stupidity of the age we live in.

That the mass of people have vulgar and uneducated tastes is nothing new. What is new is that we are forced into approval of it, and forcibly submitted to it ... we are in effect told that Yellow Man is a superior artist to Beethoven, and that almost any horrid noise made by some group of unattractive louts is our "cultural heritage" simply because a lot of people, indulging in a mixture of pot and self-hypnosis, flock to watch it....

It seems to me that there is a great number of Jamaicans who are in fear of protesting against the tastelessness and idiocy of the current pop and Reggae "culture" in case they are accused of being snobs, members of some disgraceful elite or not "genuine" Jamaicans. They should take heart and speak up, and not allow themselves to be over-run by the barbarians. (DG 8/15/82)

Though Cargill may have found them "unattractive louts" as well, it is no surprise that more tolerant Jamaicans were encouraged by the best-selling record of 1982. British-based bands from the West Indian neighborhoods of London and Birmingham enjoyed immense popularity in Jamaica, and the biggest seller of that year was "Pass the Dutchie" by Musical Youth, a group of youngsters from Birmingham. The song was a more "wholesome" rendition of the Mighty Diamonds' song "Pass the Kutchie." A "dutchie" is a large stewing pot; in the Musical Youth version it was food that was being passed about. A "kutchie," on the other hand, is a pipe for ganja smoking. Some Jamaican writers found the Musical Youth song a refreshing contrast to other popular songs. Winston Barnes of the *Gleaner*, for example, wrote that the "biggest lesson to learn from this record" was "that records that sing praises of drugs and the Rastafari faith may be shunned in preference for lover's rock and fun-oriented gimmick songs" (DG 1/9/83).

A letter to the *Gleaner* from a disgruntled user of "public transportation units" printed around election time in 1983 echoed Cargill's disgust with reggae and implied that those who enjoy reggae and ganja are of a different class than those who distain both:

> Nearly every public transportation unit, bar, etc. blares out these rude, pungent, degrading tunes defying (sic) the weed, and simultaneously defying law and order. These tunes would most insolently impute reputable professsionals as sly participants of their degrading indulgences. "Wrap up one draw fe the doctor. It haffe bun!" etc. How nauseating.... Why do passengers on public transport units tolerate the silly and abominably stupid "oral filth" played on tape en route ... we do most times behave like a pack of mindless silly jack-asses, don't we? (WG 12/19/83)

Another hit song that irked the self-styled "respectables" in Jamaica was recorded by Rita Marley and called "One Draw." It was a song about the joys of marijuana, but unlike earlier Rasta songs about the "herb," it did not dwell on the spiritual powers of the "healing of the nation." In the middle of the song was a bit of spoken dialogue in which a teacher, sounding prim and proper, asks her students how they spent their vacations. All of them, it seems, had spent their summers smoking, and they proceed to persuade their teacher to try it. This song, said to set an abominable example to children, was banned on Jamaican radio, adding to its success and popularity.

In contrast was a song by Bunny Wailer, which was not mentioned in the letters and columns in the *Gleaner*, that condemned reggae. Perhaps those critics did not have the tolerance to listen closely to the words. "Back to School," contained on an album of dance songs, seemed musically to be designed to appeal to children and used as lyrics patois forms of nursery rhymes. With a chorus of children singing back-up vocals, Wailer reviewed multiplication tables and reminded children:

> *You've got to start at A-B-C*
> *To be at the university*
> *Eenie meenie minie mo,*
> *Now here's a lesson on your radio*

Now go to school, learn the rule,
And don't you be no fool...
As busy as a bee, as cunning as a fox,
As happy as a lark,
Remember to do your homework,
And don't do it in the park...
You've gotta read and write and check and count
For you to be a star
To be able to have a bank account
To buy Mom and Dad a big posh car...
So pick up your bag with your book and pen,
'cause its back to school again!

A 1980 song by d.j.'s Michigan and Smiley proved to be prophetic and was revived for the summer of 1982. It is a warning of the evils that will befall those who do not follow the straight and narrow:

Everyday man a build explosives
The corruption of the world it exposes
Mind Jah lick you with diseases
The most dangerous diseases
Talking about the elephantitis
The other one, the poliomyelitis
Arthritis and the one diabetes
Hey Jah you fi lick them with diseases.

In 1982, an outbreak of polio alarmed the population and led to the cancellation of many annual festivities. As Jamaicans queued up for their vaccinations at health centers across the island, they sometimes sang along to the strains of that revived tune.

In sharp contrast to the d.j. style and the themes of material wealth and sexual prowess, the older reggae style had its day at the Christmas concert held in 1982, the Youth Consciousness Festival (Slinger 1983). Its main attraction was Bunny Wailer, who had spent seven years in relative seclusion, recording music but never performing in concert. Unlike others of his caliber, who have sought tours and record contracts in the United States and England, Wailer has not, to this author's knowledge, left Jamaica since he toured with the original Wailers in 1972.

The tone at the festival seems to have been celebratory and spiritual, and the music, which lasted a full twelve hours, was inspirational and somewhat nostalgic. Absent were singers who had come to be associated with the Jamaica Labour Party, such as Byron Lee and the Dragonnaires and Carleen Davis. Marcia Griffiths, another Marley associate, told the audience that the concert's purpose was "to uplift each and every one of our souls, because in this time we need a lot of upliftment" (Slinger 1983, 15). The few political notes struck included a "rap" from Peter Tosh, who told the crowd: "This moment is an event that never happened in four hundred years. We in this generation must be proud and glad, especially we who are here. This thing that is happening right now, do you know what it is? Illegal. Consciousness is illegal in a world of fantasy and illusion."

Dub poet Oku Onoura recited what was probably the most overtly political item, "Reflections in Red," with its warnings against nuclear weapon production. But Tosh's "world of fantasy and illusion" was evident right there in the stadium; the crowd sang along with Bunny Wailer's old song "Dreamland," one witness said, "as if it were a national anthem" (Slinger 1983).

It is telling that many of the songs performed at this concert were older ones, written in the early 1970s, and most of the day's popular "top ten" reggae artists, such as Yellowman, were absent. The concert seemed to be infused with a melancholy over the loss of Marley, to whom several selections were dedicated. An otherworldliness, a concentration on mystical songs, and nostalgia were also evident.

The theme of police brutality was among those that did not leave reggae music after Marley's death. After a 1978 incident in which he was beaten badly by police following a ganja arrest, Peter Tosh in particular has been associated with this theme. His 1981 recording, "Wanted Dread and Alive," is illustrated with a facsimile of a police fingerprint file form that lists Tosh's offenses as "numerous." The title song opens with a dialogue between a judge and uncooperative defendant — Tosh recites both parts — in which the defendant refuses to repeat, "So help me God," after the judge, insisting on, "So help I Jah, Rastafari."

The chorus of the song sums up Tosh's feelings about the police in two simple lines:

> Every time I see Babylon,
> My blood run cold, cold, cold.
> Every time I see the wicked men,
> My belly move, move, move.

During the Youth Consciousness Festival, Tosh, like the other performers there, sang more spiritual and lighter songs, but between songs he poked fun at his own reputation:

> "I and I have been abused, accused, condemned, incriminated, discriminated, brutalized.   And when people hear this they say, 'Peter and the police again'" (quoted in Slinger 1983).

The themes of race and class were also not uncommon in new reggae songs, but they did not seem to be developed far beyond what they had been before 1980. Tosh's "The Poor Man Feels It" on the same album is one example. A song by Michigan and Smiley characterizes "The Ghetto Man" as poor and Black, and forced to fight against his fellows:

> Tell my why the Ghettoman can't get no wuk
> Why the poorman don't have no luck
> Tell me why the blackman can't have fun
> Only the little ghettoman a fire big gun.

After 1980, both political parties occasionally embraced Rastafarian symbols and reggae music. The most outstanding example was the funeral of Bob Marley in the spring of 1981. Arranged by the government at taxpayer expense and held at the National Arena, attendance far surpassed previous state funerals, including Bustamante's and Norman Manley's. The arena was decorated with long drapes of red, green, and gold, portraits of Selassie, posters with biblical sayings, and concert backdrops. Marley lay in state while 150,000 people passed the casket. Police found it necessary at one point in the afternoon to use tear gas to disperse the crowd that was pressing to gain entrance. A month earlier, when it was clear that Marley was dying, Seaga had awarded him the Order of Merit, and a huge banner on the arena used his formal title: "Official Funeral Service of the Honourable Robert Nesta Marley, O.M." Among the groups participating were the Twelve Tribes, a Rastafarian organization with which Marley was associated; the Ethiopian Orthodox Church, into which Marley had been baptized the year before and whose archbishop for the Western Hemisphere presided over parts of the ceremony; reggae musicians, including Marley's family and band, who performed; and political leaders, who also, in their fashion, performed.

The governor general, Sir Florizel Glasspole, and Leader of the Opposition Michael Manley, read the lessons. Seaga gave the eulogy. Attendees remarked that the occasion was one of the very rare times that both Seaga and Manley had been present at the same function, and that it was the second time Marley had brought the two together — the first time more directly, at the Peace Concert in 1978.

Seaga's eulogy was dramatic. He praised Marley as "a vital part of the consciousness of this nation," whose "mission was to pursue humanity's search for justice and togetherness." Seaga found in Marley a hero of the Horatio Alger variety: "Born in a humble cottage ... he has bequeathed to us the message of his life: that with hard work and self-discipline, there is an open road to success." While Seaga may have perceived this as the message of Marley's life, it certainly was not the message of his music. As a closing, Seaga proclaimed "May his soul rejoice in the embrace of Jah! Ras Tafari!"

Seaga used the opportunity to announce the establishment of "Jamaica Park ... with gardens, murals, statues and shrines to honour the sons and daughters of Jamaica who have internationally honoured their country in the fields of culture, science or sports. Bob Marley's statue will be the first to be placed there with his guitar in hand, overlooking the playfields where little boys play...."

The story of this statue is illustrative of several elements of the complex relationship between reggae and Rastafari and Jamaican politics, notably the misplacing of some political gestures toward lower class religion and music and the hostility engendered among Jamaicans over pure representations. Seaga's announcement touched off some controversy in the *Gleaner* about whether or not a statue should be erected to honor Marley at all, much less at government expense. In one letter, the writer expounds upon the dangers that ganja poses to the health of the user, then asks: "is it wise, then, to erect a statue to the memory of the Hon. Robert Nesta Marley, a self-acclaimed ganja smoker? Will this not give wholesale licence, especially to the impressionable young, to practice this health-destroying, mind-distorting, self-abasing habit?" (DG 6/3/82).

Although sculpture and painting are not uncommon skills in the Rastafarian community, Seaga gave the commission for the statue to a Brown expatriate Jamaican without connections to that community, Christopher Gonzales. The sculpture was unveiled on the second anniversary of Marley's death, May 1983. The design, which had been approved by Seaga as minister of culture, was not wholly representative; it depicted Marley growing out of a rooted tree trunk, with a beard made of fruit. Fans who had gathered for the unveiling were not pleased; they jeered, shouted epithets, and threw missiles at the statue until Seaga ordered that it be removed to the National Gallery, where it now stands. A new statue has been commissioned, and it may yet be the first to grace "Jamaica Park." The land set aside for the park was cleared shortly after the Marley funeral, but no statues, murals, or gardens are yet in evidence. A visit to the site in 1982 revealed only a sow and two piglets appreciating the grassy field there.

The JLP government continued to memorialize Marley after his funeral. It issued a series of postage stamps with his picture and song lyrics imprinted upon them. A new performance center was built in Montego Bay and named for him. The Marley family was invited to various ceremonial occasions. The JLP's annual conference in 1982, however, revealed no use of Rasta symbols and little reggae music was played.

The PNP also venerated Marley and continued to use Rastafarian symbols. In an article in the *Barbados Sun* Manley reminisced about Marley's performances in the bandwagon concerts of 1971, long before Marley had attained international renown. He continued:

> Not so much as once did Marley compromise his
> art. He grew in sophistication, in the range of his
> concerns but never away from his roots and his
> commitments. Never did he seem to labour his
> theme.
> Here was art taking flight on wings which beat
> surely because they respond to signals longs since
> buried in the subconscious: inspiration and tech-
> nique joined in art itself." (*Barbados Sun*, 17 May,
> 1981)

In 1981, the PNP adopted a new slogan, "Redemption," the title of a song from Marley's final album (#8). At the PNP Women's Movement Conference in 1982, Rastafarian phrases and words from reggae songs were sprinkled liberally throughout the speeches, and reggae songs were played on the public address system.

The PNP arranged an event in 1982 for the presentation of the Norman Washington Manley Award for Excellence. The presention to reggae musician Jimmy Cliff was the least controversial part of the evening. The keynote speaker, on the other hand, was Harry Belafonte, who discussed the role of artists as "the protectors of history." He used the occasion to criticize the role the Reagan administration had taken in the Caribbean, in particular the Caribbean Basin Initiative:

> It is wise and important that we view carefully
> the bearer of the gift.
> Anywhere that the political and economic inter-
> ests of America have been extended, in most
> instances we have found strife, turmoil, assassin-
> ation, governments overthrown, peoples cruelly
> handled and mishandled. We have seen it in
> Argentina ... in Chile, ... all through Central
> America ... we have watched what we have done
> and those of us who call ourselves Americans with
> great pride weep because of the mischief. And
> Jamaica is now the new pawn. Jamaica will be

used one way or the other to illustrate that the American concept of domination, the American concept of you are only equal if you believe as I believe — you are only equal if you do as I say.... Then I say to you beware and be cautious of those who bring you the gifts.

The speech was broadcast live on radio and sparked angry protests from columnists and letter writers for the next several weeks. Some opposed Belafonte's making political remarks at a nonpolitical award ceremony; others felt that anyone who had made money in the United States should not criticize its government; still others called the remarks "interference" and likened them to Reagan's partisan remarks during his visit two months earlier. JLP MP Edwin Allen introduced a motion in the House to declare Belafonte persona non grata because he "engaged himself in an unwarranted and unsubstantiated attack on the Government of Jamaica and further indulged himself in making certain derogatory references to the relationship between this country and the United States of America" (DG 7/15/82). The motion was never taken to a vote.

The 1983 Election Campaigns

Seaga announced an agreement with the IMF on 23 November 1983 that was considered unusual because Jamaica had already exhausted several types of borrowing arrangements with the IMF (WG 12/12/83, 11). The new balance of payments loan agreement involved a 43 percent devaluation of the Jamaican dollar. Although Seaga couched the announcement in positive terms, the devaluation would bring on a significant cost of living increase, over and above the 18 percent increase in 1983 alone. Seaga, as one commentator put it, "seemed determined to have this election before the effects of the devaluation were worked through the economy" (Stone 1983, 61).

The PNP leaders who would be the most likely to respond to the government's announcement, Manley and P. J. Patterson, were both out of the country. Instead, the PNP's general secretary, Paul Robertson, issued the official statement the next day, which said that the party "condemns in the strongest terms the deception enacted on the Jamaican people by the Prime Minister.... In these circumstances, the only honourable thing would be for the Minister of Finance to resign. The Peoples National Party hereby calls for his resignation." (Seaga is the minister of finance as well as prime minister.) As one columnist sympathetic to the JLP, John Hearne, wrote, "Calling Mr. Seaga's character into question ... gave Mr. Seaga the justification to seize — on grounds of a moral smear — the political chance for which he had obviously been hungering" (WG 12/12/83, 13).

Seaga seized the day.   Amid a bell-ringing crowd of supporters at a mass rally that was broadcast live on radio and television, Seaga, with rather tortuous syntax, referred to the PNP statement of the day before: "Tonight I summon the people of this country to decide who has the authority to run the country.   Tonight I challenge those who challenge us to challenge that authority" (DG 11/27/83). It was Friday, 25 November; nomination day, Seaga announced, would be Tuesday, 29 November. Elections would be held 15 December.

Events did seem to fall in the JLP's favor. One of the major criticisms of Manley over the year before the election was that he was so frequently out of the country. At the time of Seaga's announcement, Manley was attending a socialist conference in Europe, providing Seaga with a double blessing. His absence and his ties with the socialists were called to the voters' attention at the same time. Seaga may have believed his own words when he told a rally at Half Way Tree Square the same weekend:

> God moves in a mysterious way his wonders to perform!   Nobody will ever convince me that destiny is not at work.... Can it be coincidence that all the things that happened in Grenada happened when an American task force with 2000 Marines, heading for Lebanon, could (be) diverted to Grenada? It is destiny at work! God moves in a mysterious way his wonders to perform!"   (DG 10/28/83, 1)

In the same speech he referred to Robertson, the author of the PNP statement that called on him to resign as minister of finance, as "some little feeble-minded person ... some midget ... some moral dwarf to question my honesty and integrity...."

By Sunday evening, PNP forces had been hastily reassembled. The National Executive Council (NEC) convened and debated the question of contesting the election. As a statement by P. J. Patterson pointed out, the entire leadership of the party "had on separate and several occasions made clear that the Party would on no account participate in an election until the new electoral list" was completed and other reforms implemented. The NEC endorsed this position; 128 voted against contesting the elections, reportedly also the Manley's position, and 14 favored contesting. Manley announced on Monday that the party would not contest. Seaga and his party, he asserted, had breached a "solemn agreement" not to hold general elections until the new voters list was completed; to use the 1980 list would disfranchise 180,000 young people and open the way to bogus voting because 100,000 dead or migrated Jamaicans were still on the rolls (DG 10/29/83).

The next day, nomination day, found most nomination centers in Kingston crowded with JLP supporters singing and ringing bells. In fifty-four constituencies the JLP candidates were unopposed, and hence were automatically considered elected. In six constituencies, the JLP candidates were challenged by either candidates from minor parties or independent candidates. Compared to 1980's 75,700 voters in the six constituencies, only about 25,500 voted in 1983. On 15 December, the Parliament of Jamaica was composed wholly of JLP members.

Even though one party boycotted and few Jamaicans voted, both parties waged campaigns. The fruits of this battle were gained in the field of public opinion rather than in parliamentary seats. There were two things in particular that the PNP wanted to influence: the relative standings of the parties in terms of percentage of popular support and public opinion on the time to hold the next general elections.

In the next section, the two parties' campaigns will be discussed. Then, the contents of the campaigns will be analyzed in terms of the same categories that guided the discussions of the four previous elections: class, race, anticolonialism, and Rastafari and reggae music.

The People's National Party Campaign

The activities of the Electoral Advisory Committee were central to the PNP's decision not to contest the election. The committee had been formed after the unanimous passage in Parliament of an amendment to the Representation of the People Act in 1979, and consisted of representatives of the parties and of three independent members. It was agreed that a new system would include certain features designed to prevent election fraud, such as photographic identification cards, thumb printing, house-to-house enumeration, and ultraviolet scanners to prevent multiple voting. Some of these features, it was agreed, were to be delayed until after the 1980 general elections.

Updating the voting list was, from the PNP's perpective, the minimum acceptable action and was the first priority of the Electoral Advisory Committee. Indeed, during the 1983 campaign period, an enumeration of voters was in progress, and the new list was scheduled for completion by July 1984.

Manley claimed that by September 1981, he had begun to doubt the intentions of the JLP government to honor its commitment to electoral reform (WG 12/12/83). The matter was discussed during the budget debate in 1982, when Manley accused the government of not acting in good faith on the question of electoral reforms. He continued, "we will not regard ourselves bound to any of the normal rules of cooperation or participation unless the solemn pledge given in 1980 is kept and adhered to in its strictest form" (DG 4/30/82). Seaga responded that the government intended to ensure that "the full programme of Electoral Reforms on which we agitated as an opposition (is) completed by us as a Government — inclusive of the photo identification card ... to ensure the elimination of bogus voting by impersonation, for the next election" (DG 5/1/82).

Indeed, the next month, the Jamaican Consulate issued a press release that reaffirmed the government's commitment; it dealt with a contract with security printers Thomas De La Rue General Services, Ltd., of England for the preparation of 1.2 million identity cards to be prepared by February 1984.

Manley's claim that the JLP broke a "solemn pledge" did not win universal sympathy. Seaga discounted it by saying that if there ever was a time when a party should not have participated, it was the JLP in the 1976 election, when so many JLP supporters had been detained. The PNP's decision on the 1983 elections, he said, showed a lack of "respect for democracy" and that the PNP feared "another beating" (DG 11/30/83, 1). Shortly after nomination day, Seaga issued a brief statement regretting the PNP decision not to participate, and added that "history will judge whether in doing so they have served their country well" (WG 12/12/83, 18).

JLP supporters emphasized other reasons for the PNP boycott. John Hearne, the *Gleaner* columnist, called it "a clear case of unpreparedness and cold feet" (WG 12/12/83, 11). Another columnist, writing under the pseudonym Paul Gordon called Seaga's statement regarding electoral reforms, quoted above, a "declaration of intent which was made a dead letter by the call on him to resign and the public impugning of his integrity." He further declared that "not to contest was, and is, a sign of cowardice" (DG 12/4/83, 14). Minister of Public Utilities Pearnel Charles likened the PNP boycott to men who "leave their wives" and "might never get a chance to go back." He also disagreed that Seaga had definitely made a "solemn pledge," and said it was the PNP that had reneged on its responsibilities (WG 12/19/83).

A number of organizations and a large part of the electorate supported the PNP viewpoint, or at least supported the call for new elections. The Jamaican Council of Churces called for a new election "as soon as possible under the new electoral system" (WG 12/12/83, 1). The Jamaica Baptist Union and the Jaycees of Jamaica concurred (*Rising Sun*, December 1983, 6). A Stone poll, the fieldwork for which was completed during the first week in December, showed that 59 percent of the respondents disagreed with Seaga's decision to hold elections on the 1980 voters list, and 70 percent believed that new elections should be held when the new list was completed (DG 12/16/83). Those polled split along party lines, with over 95 percent of supporters of each party agreeing with their party's position. They were, however, divided equally on the PNP boycott; 46 percent agreed with the decision; 47 percent disagreed. Stone reported that young people in particular were upset with and alienated by the JLP decision to hold elections with the old list (DG 12/18/83, 1).

The PNP promulgated its views in a series of mass meetings around the island for the three week period of the campaign and beyond. At a meeting at Halfway Tree Square in Kingston, for example, Manley told the crowd that "My first demand on behalf of my party is ... the minute the new system is ready ... this country must have elections the very next day. As long as 100,000 dead men in and 180,000 live men out, no elections" (DG 12/2/83).

In a major speech the day after nomination day, Manley announced that the PNP planned to start the People's Forum, which would serve as an arena for the expression of opposition opinion on government policy and major pieces of legislation. Calling the regrouping efforts of the PNP a "new beginning," Manley also announced the formation of a "shadow cabinet" of spokespersons in fifteen areas of government. Sixty constituency representatives were also named (DG 12/2/83, 1).

In response to charges that the PNP was not acting in the best interests of democracy by boycotting the elections, the People's Forum was said to reflect "the determination of the PNP to continue to discharge its responsibilities to Jamaica, to the democratic process and to the majority of people who look to it to form the next and legitimate government of Jamaica" (*Rising Sun*, December 1983, 8).

Manley emphasized that party members were not to "start trouble," an evident euphemism for political violence. "We seek no confrontation," he said at the mass meeting, "what we are going to do is within the law and within the constitution" (DG 12/2/83). It was, rather, the legitimacy of the new government that the party leader questioned: "Parliament don't have a magic by itself; it gets its authority from you. The day you're bogussed,

Parliament has no authority any more. The Parliament that is about to enter Gordon House on December 16 has no moral or political authority before the people of Jamaica ... we now have a bogus Government" (DG 12/2/83).

The People's Forum was criticized from several angles by JLP supporters. The first forum was scheduled to meet at the Pegasus Hotel, and columnist Winston Witter wrote that "the idea of a People's Forum ... to be held somewhere like the Pegasus Hotel, bears no merit for the poorer class of people whom the PNP claims to represent" (WG 12/12/83, 11). At Seaga's inauguration, he referred to the forum as the "Pegasus Parliament" and said he was certain Gordon House would "prove more interesting, rewarding, useful and purposeful" (DG 12/18/83, 1).

For the first time in several years, the PNP put a full-page advertisement in the *Gleaner*. Entitled "The Fairy Tale of 'Deliverance,'" it cited statistics on what went up: prices, the trade deficit, and the external debt; and what went down: agricultural production, the number of employed Jamaicans, and exports. "We will not live happily ever after," the advertisement predicted, and challenged the government to call elections when the new list is prepared. It went on to state that "the December 15 elections allow Edward Seaga to continue policies which will make the poor of Jamaica much poorer" (DG 12/18/83).

The Jamaica Labour Party Campaign

In the three-week campaign, the JLP set out to capitalize on those factors that had won it popularity in the past: the CBI and Grenada. It also made efforts to assuage people's fears of a "one-party state" and to put the blame for the parliamentary crisis on the PNP.

Although the CBI had been in existence for more than a year and Jamaica had already received funds through it, the implementation of the duty-free trade zones afforded President Reagan the opportunity to write Seaga a personal letter designating Jamaica as one of the beneficiaries under the act. A congressional delegation, from the House Ways and Means Committee, visited Jamaica to present the letter to Seaga. The announcement received a more prominent billing in the *Gleaner* than did Manley's announcement of the formation of the People's Forum the same day (DG 12/2/83, 1; WG 12/12/83).

The events in Grenada were likewise kept fresh in people's minds, and these were used to associate the PNP with the forces that overthrew Bishop. After the invasion, Prime Minister Seaga expelled the reporter for the Cuban news agency Prensa Latina, saying that he was involved in a plot to assassinate top leaders of the JLP. He also recited in Parliament a long list of Jamaicans who he said had traveled in Grenada, Cuba, and/or the Soviet Union. The list included many PNP supporters and, as it turned out, was inaccurate on a number of points. The climate of "witch-hunting" in which the list was presented offended even some staunch JLP supporters. Columnist Wilmot Perkins called it "ill-considered" (WG 10/21/83, 11), and economist Mark Ricketts called it "over-kill" (WG 10/21/83, 13).

As mentioned earlier, Seaga accused the PNP of disrespecting democracy by its boycott decision. He planned a number of steps to help compensate for the lack of a parliamentary opposition. He said at a mass meeting that "people based" organizations would be asked to provide representation at a higher level than the PNP's parliamentary opposition had provided (DG 11/30/83, 1). Minister of Public Utilities Pearnel Charles may have meant much the same when he told an employee group that under the new government, "the people will be the opposition" (WG 12/19/83). In his inaugural address, Seaga announced that the public would have the opportunity to participate in parliamentary debates. A particular problem arose in the case of the Senate. Ordinarily, the government nominates thirteen senators; the oppostion, eight. Seaga announced that he would nominate eight persons to the Senate "who are of national stature, having expertise in particular fields of vital interest and who are not connected to or supporters of the JLP." Given all his steps, Seaga spoke optimistically about the legitimacy of the new government: "We are poised to enter uncharted water politically but not without trepidation ... to meet this challenge with bold and creative thinking, generating exciting new political solutions which will no doubt have a bearing on the future even when the normal parliamentary form with government and opposition in Parliament is restored" (DG 12/18/83, 1)

The Use of Class Symbols and Class Conflict

References to class in the 1983 election period did not demonstrate any major shifts in the approach of the two parties. The JLP continued to avoid the issue of class divisions, and continued to stress overall national economic recovery without reference to the differential in benefits received, and hardships suffered by, different strata in society. For example, in a full-page *Gleaner* advertisement, the JLP accuses "others" of "tearing down, criticizing and undermining the economy," while "we are going ahead with a job that has to be done." The job is "nation-building" (DG 11/30/84, 24). As in 1980, unity of interests among classes is posited.

When Seaga announced the upcoming elections, he pursued this theme. He said that investors were waiting in the wings to see "how the next five years go" before making investments. "Well," he continued, "I decide we're not going to wait. I decide we want that five years now.... We want a road before us so that everybody may feel free so that they can invest because it means five more years before us that we can travel on the same road to prosperity" (WG 12/5/83).

In a nationally broadcast speech by U.S. Vice President Bush to the Jamaican Parliament six weeks before the election, he was even more explicit in asserting that the prosperity of the whole country was beneficial for all its strata, including the poor:

> Of course one of the most important considerations in choosing a path toward economic development is the condition of the very poorest members of society. As it turns out, a free economy is the best answer to their needs. When countries have adopted the free-market approach, the real incomes of the poor have risen as the country as a whole becomes more productive and prosperous. (WG 10/31/83)

A Stone poll early in the term showed that despite the JLP's victory in 1980, most Jamaicans did not consider that party interested in the plight of the poor. Only 36 percent of those polled said that the JLP was concerned, whereas 54 percent believed that the PNP was more concerned (EFE 8/31/81). Reporting the results of a recent survey of party support, Stone wrote that the public's rating of the JLP's overall performance is low. It suffers, he wrote, from a negative image of favoring the rich, laying off workers in hard times, and creating hardships for small farmers (DG 11/27/83). Elsewhere, he stated that the regular surveys demonstrate that the JLP is increasingly seen as insensitive to the needs of the poor and concerned only about the rich, businessmen, and the middle class. He attributed this to "the new pattern of conspicuous consumption taking place against the background of layoffs in manufacturing industries, inadequate employment creation ... lack of money among the majority classes and the decline in sales and earnings by higglers and small farmers" (*Gleaner Annual* 1982, 20).

It was in the PNP's interest to promote that image. The PNP's *Gleaner* advertisement, mentioned above, predicted that the JLP's policies would make "Jamaica's poor much poorer" (DG 12/18/83). In the 1982 Sectoral Debate, PNP MP Seymour Mullings accused the government of "fundamental insincerity to the cause of improving the social and material security of the working people," and of facilitating a "broad reactionary sweep against workers' rights" (DG 7/30/82).

There is evidence that the JLP has had difficulty holding onto the support of the middle and upper-middle classes, including signs of disenchantment with the government among members of organizations such as the Private Sector Organization of Jamaica and the Jamaica Manufacturers' Association, which had strongly supported the JLP in the 1980 elections. Carl Stone reported that members of the private sector felt that the JLP government was not consulting them enough on policy questions. Relations were further damaged by "corrupt practices" that plagued the issuing of trade licenses, including bribery to obtain these licenses from officials in the Industry and Commerce Ministry. He continued:

This was unfortunate for the JLP as the Industry and Commerce Ministry was expected to be the centre of close collaborative private sector linkages. Instead it became a battlefield of frustrations, accusations, and counter-accusations, and frequent quarrels between the government and the private sector. Although the private sector continued to support the government's overall ideological position and general policy goals, sharp disagreements over issues of strategy, tactics and power relations reduced private sector enthusiasm for the JLP into luke-warm support, weakened by increasing distrust of the government's intentions (*Gleaner Annual*, 1982, 36)

The Use of Race Symbols and Race Conflict

In the 1980-83 period, references to race were extremely rare, and in the 1983 campaign there were virtually none to be found. In the Prime Minister's Message on Independence Day, 1982, Seaga expressed the familiar "unity" theme in an address about nation-building:

This is not an easy thing to do: it requires a commitment to something beyond self and a steady vision of the country we want to build. It also requires that we have a clear vision about the things that unite us and that we promote these rather than those aspects of our lives — of which there are undoubtedly many in a post-colonial society such as ours -- which can so easily be exploited to engender divisiveness and hate. (Seaga 8/2/82).

Seaga may have employed other symbols, notably heroes, to appeal to the majority Black population. When Vice President Bush visited Jamaica a few days before the invasion of Grenada, Seaga requested that he discuss with President Reagan the possibility of a posthumous presidential pardon for Jamaican Black nationalist Marcus Garvey.

Bush promised that the request would receive "highest consideration" (DG 12/4/83). On the same visit, Bush and Seaga took part in a ceremony honoring the slave rebellion leader Sam Sharpe in Montego Bay (WG 10/31/83).

Although former Prime Minister Hugh Shearer is minister of foreign affairs, Seaga seemed to have taken on the role of clarifying Jamaica's actions in Grenada and in some other aspects of foreign policy. However, one subject seems to be left strictly to Shearer: South Africa. For example, Shearer issued a statement on International Day for the Elimination of Racism condemning apartheid as "the most vicious form of racism ... a crime against humanity, a crime against the conscience and dignity of all mankind." He further condemned South Africa's actions in Namibia, which he said "expose a determination ... to frustrate the inalienable right of the people of Namibia to self-determination and independence" (Jamaican Consulate Release, 3/31/83).

Racial groups within Jamaica remained a little-mentioned topic in political statements. The PNP may have shied away from such references because the party had been criticized so strongly and effectively in 1980 for fostering "divisiveness." Only the Workers Party of Jamaica has pointed out with some regularity the different standards of living among racial groups. In its statement on Seaga's first IMF agreement, for example, it said that the pact would increase economic hardships for the Black majority, while a 5 percent minority of Jamaicans would grow richer and stronger (EFE 4/26/81).

Anticolonialism and Anti-imperialism

As is obvious from the first part of this chapter, fear of Cuba and of communism remained stronger than anti-imperialism in Jamaican politics. The fears were fostered by the JLP, which combined it with efforts to implicate the PNP in "international communist" plots. Surveys showed that while anticommunism dwindled around mid-term of the JLP government — when 48 percent opposed Jamaica's break with Cuba (EFE 11/83) — its strength was renewed when Maurice Bishop was killed in Grenada, evidently by individuals claiming to be Marxists-Leninists.

The JLP seized the incident immediately, before the invasion, to draw parallels between the situation in Grenada and "what might have been" in Jamaica.   A JLP statement issued then said:

> The Bishop regime was part of an international conspiracy spearheaded by Cuba, designed to enslave the people of the Caribbean.... The events in Grenada have followed established patterns that have been adhered to in several preceding government takeovers ... it is our duty to learn from them in order to ensure that the same thing will not happen here.

The statement goes on to say that Cuba had planned much the same chain of events in Jamaica during Manley's last term:

> What happened in Grenada could easily have happened here but fortunately, the innate good sense of the Jamaican people saved the day. Let us not be complacent, however, believing the threat has vanished. The Victory of 1980 has merely delayed the time-table, and the security of Jamaica is not any less threatened now than it was then. (WG 10/31/83, 7)

A *New York Times* report on the campaign noted that at a JLP rally in West Rural St. Andrew, one of the six contested seats, the organizers "warmed up the already sympathetic crowd" by showing an American-made videotape called "The Liberation of Grenada" (11 December, 1983, 2E).

JLP advertisements also stressed the anticommunist theme.   Juxtaposed with "improved relations with the United States" in a list of achievements are the words "Gone are the fears of foreign domination and alien ideology" (DG 11/30/83, 24).   The ideologies of the United States are obviously not considered "alien";   as Bush pointed out in his speech before the Grenada invasion, "In an historical sense, Jamaica and the U.S. are brothers, united in a common experience and shared values.... Jamai-

ca and the United States are true collaborators" (WG
10/31/83, 13). This bring to mind another parallel with the
1960s. When Bustamante mobilized forces against the
West Indies Federation, he claimed that the federation
would cause Jamaica to be dominated by Trinidad and
Tobago. The JLP began using the slogan "freedom" in this
context. The demise of the federation may have opened up
each island to further economic exploitation by the large
industrialized countries, but Jamaica was certain of its
freedom from Trinidadian hegemony.

As is evident in the above account of the PNP's first-
term opposition, anticommunism was a factor in pushing
the party toward more centrist positions. Manley tirelessly
denied that the party was communist. However, he was
not apologetic about the party's cordial relations and his
own friendship with Fidel Castro, and before the Grenada
invasion reiterated his position that diplomatic relations
with Cuba would be reestablished were the party to form
the next government. This was "viewed with alarm" by the
JLP (WG 10/31/83, 7).

Concerning the role of the United States in Jamaican
politics, Manley frequently repeated his conviction that the
Central Intelligence Agency helped to defeat the PNP
through a destabilization process and a campaign of violence and "disinformation." His book, published in 1982, is
the most thorough statement of his argument (Manley
1982). In an appearance in New York City Manley declared, "I've always made it clear that we have never found
the 'smoking gun,'" but he said incidents of violence to
scare away tourists stopped "almost instantly after the
election" (*Daily Challenge* 9 March, 1983). As mentioned
earlier, Manley accused the Seaga government of pandering
to United States preferences when it broke relations with
Cuba in 1981.

One item that had gained significance as a symbol of
anticolonialism or anti-imperialism was the kariba jacket
or guayabera shirt, as described in previous chapters. The
Gleaner's regular cartoonist, a Syrian who supports the
JLP, usually depicts "communists" (e.g. WG 10/21/81, 12)
and PNP members (e.g. DG 12/2/83, 8) with karibe jackets.
In early 1982, probably in an effort to harass the single
PNP MP who consistently dressed in this way, D. K. Dun-

can, the speaker of the House declared a parliamentary dress code. As of April 7, MPs, visitors, and journalists were required to dress "with propriety," operationally defined as no short sleeve karibas and no guayabera shirts (EFE 3/27/82).

In other ways, the JLP did not shy away from symbols of colonialism. Cultural activities included a restoration of so-called Great Houses and artifacts of European plantation life (DG 6/19/82). One JLP member close to these developments said that these restorations celebrate both the European and African heritage of Jamaica; they are of European design but were executed by African slave artisans (#29).

A related incident was a disagreement over the name of a park in the parish of Trelawny. It had long been called Victoria Park, named after the nineteenth-century British monarch. Under the PNP, its name had been changed to Uriah Rowe Park, commemorating a Black PNP member who was the first mayor of the town of Falmouth. When the JLP council voted to revert to the park's original name, the PNP accused it of being infiltrated by "a vestige of old colonialism" (EFE 12/4/83).

Rastafari and Reggae

There was very little use of Rastafarian words and symbols and of reggae music in the 1983 campaign. Accounts of mass meetings make no mention of musicians performing live to attract an audience, nor were there special concerts organized by the parties. The sole use of reggae lyrics found was Seaga's statement that the PNP boycotted the election because it feared "another beating. Dem draw bad card," he said, a reference to the popular song of 1980 (DG 11/30/83, 1).

Two catchwords that had significance for Rastafarians, the JLP's "Deliverance" and the PNP's "Redemption," had both been abandoned. The tapes of party songs and some compatible reggae songs had become a routine opening for party meetings, but respondents could not recall any new songs added to the repertory.

Results

As Jamaicans learned only after the one-party government was already a "given," the new voters list would have
been extremely favorable for the PNP.   Carl Stone's
survey, conducted after nomination day, found that, with
the 1980 voters list, 51 percent supported the JLP and 49
percent the PNP.   However, of those who would be on a
new voters list, only 45 percent would support the JLP and
55 percent the PNP (FFJ Newsletter, February 1984).

The most important results of the election may have
been the revitalization of the PNP.   Manley had been
accused before the election of not seeming to want to take
power, preferring a quiet opposition and a multitude of
international speaking engagements.   With a new network
of constituency representatives, a true shadow cabinet, and
a procedure for regularly and systematically generating
and publicizing views in opposition to the government, the
party stands in a far better position than it did at the end
of 1980.

The JLP, on the other hand, has made the obvious short-
term gain of holding a monopoly on state power and
prestige.   On the other hand, it has offended the fierce
attachment to the forms of the electoral process that,
ironically, the JLP itself so carefully inculcated among
Jamaicans since 1978.

What remains unclear is when the next elections will be
held. Although Seaga said he wanted to give investors five
more years of the same government (WG 12/5/83), he is by
no means bound to wait the full term before dissolving
Parliament again. When he chooses to do so will depend on
two factors. First, the government's popularity may decline as Jamaicans feel the full effects of devaluation.
The government's national and international prestige may
suffer if Jamaicans continue to feel that the 1983 elections
were a violation of their democratic rights. It is probable
that, in the case of declining popularity, Seaga will resist
calling elections that he perceives his party will lose until
a certain threshold is reached, beyond which the government's legitimacy would increasingly be called into question and earlier elections would be the only way to ease

tensions. Second, what happens in Jamaica is somewhat dependent on the outcome of the 1984 presidential election in the United States. A Republican victory would assure Seaga of continued support from the United States. A Democratic victory may create an atmosphere more tolerant of change in the Jamaican government.

In any case, the 1983 election left many Jamaicans and others in the Caribbean dismayed and anxious, though in disagreement about who was at fault. The Trinidad and Tobago newspaper *Express* called it "a pyrrhic victory," curiously the same words Fidel Castro used to describe the U.S. invasion in Grenada, and "a most unhealthy political development for Jamaica" (DG 12/2/83). A similar boycott by the opposition had taken place in Trinidad in 1971, resulting in a new opposition forming when two government members abandoned their party to form a new one.

Jamaica's Anglican Bishop Neville DeSouza found a certain irony in the one-party government, which, he said, was "not the desire of Jamaicans nor desirable from any standpoint. We went to Grenada to help them preserve the democratic way of life and found that within a month we could well have presided over the demise of ours" (WG 12/26/83).

8

Conclusion:
Symbolic Politics, Conflict and Democracy

This book began with the questions: Why did Jamaican
political parties use Rastafarian symbols and reggae music
in their electoral campaigns? To what extent did they do
so? How did their use of symbols change over five elections? Which of the available symbols did they use? One
possible reason that politicians used the symbols may be
that they helped to attract the support of groups that are
formed by the social structures in every postcolonial,
plural society, and that are severally vying for a voice in
the affairs of government. If so, the changing use of
Rastafarian symbols and reggae music over seventeen
years will be able to shed some light on the changing
salience of social groups formed by divisions within the
society.

In this chapter, the changing salience of class and race
will be discussed first. Second, the relative prominence of
anticolonialism will be explored. Finally, the political role
of Rastafari and reggae over the years will be presented,
including the importance of these in the future of Jamaican politics.

The Salience of Class and Class Conflict

One difficulty in the design of this study lay in the
attempt to distinguish symbols of race and of class in a
society in which racial strata and socioeconomic classes
coincide to the extent that they do in Jamaica. In this
social structure, which Hoetink calls "horizontal layering"

290

(1972, 29), race and class labels are often used interchangeably in ordinary speech.   A symbol whose overt
referent is racial may be imbued with a deeper meaning
referring strictly to class. Nevertheless, some brief comments can be made about the changing salience of class
symbols in the five Jamaican elections.

When Jamaica held its first election as an independent
nation, the Jamaica Labour Party had a reputation for
representing the poor or the "small man," but it also
traditionally had received the support, electoral and financial, of the wealthiest section of the society. The JLP's
1967 electoral propaganda intimated that the party could
represent the interests of all classes in society. Some
Labour Party leaders were known as champions of the poor,
notably Bustamante, who did not run for Parliament but
who remained titular head of the party, and Seaga, who
was credited with introducing the term "have-nots" to
Jamaica and who represented one of the poorest urban
constituencies in Jamaica.

The People's National Party was the reputed representative of the middle class and those who aspired to be middle
class, that is, the better-off sections of the lower class.
The PNP systematically introduced notions of class and
class conflict into its electoral propaganda of 1967, asserting that the JLP was governing in the interests of the
wealthy. The party made several specific promises that
were in the interest of the lower class, such as a minimum
wage law. The PNP, well aware that Bustamante was
known as a supporter of the causes of the poor, took
advantage of his resignation from active politics to imply
that the JLP would be a different party without him.

In 1967, only one Rastafarian symbol was used in connection with the question of class interests, and that
appeared in a letter to the *Gleaner* rather than in the
partisan propaganda proper.

In 1969, members of the radical organization Abeng tied
issues of race and class and introduced symbols of Rastafari. It addressed the problems of unemployment, poverty,
and the role of foreign capital in Jamaica, and popularized
the term *sufferers*. It was during this period that Rastafari
became popular among youths of the middle class and of
the better-off sections of the lower class.

In the 1972 election campaign, issues of class received much wider attention than in the previous election. The PNP made a concerted effort to associate itself with the interests of the lower class, and used Rastafari and reggae toward this end. The JLP's claim that its government had brought progress and prosperity to Jamaica was met with the PNP's charge that the government had not distributed the wealth but, instead, had used it to enrich government ministers personally. It was those who had grown rich on corruption who were the target of Manley's attacks, not the indigenous or foreign upper class as a whole. The corrupt rich were the group that Manley menaced with the Rod of Correction, a symbol that resonated profoundly with the Rastafarians.

Beside stirring up anger against the corrupt rich, Manley declared himself a "Sufferers' man" and promised a government that would solve the problems of sufferers. The term itself was popularized by the Rastafarians, and Manley presented it frequently in connection with other Rastafarian symbols and reggae music, such as the song whose title became the PNP's main slogan, "Better Must Come." Although the party did not express a consistent ideology of class conflict, its candidates promised that the poor would enjoy more material goods and a more equitable distribution of wealth under a PNP government.

Perhaps in reaction to the formidable attacks from the PNP, the JLP placed more emphasis in this election than in 1967 on what the government had done for the poor, including a national insurance scheme that provided pensions for some of the elderly, and the greater availablility of secondary school places for the children of the poor. But the Labour Party still did not tie itself to the interests of any one group, as Manley had done with the "sufferers." Instead, the JLP accused the PNP of fostering "class hatred," and claimed that the JLP government could improve the condition of the poor without antagonizing the well-to-do.

Although one Labour supporter described the PNP in a letter to the *Gleaner* as the party of the middle class, it was clear that this characterization was eroding. The JLP propaganda itself did not level this charge at the PNP, as Bustamante had done in elections before the country gained independence.   The JLP did not use Rastafarian symbols or reggae music in 1972 in connection with any issues of the lower class in its national campaign.

By 1976, the PNP had adopted a more or less coherent philosophy to guide policy decisions: democratic socialism. A majority of voters understood democratic socialism to mean a commitment to the needs and interests of the poor. Interest in the questions of class and class conflict reached its highest point in this election. The PNP emphasized the benefits to the poor of the programs and legislation that the government had introduced in its first term, and extended its analysis of class conflict beyond simply contrasting the life chances of the poor with those of the corrupt rich as it had done in 1972.   To continue the programs that benefited the poor, the PNP admitted that other parts of society would have to make sacrifices. The party stopped short of condemning capitalists as a class, but defined capitalism as a system that brought economic prosperity to the few while the many suffered.   The candidates of the PNP characterized the JLP as the party of capitalists "who resist change" and who want to "free up the rich so they can exploit the poor." Manley condemned those who had fled Jamaica to avoid paying the higher taxes that his government had imposed, but businessmen who worked "within the bounds of the national interest and the rights of the people" were welcomed under democratic socialism.

The PNP used commissioned Rastafarian music as a frame in which to advertise the programs it had introduced for the benefit of the poorest section of the lower class, but did not use noncommissioned music as directly as it had in 1972.   Party members continued to use Rastafarian words and began to dress in ways similar to the Rastafarians, but campaign officials considered that reiterating the party's record of programs was the best way to convey its commitment to easing the lives of the poorest in the society.

The JLP, again, repeated the charge that the PNP was fostering class hatred. Some JLP supporters accused the PNP of "pampering the proletariat" and of mismanaging the finances of government. The JLP overestimated the electorate's fear of socialism and tried to promote it by presenting democratic socialism as a system under which everyone would be uniformly poor. The sole direct statement on classes by the JLP claimed that the party would try to build a stronger middle class by "lifting the poor high-up." That is the extent of the JLP's references to class as well as the only use of a Rastafarian symbol (the phrase *high-up*) in connection with class in the JLP materials.

In 1976 both parties used reggae music as a way of drawing crowds of lower class people to mass outdoor meetings. The PNP had the edge over the opposition party in that respect, because it had used reggae music and hired many musicians in the previous election. The government planned a concert with Bob Marley as headliner, and this performance was made accessible to the urban lower class; it was a free concert held near downtown Kingston. When Marley was shot by gunmen several days before the concert, the PNP implied that the JLP was responsible for the shooting and that the JLP wanted to prevent "the masses" from enjoying the concert.

In 1980, the PNP accused the JLP of wanting to "slip up beside those with money." By that time, it seemed like a good idea to most Jamaicans. The economy had undergone an unprecedented period of "negative growth"; economic austerity measures imposed by the IMF agreements, and shortages of all imported goods had taken a heavy toll of the PNP's popularity. In 1980, unlike 1976, the JLP succeeded in convincing the electorate that socialism was causing poverty. The Labour Party laid all of Jamaica's economic troubles at the doorstep of PNP mismanagement, and implied that the government's attention to foreign policy matters was distracting it from the plight of the poor at home. JLP graffiti artists scrawled "The Poor Can't Take No More" on walls around Kingston, and candidates promised that when the JLP formed the government, money would "jingle in your pockets."

The JLP used two Rastafarian songs in the 1980 election campaign in relation to class interests; both were concerned with food shortages. The party's supporters paraphrased a line from the song that contained the PNP's slogan "Stand Firm" to imply that if the PNP were reelected people would have no food to eat. Second, the JLP made extensive use of a reggae song by a Rastafarian singer about the food shortages and their devastating effects on the poor.

The PNP was on the defensive in the 1980 election, and still emphasized the programs, instituted in its first term, that benefited the poor.   Many of the programs had suffered severe cutbacks under the terms of the IMF agreements.   The party used the National Heroes as symbols that highlighted the government's commitment to the struggles of the poor, and tried to present the JLP as the party of exploitative capitalists. The PNP used few Rastafarian symbols and reggae music in this election, in direct association with its policies toward the lower class.

Three years later money still failed to jingle in many Jamaican pockets, and relief was not in sight. The JLP continued with the tone set by Bustamante, enlisting United States Vice President George Bush's assistance in convincing the electorate that the interests of all classes could be served simultaneously, and that a free market economy was the only way this feat could be accomplished. The PNP continued, in turn, to accuse the government party of lack of concern about the poor.

In summary, references to class and to class conflict increased in importance through 1976, when the actual class coalitions supporting the two parties changed significantly, and when the PNP lost many of its middle- and upper-class supporters. Once the party of the middle class, the PNP has clearly effected a change in that image. Up to the 1983 election, public opinion polls demonstrated that most people continued to define the PNP as the party "most interested in the poor."

Rastafarian symbols and reggae music were used most effectively to associate the political party with the interests of the lower class in two elections, by the PNP in 1972 and by the JLP in 1980. In both cases, it was the victorious opposition party that used the symbols and music most effectively in this way, and in both cases, the music used was not specifically commissioned but was original reggae music that took on political meaning after the fact of its production.

How will references to class figure in future campaigns? The parties' images seem firmly entrenched now, and such an image as the JLP has with regard to class relations will probably not work to its advantage. A survey in 1981 of Jamaican lower class youths aged thirteen to eighteen years sheds light on what may be expected of the newest voters in the elections to come: only 14 percent of these youths believed that Jamaica was a democratic country. In further exploration of this curious finding, Carl Stone discovered that a majority of the youths defined democracy as a means of adapting government to the needs of the poor.   About 30 percent responded that Jamaica was definitely not democratic because the poor had no real voice in government.   Significantly, 40 percent thought that communism was "a good thing," and believed that it helped poor people and thus represented "true democracy" (EFE 9/9/81).

The promises of "deliverance" made by the JLP in its 1980 campaign were easily believed at the time. The fragile economy of Jamaica is easily affected by the vagaries of the world economy; a discovery of bauxite in Sardinia, a decision made in a comfortable board room thousands of miles away — any number of locally uncontrollable incidents can leave thousands of workers redundant, cause a substantial increase in the external debt, and make economic plans obsolete overnight. Such are the circumstances that each successive government in Jamaica has appealed to the electorate to understand, and that each successive opposition party has called a cover-up for mismanagement. As the promises of "deliverance" for the poor fade against the realities of the Jamaican economy, the poor will reinvest their hopes. The PNP, which, on this issue, already is ahead in popular opinion, will doubtless try in future elections to rekindle hopes that "better must come."

The Salience of Race and Racial Conflict

The Rastafarians were clearly in the vanguard of racial consciousness in the early to mid-1960s. Some informants perceived that Black power philosophy was imported from the United States and "legitimated" Rastafari in Jamaica (e.g. #14), yet the "Twenty-one Points" and the campaign of Ras Sam Brown predated the heightened activity of the

American Black power movement. But the Rastafarians' influence was minimal in the early 1960s. Ras Sam Brown, an independent candidate in the Blackest and poorest constituency in Jamaica, lost miserably in 1962, as did his Brown PNP opponent, to a White candidate.

References to race in 1967 were rare and indirect. Neither party questioned the validity of the national motto, "Out of Many, One People." Martin Luther King, Jr., had given an address at the University of the West Indies in Kingston two years before the elections, and the PNP adopted at least one of the songs popularized in the American civil rights movement. There is evidence that symbols with an African resonance, such as the name "Burning Spear," were used locally, especially in the Western Kingston constituency, by both the PNP and the JLP candidates. On the national level, only the JLP referred to Africa, first when the party's advertisements highlighted visits of African leaders, including Haile Selassie, to Jamaica during the Labour Party's tenure in office. Second, the JLP also promised to explore the possibility of Jamaicans migrating to Africa for employment, a significant promise given the high degree of interest in repatriation among Rastafarians at the time. The only reference to South Africa and apartheid was also in the JLP materials.

The period between the 1967 and 1972 elections saw a spread of the Black power movement throughout the Caribbean, influenced in large part by writers and activists in the United States. The JLP government, eager to present Jamaica to the West as a stable, orderly, and nonrevolutionary nation in which one could safely invest one's capital, was not sympathetic. The government banned both imported Black power literature and Jamaican reggae songs that were even mildly critical of the government. When it banned a young radical professor and black nationalist, Walter Rodney, university students marched in protest and sparked riots in downtown Kingston. Among Rodney's "subversive activities," according to the government, was associating with Rastafarians.

Abeng, a radical newspaper that was published by sympathizers of Rodney's cause, espoused Black nationalism and associated reggae and Rastafari with that philosophy.

Several former members of the organization that published the paper worked in the PNP's 1972 campaign.

Informants reported a strong association between the PNP's 1972 campaign and Black nationalism. The association may have begun when the JLP, in an attempt to discredit the opposition PNP, blamed it for the Rodney riots. Manley supported some of the causes of the Black nationalists, such as the proposal to teach African history in Jamaican schools, and praised the concept of "Black power." The PNP freely adopted the slogans of the American Black power movement for use in its own campaign; however, the party avoided direct, overt references to Black nationalism.

The PNP's use of Rastafarian symbols and reggae music was closely associated with their use in *Abeng* and with Black nationalism. The first song the party adopted in this period was "Everything Crash," which had been discussed in *Abeng*, and in the campaign one physical prop candidates used was the *abeng*, or cow-horn, itself. The Rod of Correction was reputedly of African origin, and its threatened use was not inconsistent with the way such rods were used in premissionary slave religions.

The JLP did not seem to make a special appeal to Black voters qua Black voters in 1972. One JLP candidate used a slogan that a PNP candidate had used in the 1969 by-election, "Young, Gifted and Black," but the primary thrust of the Labour Party's advertisements was to discredit and deplore the PNP's "injecting race into the campaign." They also tried to appeal to voters' fears of the militancy of Black power. The Labour Party did not use Rastafarian symbols in 1972 in connection with racial divisions, except in a negative way, to try to convince the electorate that the PNP wanted to set up an anti-Christian government.

The parties faced a different set of racial issues in 1976: a White man had been chosen leader of the Labour Party. The PNP government's first term in office had been characterized by the institution of a number of social programs to benefit the poorest section of the lower class, a group overwhelmingly Black. Some informants said that the PNP could now afford to abandon Black nationalism. But, perhaps because the leader of the opposition was an easy target, the PNP's unofficial campaign (i.e. unsigned leaflets) accused the JLP of representing only White and, more specifically, Syrian interests.

While race was important in the PNP's 1976 campaign, Rastafarian symbols were not used as referents to racial issues. The unofficial leaflets referred to race directly; the official campaign concentrated on reminding voters of the government's support of African liberation struggles and its repeal of the ban on books written by Black nationalists.

The JLP studiously avoided overt statements on race in 1976. The party did stress the fact that Seaga had brought Garvey's remains to Jamaica, and emphasized Seaga's achievements in the field of culture, including music promotion, in an effort to associate the JLP with the cultural interests of Blacks. Thus the party referred to races in Jamaica as cultural groups, but did not acknowledge conflict based upon race. Rather, it tried to present Jamaica as a unified if not quite homogeneous nation. The party's own lack of unity sometimes made that presentation difficult.

The Labour Party used a number of Rastafarian words and phrases in 1976, and may have directed these toward Black audiences. But it did not use the symbols to mask issues of race. Rather, JLP activists recognized that focusing on racial conflict would clearly not be in the interests of their party. They also perceived that Seaga, as a White man, would be seen as patronizing if he used Rastafarian symbols frequently; however, he sometimes used Rastafarian phrases in his campaign speeches.

The JLP's attempts to present the country as united despite racial differences proved to be more successful in 1980. Propaganda against the PNP's "racism" ran high and the PNP's song that called attention to Seaga's foreign birth was frequently vilified as racist.

In the 1980 election campaign, the ambiguity of cultural nationalism as a tool of propaganda was exposed. The PNP had been associated with Black nationalism more strongly than the JLP, and in the campaign, JLP supporters used Black nationalism against the incumbent party. As part of its anticommunist stance the JLP stressed Garvey's conflicts with communists, and one JLP supporter called on the defunct Black Panther Party to legitimize anti-Cuban sentiments. The JLP made effective use of an alternative set of symbols — Revivalism —to demonstrate the "Black" qualities of its leader

The PNP, clearly on the defensive, continued to remind the electorate of the government's support of African liberation movements and to assert the continuity between the struggles of Marcus Garvey and other Black Jamaican heroes and the present PNP government. Some factions of the PNP continued to use Black nationalist rhetoric, but the party evidently overestimated the voters' reluctance to vote for a party led by a White man.

References to race in 1983 were limited to an occasional oblique mention of Marcus Garvey or a brief condemnation of apartheid. The current state of domestic race relations was not alluded to in the major statements of the two mainstream parties.

In summary, race was most important in the election of 1972, when Black nationalism was fresh in the minds of the voters. The PNP used Black nationalist symbols frequently in that election, and the party's use of Rastafarian symbols was geared to reach voters with Black nationalist sentiments. Throughout the five elections, the JLP avoided the issue of racial conflict, with the exception of some use of Black nationalists' anticommunism in 1980.

The uncontested election in 1983 brought as few references to race to the fore as in 1967. But that fact, as was seen in the aftermath of the latter election, is no reason to believe that the issue of racial inequality is dead. Just as the uprisings of 1968 were sparked by developments among Blacks in the United States, so too the campaign of the Reverend Jesse Jackson in 1984 may affect political trends in Jamaica. The Jamaican electorate cannot but be affected by a Black American mainstream politician conducting a fairly successful campaign, particularly one that has been as international in scope as Jackson's has been.

As mentioned in chapter 1, for each contested election the candidates' pictures in the *Gleaner* were coded for racial phenotype. Race was seen, as Jamaicans define it, as a continuous variable, coded from 1 (White) to 5 (Black). The results of this exercise are presented in Table 8.1. Several points need to be made about the results. First, it is noteworthy that Corporate Area candidates tend to be

lighter than rural candidates. This is not surprising; the
Brown and White population is concentrated in the Corporate Area (Francis 1963).   Second, aside from the urban-
rural differences that are consistent for both parties, the
most striking difference is the change in the color of PNP
candidates in 1980, when the PNP selected a greater
number of darker candidates to stand in the election than
either party had ever done before.

Table 8.1
Mean Racial Scores for
Parliamentary Candidates 1967 – 1980
(5 = Black; 1 = White)

	1967 (N)	1972	1976	1980
PNP				
Total	3.25(53)	3.30(53)	3.50(60)	4.18(60)
Corporate Area	2.54(11)	2.82(11)	3.10(15)	4.13(15)
Rural	3.42(42)	3.43(42)	3.64(45)	4.20(45)
JLP				
Total	3.17	3.26	3.43	3.30
Corporate Area	3.27	3.00	2.80	2.66
Rural	3.14	3.33	3.64	3.51
Winners				
Total	3.40	3.37	3.25	3.42
Corporate Area	3.26	2.09	2.67	3.20
Rural	3.42	3.37	3.44	3.49

Source: Photographs in the *Daily Gleaner*, 1967 – 1980.

This second observation may be interpreted as a delayed effect of the PNP's commitment to the cause of Black nationalism a decade earlier. The efforts that the party made in the period before the 1972 election to demonstrate its commitment to change in the status of Blacks in Jamaica, and the grass-roots organizing techniques that the party adopted at that time may have attracted a new group of activists who reached the level of candidate material only in 1980.

A third aspect of the results to be noted is the trend in the JLP's Corporate Area candidates. In 1967, the JLP candidates were nearly the same as the PNP's as far as racial phenotype is concerned. While the JLP's rural candidates remained basically the same over the years, the trend for the Corporate Area was toward more lighter-skinned candidates. As party leader, Seaga had the prerogative to draw into the higher ranks the party activists with whom he was personally associated. The individuals whom Seaga has brought into the higher ranks of the party have been more frequently White or Brown than Black.

The Salience of Anti-Colonialism

In chapter 1 the possibility was raised that political parties may have used Rastafarian symbols and music, as a pseudotraditional culture, to demonstrate to the voters how different the power of the JLP or the PNP was from that of the old colonial order. In the course of the research it was found that anti-British sentiment was not particularly strong, but the tangential questions of foreign ownership, foreign influence, and imperialism were provocative ones.

In the 1967 election, the PNP tried to convince the electorate that the JLP was "traveling the same colonial road" as Jamaica's first government in independence. But the accusation probably did not ring true because of Bustamante's early struggles with the colonial government of the late 1930s. The anniversary of his release from detention was celebrated shortly before the election; the party and the union apparently strove to keep the memories fresh. But at the same time, Bustamante was on warm terms with the British, including the former governor who had detained him. Busta had been knighted in 1953. The JLP did mention in its advertisements, however, that its foreign policy had had an anticolonial focus.

The 1972 election saw relatively little interest in the issues of postcolonialism, such as foreign ownership of economic enterprises, on the part of the political parties, although Rastafarian music that was used by the PNP referred to the period of colonialism and slavery as not different from the current "Babylon." Both parties supported the idea of bringing more economic enterprises under Jamaican control; the JLP promised to do this "the Jamaican Way: Gradually." Although *Abeng* had criticized the degree to which enterprises in Jamaica were under foreign control, neither party dwelt on its program to alter that state of affairs.

By 1976 "imperialism" was firmly rooted in the PNP's vocabulary. Manley's friendship with Fidel Castro and his open admiration of the Cuban government was justified with reference to the fact that both Cuba and Jamaica had had the experience of colonial domination. Manley boasted that his government had put the multinationals "under heavy manners" with the bauxite levy, and emphasized Jamaica's participation in the struggle of the entire Third World for a new international economic order. The PNP accused the developed world of interference in Jamaica's internal affairs. "C.I.A. Out!" was the graffito of the day; similar sentiments were expressed in reggae music produced by Rastafarians. The PNP reminded the electorate of the benefits of Cuban friendship with a song that also used Rastafarian symbols. Bob Marley was said to be an anti-imperialist singer whom the JLP had tried to silence. Nonetheless, there was some ambivalence on the part of Rastafarians toward Cuba, which had supported the revolution in Ethiopia. Probably the strongest symbol of anti-imperialism and anticolonialism used by the PNP was its abandonment of jackets and ties.

The JLP's "program" for 1976 was called "nationalism," but the party emphasized that it would change the degree of foreign control over economic enterprises by "moral suasion" rather than force. The JLP considered reggae music an appropriate symbol in itself of nationalism, in that it was a truly Jamaican cultural product. Enjoyment of some of that music by then had spread into the middle class; therefore it resonated well with the "unity" theme of the JLP.

In 1980 the parties were decidedly polarized about the question of foreign influence and capital in Jamaica. Seaga said that one of Jamaica's greatest assets was its physical proximity to the United States, and promised to make a concerted effort to attract foreign capital. The PNP, on the other hand, was embittered and divided after its experience with the International Monetary Fund, and some of its candidates were outspokenly anti-American. By 1980, the parties' stands on the issues had become so clear-cut and conspicuous that symbols would have been redundant.

The three years after that election did not bring many new developments to the parties' positions, except that the JLP's position shaped policy and hence its results were visible for the first time since the new leadership took control over the party. Abandoning hope of bringing economic enterprises more under local control — even "the Jamaican way: Gradually" — the JLP embarked on an ambitious effort to attract foreign investors, through improved relations with the ruling class of its northern neighbor. The U.S. Business Committee on Jamaica and the provisions in the Caribbean Basin Initiative legislation for tax breaks for investors were parts of the plan.

The JLP carefully tried to channel the Jamaicans' high regard for independence into a desire to be free from the "alien ideology" represented by Cuba and, until October 1983, by Grenada. It used the emotionally laden word *enslave* to describe Cuba's designs for the Caribbean. Jackets and ties became de rigueur, and were required attire in the JLP-dominated Parliament. The PNP, in contrast, repeatedly reiterated its support for Cuba, the Bishop government in Grenada, the Sandinista government in Nicaragua, and the rebels in El Salvador, and, equally often, denied that it would want to form a government in Jamaica similar to any of these.

It is interesting to note that while anti-Cubanism and anticommunism virtually permeated Jamaican institutions, in all the research represented in this book, never once was an anticommunist or anti-Cuban phrase located in a reggae song. Around the 1976 election, several reggae songs took an anti-American perspective, particularly condemning the Central Intelligence Agency, but no reggae song could be found that was critical of the Cuban or Grenadian governments or of communism in general.

In summary, the issues of foreign control and ownership reached a peak in 1980, and the two parties continue to be polarized on these grounds. New trends in foreign ownership were eclipsed in 1983 by the issue of electoral reform; the PNP only obliquely referred to these trends as part of the JLP's overall economic policies.

Rastafari and Reggae in Jamaican Politics

In chapter 1 the question was posed: "Why would a political party identify itself with a millenarian cult, whose beliefs are sharply at odds with a majority of the electorate, and whose membership never exceeded about 3 percent of the population?" It is now time to begin to answer that question.

As we have seen, although the vast majority of the population of Jamaica would hardly accept the idea that Haile Selassie is the Messiah, the Rastafarians are far from isolated. They have long been in the vanguard of protest against a society whose historic racial divisions have persisted despite democratic institutions and in which wealth is concentrated in the hands of a very few.

Given Jamaica's history of protest, it is hardly surprising that protest in modern Jamaica is expressed through the forms of religion and music. These two outlets had long been the almost exhaustive "repertoire of contention" (Tilly 1977) of the descendants of Jamaican slaves. Throughout Jamaica's history, protest movements of the Black and poor were led by religious leaders, and music was always an integral part of the religion of the Black and poor. Religious and musical expression were the only forms tolerated by an extremely repressive colonial society.

The late 1960s saw a resurgence of the power of religion and music as a form of protest against the injustices of a divided society. The fusing of a new form of recorded popular music — reggae -- with the older cult of Rastafari enabled the Rastafarians to reach mass audiences and lent reggae meaning and purpose beyond entertainment. That fusion, in conjunction with imported ideas of Black power and the older Jamaican Black nationalism, presented a new history, a new vision of the past, as well as a vision of a potential new social order. The JLP government at the time recognized its precarious position in the face of such a vision, and took steps to lessen its impact. But the repression only served to strengthen the movement.

The concept of "preparation" with regard to negotiated independence from the colonial empire rings true in the case of Jamaica. The Brown stratum that had inherited power in that nation seemed to have carefully and deliberately gone about the business of showing the Western world how well-prepared it had been for independence. Part of this preparation was a shunning of radicalism, especially after the Cuban revolution. Another aspect of it involved the denial of potentially disruptive aspects of society: hence, the myth of racial harmony that the founders of Jamaican independence so warmly embraced.

The JLP government of 1962-72 exemplified these trends. Its Black ministers had no sympathy for concepts of Black power; Rastafari was considered subversive; reggae music pleading for food for the hungry was not permitted to be played on the radio. The government seemed to have the forms of mature nationhood without the substance; like the bar graphs in its advertisements that had no relation to the numbers they were supposed to represent, the JLP had only the trappings of sophistication in government, including sybaritic ministers mouthing platitudes similar to those of the colonial administrators who preceded them.

Rastafari, coupled with the medium of reggae music, posed a challenge to Brown stratum hegemony that pointed out the inequities generated by colonialism and maintained by the independent government. It exposed the myth of harmonious multiracialism. It asserted a moral authority that recognized the perpetuation of poverty as a criminal act, for which the Jamaican elite would be held responsible. Although Rastas were never strong numerically, their subculture served as an organizing principle for relevant social groups in the society.

The Rasta challenge and the JLP's repression of it created an atmosphere to the PNP's advantage in 1972, and that party used it to the fullest. It appropriated particularly those aspects of the challenge that were linked with the Rastafarian moral authority. "Joshua's" promise was one of social justice, an end to oppression, punishment for the corrupt, and a "spiritual and moral rebirth." The PNP, as the opposition political party, could pose as a critic of the "system" while gaining power within it.

The PNP seized the opportunity in 1972 to link itself with the Rastafarian moral authority, and for some politicians it may have been a cynical manipulation of emotionally loaded symbols. But in the process of co-opting dissent, the PNP changed. The party recruited individuals who had been involved in the Black power movement, individuals who were not only more adept in the use of the symbols but were committed to the ideas the symbols condensed and represented.

The PNP's first term was a sharp contrast to the "well-prepared" governments before it. Efforts were directed toward improving the life chances of the very poor: the illiterate, the domestic worker, the chronically unemployed. The wealthy were called upon to sacrifice by paying higher taxes, by forgoing expensive trips abroad, and by doing without imported luxuries. Through these efforts, the Manley government deflected the problem of racial tensions and channeled the frustrations of a racially divided society into expressions of class conflict. The Black nationalism-oriented recruits of 1972 had, by 1976, evolved a set of government priorities based on "deep reforms" of the economic structure of society: democratic socialism. But in the PNP's second term, the more radical program of the younger members of the party was put under the "heavy manners" of International Monetary Fund agreements. The social and economic reforms it had planned were postponed; the ones it had already instituted were cut back.

In addition to the impact of economic austerity policies on the very poor, the PNP also lost its ability to link itself with the moral authority that it had had in 1972. A number of incidents, in particular the Green Bay killings, connected the PNP with the political violence that was afflicting the poorest neighborhoods in Kingston and destroyed the relatively clean record with respect to violence that it had enjoyed in 1976. Criticism of the government from some Rastafarian circles, mild during the first term, became bitter in the second term, especially after the peace truce that they had supported was broken. Contrary to expectations, the PNP had not fundamentally altered "Babylon."

By 1980, the Rastafarians themselves had lost some of their influence on the symbols of political parties. Many were now successful artists who spent more time abroad than in Jamaica. They had been courted by politicians of both parties for eight years; one informant described them as "spent." Those who still denied Selassie's death were increasingly isolated and by definition withdrawn from society. A number spent the 1980 preelection period appealing to the British High Commission for a "Bill of Repatriation" from the queen. Those who accepted Selassie's death faced an unavoidable crisis of faith. The dream that some Rastas entertained of truly taking power in society was dead.

The JLP of 1980 advocated free enterprise, foreign investment, technical expertise, and Jamaican unity. With that program, and with a White, foreign-born Harvard graduate leading the party, the JLP had a strong need to associate itself in some way with the lower-class Blacks who make up a majority of the electorate. Rastafarian symbols were inappropriate for that party at that time, partly because of their longer association with the PNP but, more importantly, because the program that the JLP promised did not resonate with the concerns of Rastas.

Seaga showed that he was adept in the use of other symbols of the Black lower class. Revival cults, a subject that Seaga knows intimately, partly took the place of Rastafari in providing political symbols and music. The Evangelical churches supplied the JLP with a moral argument, however unfounded, for anticommunism. Seaga's long association with Jamaican music enabled him to present himself as a promoter and protector of lower-class culture. The ideas and symbols of Black nationalism, especially National Hero Marcus Garvey, were redefined to highlight, or to invent, their anticommunist aspects. The redirection of these symbols is a classic example of the ambiguous nature of political symbols generally; their multiple and vague meanings make them flexible enough to support contradictory positions.

By 1983, a further decline in the active influence of Rastafari and reggae was evident. The subculture's major leader, Bob Marley, was dead at age thirty-six. The newest artists avoided politics, considering partisan issues too dangerous to handle in recorded songs. Some of the older artists turned more to the spiritual aspects of Rastafari. There seemed at the same time to be a resurgence in expressions of disgust toward reggae and Rastas on the part of the upper-middle class, which registered its dislike for the subculture in the *Gleaner* in stronger terms than had been used since the 1960s.

But at least one survey showed that Rasta was still strong in the minds of the youth of Jamaica. In the study of lower class youths by Carl Stone cited above, almost half favored Rastafari, believing that the subculture aided in preserving the culture of Blacks in Jamaica (EFE 9/9/81).

The symbols that the JLP depended upon in 1980 did not all become a permanent part of the party's representation of itself to the general public. Despite Seaga's controversial participation in a Revival Table in 1981, it is the Harvard scholar, not the Revivalist shepherd, who occupies Jamaica House now. The Jamaican government, again, seems "prepared" and "mature:" its prime minister has a cordial relationship with the president of the United States; his government moved the country out of "the age of innocence" when, as *Gleaner* editor Hector Wynter said, it showed its readiness to "sacrifice young people" (WG 10/21/83, 7).

The symbols that are used to present the image of mature government mask the sordid side of maintaining power and controlling communities. By the time of the invasion of Grenada, the "age of innocence" was certainly long over; since the 1960s Jamaica's political parties have sacrificed their lower-class youth to "tribal" violence. Because the election was uncontested, there was little violence around election time in 1983, but several months later the volatile network of street politics became visible again when violence erupted in some of the poorest neighborhoods in Kingston. Street-gang supporters of the JLP in a housing project known as "Rema" apparently became disenchanted with the payoffs available from their party of loyalty. They opened talks with members of a gang in neighboring Arnett Gardens, known as "Concrete Jungle," which supports the PNP. Gunmen — armed with M16's and AK47's — from Tivoli Gardens, in Seaga's constituency, invaded Rema, shouting, "Where are the rats?" They sparked off a thirty-six-hour gun battle that left ten dead, scores injured, and many more homeless. Seaga, Pearnel Charles, and the deputy police commissioners negotiated the peace, posing for photographs with gang leaders as they all drank tepid beer to celebrate the "truce." Only one weapon was captured.

It is difficult to reconcile the presence and power of street gangs organized along partisan lines, armed with sophisticated weapons, and adept in the arts of intimidation with the view expressed by U.S. Vice President Bush that Jamaica is blessed "with a thriving democracy that serves as an inspiration to all in the Caribbean" (WG 10/24/83).

Many words have been spoken and written in the last two years about democracy in the Caribbean, but many have failed to address the spirit of democracy — the voice of the people in the affairs of their government — and focused rather on the trappings of democracy, the arrangements and behaviors in the Third World that can be said to be analogues to those of the institutions of democracy in economically advanced countries. Jamaicans, said Bush, "have been steadfast in (their) commitment to democratic traditions" (WG 10/24/83). Jamaicans can be said to have a free press: a single newspaper company whose editor-in-chief is a former political party chairman. Jamaicans have free elections, but gunmen with rifles persuade their neighbors to vote for the party of the gunmen's choice.

Into the maze of symbols, forms, and appearances that make up Jamaican political culture, the Rastafarians entered, with an ambitious rewriting of history, a demand for deep social change, a self-righteous anger over injustice and inequity, and King Alpha's song of redemption. Politicians could not but listen. "If them no use Rasta," said Bob

Marley of politicians, "no go. Rasta have the conscience of society." The Rastas' challenge to the social order paved the way for a political philosophy that aimed to loosen the bonds of a rigid racial hierarchy and a severely unequal economic structure, and hence made an undeniable contribution to the priorities of government in the 1970s.

Was the influence of this challenge buried along with its most outstanding spokesperson? The evidence presented in this book indicates that it could not have been. Self-styled "strangers in a strange land," dubbed by academicians "the most alienated" of Jamaicans, the challenge of the Rastafarians resonated with the most profound currents of Jamaican society. As long as the inequity of "economic freedom," the injustice of ethnic advantage, and the hypocrisy of symbolic democracy thrive in Jamaica, the challenge shall live.

Bibliography

A list of other sources is given following the bibliography.

Allum, D. "Legality vs. Morality: A Plea for Lt. Raffique Shah." In *The Aftermath of Sovereignty*, ed. L. Comitas and D. Lowenthal. Garden City, N.Y.: Anchor/Doubleday, 1973.

Augier, F. R., and S. C. Gordon. *Sources of West Indian History*. London: Longman, 1962.

Austin, Diane J. "Symbols and Ideologies of Class in Urban Jamaica: A Cultural Analysis of Class." Ph.D. diss., University of Chicago, 1974.

Ayearst, Morley. "A Note on Some Characteristics of West Indian Political Parties." *Social and Economic Studies* 3 (September 1954.)

Bahadoorsing, Krishna. *Trinidad Electoral Politics: The Persistence of the Race Factor*. London: Oxford University Press, 1968.

Barrett, Leonard. *The Rastafarians*. Boston: Beacon Press, 1977.

Beckford, George, and Michael Witter. *Small Garden ... Bitter Weed*. Morant Bay: Maroon Publishers, 1980.

Bibliography 313

Bell, Wendell. *Jamaican Leaders.* Berkeley and Los Angeles: University of California Press, 1964.

Bennett, George, and Carl Rosenberg. *The Kenyatta Election: Kenya 1960 to 1961.* London: Oxford University Press, 1961.

Bigelow, John. *Jamaica in 1850.* Westport, Conn.: Negro Universities Press, 1970; first published 1851.

Birhan, Iyata Farika. *The Rasta Dictionary.* 1980.

Blanshard, Paul. *Democracy and Empire in the Caribbean.* New York: Macmillan, 1947.

Campbell, H. "Rastafari: Culture of Resistance." *Race and Class* 22 (Summer 1980): 1-22.

Cashmore, Ernest. *Rastaman: The Rastafari Movement in England.* London: Allen and Unwin, 1979.

Charles, Pearnel. *Detained.* Kingston: Kingston Publishers, 1978.

Chevannes, A. Barrington. "The Repairer of the Breach: Reverend Claudius Henry and Jamaican Society." In *Ethnicity in the Americas,* ed. F. Henry. Hague: Mouton, 1976.

Chief Electoral Officer. *Report on the 1967 Election.* Kingston, 1967.

Chief Electoral Officer. *Report on the 1972 Election.* Kingston, 1972.

Chief Electoral Officer. *Report on the 1976 Election.* Kingston, 1976.

Clark, S. *Jah Music: The Evolution of the Popular Jamaican Song.* London: Heinemann, 1980.

Coleman, J. "The Politics of Sub-Saharan Africa." In *The Politics of Developing Areas,* ed. G. Almond and J. Coleman. Princeton: Princeton University Press, 1960.

Courlander, Harold, and Remy Bastien. *Religion and Politics in Haiti: Two Essays.* Washington, D.C.: Institute for Cross-Cultural Research,1966.

Craton, Michael, and James Walvin. *A Jamaican Plantation.* Toronto: University of Toronto Press, 1970.

Curtin, Phillip. *Two Jamaicas.* (Westport, Conn.: Greenwood, 1955).

Davis, C.L. "The Mobilization of Public Support for an Authoritarian Regime: The Case of the Lower Class in Mexico City." *American Journal of Political Science* 20 (November 1976): 653-70.

Davis, Stephen, and Peter Simon. *Reggae Bloodlines: In Search of the Music and Culture of Jamaica.* Garden City, N.Y.: Anchor, 1977.

Deschen, S. "On Religious Change: The Situational Analysis of Symbolic Action." *Comparative Studies in Society and History* 12 (1970): 260-74.

Depres, Leo A. *Cultural Pluralism and Nationalist Politics in British Guiana.* Chicago: Rand McNally, 1967.

Deutsch, Karl. *Nationalism and Social Communication.* Cambridge, Mass.: MIT Press, 1953.

Director of Elections. *Report -- General Election 1980.* Kingston.

Duncan, Donald Keith. Public address, Columbia University, 1980.

Edwards, D.T. "Small Farming in Jamaica: A Social Scientist's View." In *Work and Family Life: West Indian Perspectives,* ed. Lambros Comitas and David Lowenthal. Garden City: Anchor, 1973.

Elder, J.D. "Evolution of Traditional Calypso of Trinidad and Tobago: A Socio-Historical Analysis of Song Change." Ph.D. diss., University of Pennsylvania, 1966.

Foner, Eric. *Nothing But Freedom: Emancipation and Its Legacy.* Baton Rouge: Louisiana State University Press, 1983.

Francis, O.C. *The People of Modern Jamaica.* Kingston: Department of Statistics, 1963.

Friedrich, Paul. "Revolutionary Politics and Communal Ritual." In *Political Anthropology,* ed. M.J.Schwartz, Chicago: Aldine, 1966.

Garrison, Len. *Black Youth, Rastafarianism and the Identity Crisis In Britain.* London: Afro-Caribbean Educational Resources, 1979.

Garvey, Amy Jacques. *Garvey and Garveyism.* New York: Collier Books, 1963.

316   Race, Class, and Political Symbols

Girvan, Norman. *Foreign Capital and Economic Under-development in Jamaica.* Kingston: Institute for Social and Economic Research, 1971.

Gleaner Company. *Geography and History of Jamaica.* Kingston: Gleaner Company, 1973.

Gonsalves, Ralph. "The Rodney Affair." *Caribbean Quarterly* 25 (September 1979): 1-24.

Gronseth, Evangeline C. "Patterns of Mobility in Post-Independence Jamaica." Ph.D. diss., Columbia University, 1978.

Hammond Almanac. Maplewood, N. J.: Hammond, 1979.

Hayes, Lorrel. Interview with Edward Seaga. *Daily Gleaner,* 28 September 1980.

Hearne, John. "Introduction." In *The Search for Solutions,* by Michael Manley. Oshawa, Canada: Maple House Publishing Company, 1976.

Hebdige, Dick. *Subculture: The Meaning of Style.* (London: Methuen, 1979.

Hoetink, H. "National Identity, Culture, and Race in the Caribbean." In *Racial Tensions and National Identity,* ed. Ernest Q. Cambell, Nashville: Vanderbilt University Press, 1972.

Hughes, Colin A. "Fair and Equal Constituencies: Australia, Jamaica and the United Kingdom." *Journal of Commonwealth and Comparative Politics* 16 (November 1978): 256-71.

Hurwitz, Samuel, and Edith Hurwitz. *Jamaica: A Historical Portrait.* New York: Praeger, 1971.

Jamaica Information Service (JIS). *An Official Handbook, Jamaica.* Kingston: 1971.

Jamaica Labour Party. "People Program." In *Perspectives on Jamaica in the 1970's,* ed. C. Stone and A. Brown. Kingston: Jamaica Publishing House, 1981.

------. "Change Without Chaos." Kingston, 1980. (Election Manifesto.)

------. "The Jamaica Decision." Videotape, 1982.

James, C.L.R. *Party Politics in the West Indies.* San Juan, Trinidad, 1962.

Key, V.O. "A Theory of Critical Elections." *Journal of Politics* 17 (1955): 3-18.

Kilson, Martin. *Political Change in a West African State.* Cambridge: Harvard University Press, 1966.

King, S., and R. Girling. "Caribbean Conflict." *NACLA Report on the Americas* 12 (May 1978): 3-36.

Kitzinger, Sheila. "The Rasta Brethren of Jamaica." In *Peoples and Cultures of the Caribbean,* ed. M.M.Horowitz. Garden City, N.Y.: Natural History Press, 1971.

Kopkind, Andrew. "Trouble in Paradise." *Columbia Journalism Review,* March 1980, pp. 41-50.

318   Race, Class, and Political Symbols

Lacey, Terry. *Violence and Politics in Jamaica 1960-1970: Internal Security in a Developing Country.* London: Frank Cass, 1977.

Landis, Fred. *Psychological Warfare in the Media.* Kingston: Press Association of Jamaica, 1980.

Lewis, Bernard. *History Remembered, Recovered, Invented.* Princeton: Princeton University Press, 1975.

Lewis, Gordon. *The Growth of the Modern West Indies.* London: MacGibbon and Kee, 1968.

Lewis, Rupert. "Black Nationalism in Jamaica in Recent Years." In *Essays on Power and Change in Jamaica.* ed. C. Stone and A. Brown. Kingston: Jamaica Publishing House, 1977.

Lewis, Vaughan. "Issues and Trends in Jamaican Foreign Policy, 1972 to 1977." In *Perspectives on Jamaica in the 1970's,* ed. C. Stone and A. Brown. Kingston: Jamaica Publishing House, 1981.

Lewy, Gunther. *Religion and Revolution.* New York: Oxford University Press, 1974.

Lindsay, Louis. "The Myth of Independence: Middle Class Politics and Non-Mobilization in Jamaica." Kingston: Institute for Social and Economic Research, 1975.

Lowenthal, David. *West Indian Societies.* New York: Oxford University Press, 1972.

Manley, Michael. *The Politics of Change.* London: Andre Deutsch, 1974.

——. *A Voice at the Workplace.* London: Andre Deutsch, 1975.

——. "Not For Sale." San Francisco: Editorial Consultants, 1976a. Address to the 38th Annual Conference of the People's National Party, 19 September 1976.

——. *The Search for Solutions* Oshawa, Canada: Maple House Publishing Company, 1976b.

——. *Jamaica: Struggle in the Periphery* London: Writers and Readers Publishing Cooperative Society, 1982.

——. "Grenada in the Context of History." *Caribbean Review* 12 (Fall 1983).

Mintz, Sidney. "The Caribbean as a Socio-cultural Area." In *Peoples of the Caribbean.* ed. M. M. Horowitz. Garden City, N.Y.: Natural History Press, 1971.

Morales Padron, Francisco. *Jamaica Espanola.* Seville: Escuela de estudios hispano-americanos de Sevilla, 1952.

Morris, Mervyn. *On Holy Week.* Kingston: Sangsters, 1977.

Moskos, Charles C. *Sociology of Political Independence: A Study of Nationalist Attitudes among West Indian Leaders.* Cambridge, Mass.: Schenkman, 1967.

Munroe, Trevor. *The Politics of Constitutional Decolonization: Jamaica 1944-1962.* Kingston: Institute for Social and Economic Research, 1972.

Nettl, J.P. *Political Mobilization.* London: Faber and Faber, 1967.

Nettleford, Rex. *Identity, Race and Protest in Jamaica.* New York: William Morrow, 1972.

Nettleford, Rex, ed. *Norman Washington Manley and the New Jamaica.* New York: Africana Publishing Company, 1971.

New World. Kingston: New World Collective, October 1965.

Noyce, John L. *The Rastafarians in Britain and Jamaica.* Brighton: University of Sussex Press, 1978.

O'Gorman, Pamela. "An Approach to the Study of Jamaican Popular Music." *Jamaica Journal* 6 (December 1972): 50ff.

Owens, Joseph. *Dread: The Rastafarians of Jamaica.* Kingston: Sangsters, 1976.

------. "Literature on the Rastas 1955-1974." *Savacou* (1975).

Panton, Earl. "The Calabash Hour." Weekly radio broadcast on WHBI-FM, New York City.

People's National Party. "Manifesto." In *Perspectives on Jamaica in the 1970's,* ed. C. Stone and A. Brown, Kingston: Jamaica Publishing House, 1981.

------. "The 1980 Election Manifesto." Kingston, 1980.

Phillipo, James. *Jamaica: Its Past and Present State.* London: Dawsons, 1969; first published 1843.

Phillips, Peter. "Jamaican Elites: 1938 to Present." In *Essays on Power and Change in Jamaica*, ed. C. Stone and A. Brown. Kingston: Jamaica Publishing House, 1977.

Planno, Mortimer. Videotape interview by Lambros Comitas, 1969.

Pool, Ithiel de Sola. *Symbols of Internationalism*. Stanford: Stanford University Press, 1951.

Pye, Lucian. *Aspects of Political Development*. Boston: Little, Brown, 1966.

Reid, S. "An Introductory Approach to the Concentration of Power in the Jamaican Corporate Economy and Notes on its Origins." In *Essays on Power and Change in Jamaica*. ed. C. Stone and A. Brown. Kingston: Jamaica Publishing House, 1977.

Robotham, Don. "Agrarian Relations in Jamaica." In *Essays on Power And Change in Jamaica* ed. C. Stone and A. Brown. Kingston: Jamaica Publishing House, 1977.

Rodney, Walter. *The Groundings with My Brothers*. London: Bogle L'Ouverture, 1969.

Rosenblum, Walter A. *Political Culture* New York: Praeger, 1975.

Schaffer, B. "The Concept of Preparation." *World Politics* 18 (October 1965): 42-67.

Seaga, Edward. "Revival Cults in Jamaica." *Jamaica Journal* 3 (1969): 289-302.

Sewell, Lileth. "Music in the Jamaican Labour Movement." *Jamaica Journal*. Kingston, Institute of Jamaica, 1978.

Sigmund, Paul E. *The Ideologies of Developing Nations*. New York: Praeger, 1967.

Simpson, George. "Jamaican Revivalist Cults." *Social and Economic Studies* 4 (1955): 133–49.

------. "Political Cultism in West Kingston." *Social and Economic Studies* (1955).

------. *Religious Cults in the Caribbean: Trinidad, Jamaica Haiti.* Rio Piedras: University of Puerto Rico, 1970.

Singham, A.W., and N.L. Singham. "Cultural Domination and Political Subordination: Notes towards a Theory of the Caribbean Political System." *Comparative Studies in Society and History* 15, no. 3 (1973).

Slinger, Penny. "Youth Consciousness Festival." *Everybody's Magazine*, March 1983.

Small, Richard. "Introduction." In *The Groundings with My Brothers*. by Walter Rodney. London: Bogle L'Ouverture, 1969.

Smikle, Patrick. Personal communication, 1982.

Smith, Michael G. *Framework for Caribbean Studies* Kingston: University of the West Indies, 1955.

------. *Plural Society in the British West Indies.* Berkeley and Los Angeles: University of California Press, 1965.

------. "Institutional and Political Conditions of Pluralism." In *Pluralism in Africa,* ed. Leo Kuper and M. G. Smith. Berkeley and Los Angeles: University of California Press, 1969.

Smith, Michael G., Roy Augier, and Rex Nettleford. "Report on the Rastafari Movement in Kingston, Jamaica." Kingston: Institute of Social and Economic Research, 1960.

Smith, Raymond T., "Social Stratification, Cultural Pluralism and Integration in West Indian Societies." In *Caribbean Integration,* ed. S. Lewis and T. G. Matthews. Rio Piedras: Institute of Caribbean Studies, 1967.

Stephens, Evelyne, and John Stephens. "Democratic Socialism in Dependent Capitalism: An Analysis of the Manley Government in Jamaica." Paper presented at the meetings of the New York Political Science Association, April 1983.

Stephens, John. Personal communication, 1982.

Stone, Carl. "Bauxite and National Development in Jamaica." In *Essays on Power and Change in Jamaica,* ed. C. Stone and A. Brown, Kingston, Jamaica Publishing House, 1977.

------. "Class and the Institutionalization of Two-Party Politics in Jamaica." *Journal of Commonwealth and Comparative Politics* 14 (July 1976): 177-96.

Stone, Carl. Personal communication, 1983.

------. "The Jamaican Reaction: Grenada and the Political Stalemate." *Caribbean Review* 12 (Fall 1983).

Stone, Carl, and Aggrey Brown, eds. *Essays on Power and Change in Jamaica.* Kingston: Jamaica Publishing House, 1977.

------. eds. *Perspectives on Jamaica in the 1970's.* Kingston: Jamaica Publishing House, 1981.

Thelwell, Michael. *The Harder They Come.* New York: Grove, 1980.

Tilly, Charles. "Repertoires of Contention." In Mayer N. Zald and John D. McCarthy, *The Dynamics of Social Movements.* Cambridge, Mass.: Winthrop, 1979.

Toure, S. *Independent Guinea: Articles and Speeches.* Moscow: 1960.

U. S. Department of State, "Background on the Caribbean Basin Initiative," March 1982.

Walters, E. "Reggae as Feedback." Lecture, Visual Arts Research and Resource Center, New York City, 1981.

White, G. "Rudie, oh Rudie." *Caribbean Quarterly.* 13 (September 1967). 39-45.

Williams, Eric. *British Historians and the West Indies.* New York: Africana, 1972.

Sources

Documents

I.	Michael Manley, 1969 Budget Speech.
II.	Unofficial pro-PNP poster, 1976.
III.	Michael Manley. internal party speech, 1973.
IV.	PNPYO Leaflet, 1976.
V.	PNP Notes for Canvassers, 1976.

VI.	Unofficial pro-PNP leaflet, 1976.
VII.	Unofficial pro-PNP leaflet, 1976.
VIII.	Unofficial pro-PNP leaflet, 1976.
IX.	Unofficial pro-PNP poster, 1976.
X.	PNPYO Newsletter, 1973.

Newspapers

Daily Gleaner, Sunday Gleaner, Star, Jamaica Weekly Gleaner, Gleaner Annual (Kingston: Gleaner Company)

Daily News, Sunday Sun (Kingston: Daily News, Ltd.)

Abeng (Kingston: Abeng Collective)

New York Times

Barbados Sun

Friends for Jamaica Newsletter (New York)

Rising Sun (PNP)

Struggle (WPJ)

Daily Challenge (Brooklyn, New York)

Other Sources

EFE, Spanish News Agency

Everybody's Magazine

Appendix

Respondent Characteristics

Number	Race	Class Origin	Current Occupation	Rasta?	Political Affiliation
1.	Black	Lower	Clerk	Yes	None
2.	Black	Lower	Driver	Yes	None
3.	Black	Lower	Guard	No	None
4.	Black	Lower	Journalist	No	PNP
5.	Brown	Middle	Journalist	No	JLP
6.	Brown	Middle	Journalist	No	PNP
7.	Brown	Middle	Journalist	No	PNP
8.	Brown	Middle	Party officer	No	PNP
9.	Brown	Middle	Educator	No	JLP
10.	Black	Middle	Educator	No	PNP
11.	Brown	Middle	Journalist	No	PNP
12.	Brown	Middle	Educator	No	JLP
13.	Brown	Middle	Student	No	PNP
14.	Brown	Middle	Journalist	No	JLP
15.	Brown	Middle	Filmmaker	No	PNP
17.	White	Middle	Writer	No	JLP
18.	Black	Lower	None	Yes	None
19.	Black	Middle	Journalist	Yes	None
20.	Brown	Middle	Public Relations	No	PNP
21.	Black	Middle	Educator	No	WPJ

Number	Race	Class Origin	Current Occupation	Rasta?	Political Affiliation
22.	Black	Middle	Educator	No	PNP
23.	Brown	Middle	Clerk	No	Not known
24.	Black	Lower	Advertising	No	JLP
25.	Black	Middle	Public Relations	No	PNP
26.	Brown	Middle	Translator	No	PNP
27.	Black	Middle	Musician	No	Not known
29.	Black	Middle	Government Minister	No	JLP
30.	White	Upper	Public Relations	No	None
31.	Brown	Middle	Government Minister	No	JLP
32.	White	Upper	Manager	No	JLP
33.	Black	Middle	Dancer	No	PNP
34.	Brown	Upper	Party officer	No	PNP
35.	Black	Lower	Rasta leader	Yes	None
36.	Brown	Lower	Musician	Yes	Not known
37.	Black	Lower	Musician	Yes	Not known
38.	Black	Lower	Craftsman	Yes	Not known
39.	Black	Middle	Student	No	PNP
40.	Black	Middle	Educator	No	WPJ

Note: Numbers 16 and 28 are invalid, due to duplication.

Index